MORE LITERARY ESSAYS

Photograph by Alan Daiches

DAVID DAICHES, who is now Professor of English and Dean of the School of English and American Studies at the University of Sussex, has also taught at Edinburgh, Oxford, Cambridge, and, in the United States, at The University of Chicago and Cornell. He has published some twenty books which include *The Novel and the Modern World* (Chicago, 1960), *Robert Burns, Critical Approaches to Literature, A Critical History of English Literature, John Milton,* and *A Study of Literature.*

MORE
LITERARY ESSAYS

BY

DAVID DAICHES

THE UNIVERSITY OF CHICAGO PRESS

The University of Chicago Press, Chicago 60637
Oliver & Boyd, Edinburgh and London

Library of Congress Catalog Card Number : 68–16688

Printed in Great Britain

Preface

THESE ESSAYS represent for the most part a return to themes on which I have written earlier, in my original collection of *Literary Essays* and elsewhere. The range of interests is identical with that covered in the earlier volume. Most of the essays have either appeared in periodicals or were originally given as public lectures in various parts of the world. I have to thank the Editor of *Commentary* for permission to use "Presenting the Bible" and "The Book of Job" and the Editors of *Encounter* for permission to use "Cultivated Innocence" and "Mark Twain as Hamlet". Three of the essays have previously appeared in other collections. The essay on Hugh MacDiarmid first appeared in *Hugh MacDiarmid: A Festschrift*, edited by K. D. Duval and Sydney Goodsir Smith (Edinburgh, 1962), that on Yeats first appeared in the collection of Yeats criticism *In Excited Reverie*, edited by A. N. Jeffares and K. G. W. Cross (1965), and that on Burns in *Restoration and Eighteenth Century Literature*, edited by Carroll Camden (University of Chicago Press, 1963). The biographical sketch of Sir Herbert Grierson was written at the request of the British Academy and first appeared in the *Proceedings of the British Academy*, Vol. XLVI.

Acknowledgments are due to Mr M. B. Yeats and the Macmillan Company for permission to quote from William Butler Yeats: *Collected Poems*; also to the Macmillan Company for permission to quote from Hugh MacDiarmid: *Collected Poems*.

DAVID DAICHES

The University of Sussex
March 1967

Contents

1. Myth, Metaphor, and Poetry 1

2. Misunderstanding as Humour: An Aspect of the English Comic Tradition 19

3. Language and Action in Marlowe's *Tamburlaine* 42

4. Imagery and Meaning in *Antony and Cleopatra* 70

5. Some Aspects of Milton's Pastoral Imagery 96

6. Carlyle and the Victorian Dilemma 115

7. Yeats's Earlier Poems : Some Themes and Patterns 133

8. Sir Herbert Grierson 150

9. The Identity of Burns 164

10. Hugh MacDiarmid : The Early Poems 184

11. Lincoln and Whitman 211

12. Cultivated Innocence 231

13. Mark Twain as Hamlet 238

14. Presenting The Bible 248

15. The Book of Job 268

I

Myth, Metaphor, and Poetry[1]

It is some time now since the study of poetry became involved with
the study of myth. The modern concern with the differentiating
qualities of the literary use of language and the modern insistence
that poetic discourse is different in kind from factual or scientific
communication has led literary critics to ponder over the nature of
myth and its relation to poetic ways of knowing and creating. At the
same time anthropologists, psychologists, and others have been
building up a vast though not always self-consistent body of knowledge and opinion about the origin, nature, and function of myth.
When the literary critic avails himself of this body of knowledge, as
he has done so often in recent years, the result is sometimes helpful,
sometimes confusing. Sometimes we feel rather taken aback by the
bold assimilation of poetic, mythical, religious, and mystical discourse
of the kind that, for example, the distinguished American philosopher
and poet, Philip Wheelwright, goes in for. In the opening of his book,
The Burning Fountain : A Study in the Language of Symbolism, Mr
Wheelwright tells us of Wannemunne, the goddess of song in Estonian
legend, and remarks : "To listen for the voice of Wisdom, or the
Muse, or Wannemunne, or Conscience, or Christ, means standing
ready to be guided by an imperative not wholly of one's own making,
yet to which one's psyche responds at a level of depth. It is an
apprenticeship in singing the full song." And by "the full song" Mr
Wheelwright means expressive or depth language as distinct from
mere literal language. But this identification of saint, seer, and poet—
and Mr Wheelwright talks of the three together in this same chapter
as representing a single way of knowing and expressing—is merely a
gesture intended to alert the reader to the existence of methods of
knowing and discoursing other than the scientific one. Such an alerting

[1] The G. H. Edmonds Memorial Lecture, Royal Society of Literature, June 1961.

may be necessary ; it may indeed be a prerequisite to any full exploration of the nature of poetry or of imaginative literature in general ;
nevertheless, we must make distinctions if we are to advance understanding. To reduce great works of literature to a few basic and
recurring myths, even when the process is done with the dazzling
brilliance of Mr Northrop Frye in his impressively original work, *Ana-
tomy of Criticism*, is to risk blurring the distinction between the work
itself and its paraphrasable plot. *King Lear* is not a myth, though
we may trace mythical patterns in it ; it is not a myth, even though
the presence of mythical patterns in it may help to explain the pro-
fundity and universality of the tragedy which is the theme of the play.
And *Paradise Lost* is not a myth, though it derives its plot from one of
the greatest myths of all and includes many other elements from myth.

These distinctions are obvious ; I shall try and explore some of
their implications later. What I want to note first, however, is the
fact that interest in myth has been pressed on literary critics by their
need to emphasise the basic difference between—to put it crudely—
poetry and science. The difference is not, of course, a modern discovery, any more than the relation between the poetic and the primitive
is a modern notion. Matthew Arnold, in a famous essay on poetry,
wrote : "Our religion has materialised itself in the fact, in the supposed
fact ; it has attached its emotion to the fact, and now the fact is failing
it. But for poetry the idea is everything ; the rest is a world of illusion,
of divine illusion. Poetry attaches its emotion to the idea ; the idea *is*
the fact." This, I suppose, sounds too familiar and hopelessly over-
simplified to modern critical ears. (For one thing, Arnold clearly does
not mean "idea" in any philosophical sense when he uses that term.)
More than forty years after Arnold's essay Ogden and Richards wrote
in *The Meaning of Meaning*: "A poem . . . has no concern with
limited and directed reference. *It tells us, or should tell us, nothing.*
It has a different, though an equally important and far more vital
function—to use an evocative term in connexion with an evocative
matter. What it does, or should do, is to induce a fitting attitude to
experience." And in his *Principles of Literary Criticism* Richards
stated that "in its use of words poetry is just the reverse of science".
The process of distinguishing between poetic and scientific discourse
has continued steadily through the last seventy-five years. And the
notion that poetry is essentially a primitive mode of expression, akin
to myth, goes back at least to the eighteenth century ; I need cite only

John Brown's *Dissertation on the Rise . . . of Poetry and Music,*
published in 1763, which recommends a study of the "principles of
savage nature" as a method of investigating the nature of poetry. And
Shelley, in his *Defence of Poetry,* written in 1821 though not published
until 1840, asserted that "poetry is cognate with the nature of man".
He went on to equate primitive language with the poetic use of
language. "In the youth of the world, men dance and sing and imitate
natural objects, observing in these actions, as in all others, a certain
natural rhythm or order . . . [The language of primitive man] is vitally
metaphorical; that is, it marks the before unapprehended relations
of things and perpetuates their apprehension, until the words which
represent them become, through time, signs for portions or classes
of thoughts instead of pictures of integral thoughts." And again:
"In the infancy of society every author is necessarily a poet, because
language itself is poetry." The line from this kind of statement to
Maud Bodkin's *Archetypal Patterns in Poetry* is not difficult to trace:
but between Shelley and Maud Bodkin criticism has become involved
in anthropology and psychology, with a marked difference in the
degree of documentation and particularisation required of any critic
who would venture the kind of generalisation that Shelley so readily
indulged in.

When I say, then, that our age has rediscovered myth, I am not
saying that our age is the first to relate myth and poetry, nor am I
saying that not until the twentieth century did literary critics feel the
need to separate poetic from scientific discourse and relate the former
to those other kinds of non-scientific ways of knowing and communicating we know as mythology and religion. It is a question of
degree and of emphasis. Modern literary criticism is on the whole
more committed to an affiliation of poetry, myth, and religion than
the criticism of any other age has been. It is not so much that we
seek to salvage, with Matthew Arnold, the poetic truth of mythological
or religious formulations that can no longer be literally believed in.
The modern literary critic is less concerned to prove that the Bible
may be untrue as historical fact but remains important and valuable
as poetic statement—and that was Arnold's position—than to use
analogies between religion, myth, and literature so as to illuminate
the nature and value of poetic discourse. Does it help us in examining
imaginative literature to look at myth and religion and to seek common
ways of knowing and communicating in all three?

Before I try to answer this question, I think I should acknowledge the existence of a paradox that may already have occurred to many of you. What we call the "New Criticism" is committed to an analytic sophistication, a belief in ironic complexity as the essential element in poetic discourse, that would seem to be far removed from any view of poetry as representing a primitive way of knowing and expressing. The reduction of all poetry to paradox, and the reduction of all imaginative literature to myth are surely incompatible procedures. There seems to be a simple contrast between *naïveté* and sophistication. It seems to me that the paradox exists only when we really try to reduce all poetry to paradox and all imaginative literature to myth. Obviously, such wholesale reduction is preposterous. (Though to say that it is preposterous does not mean that no modern critics are incapable of it.) What we are, or what we ought to be, seeking here are helpful analogies. We may be able to understand better the nature and the differentiating qualities of the poetic use of language if we look at the way language is used in the telling of myths and in the communication of religious attitudes. We might almost say that in mentioning in the same breath—as Mr Wheelwright does—saint, seer, and poet we are using language poetically or metaphorically. The identification, even the association, of these three is not a literal truth, but rather a teasing and suggestive metaphor. I do not say, not a literal truth but *only* a teasing metaphor, because to phrase it in that way would be to declare myself a believer in literalism as the only wholly adequate method of discourse. I would rather say: not a literal truth, but *more* than a literal truth, a metaphor.

Before the argument can be carried any further some clarification is necessary. I have up till now used the term "myth" as though we were all agreed on what it means. But what is myth? One's answer to this question depends on the angle from which one approaches it. The anthropologist gives his answer in terms of human behaviour rather than in terms of man's ways of knowing. In an essay on "Myth and Ritual" contributed to a symposium on myth brought out by the American Folklore Society in 1955, Lord Raglan remarked that in order to explain what a myth is "it is perhaps only necessary to say that in the view of many modern students it is simply a narrative associated with a rite". After further discussion he extended his definition to say that "myth is not merely a narrative associated with a rite, but a narrative which, with or without its associated rite, is believed to confer life". On this view, the ritual comes first, and the myth is a *post hoc* explanation of the ritual. But the ritual acts out something of central importance to the welfare of man, and the myth associated with the ritual, in the words of S. H. Hooke,[2] "embodies a truth of profound emotional significance, a situation, moreover, which is in its nature recurrent, and which calls for the repetition of the ritual which deals with the situation and satisfies the need evoked by it". Ernst Cassirer seems to hold a similar view— I say *seems* because there appear to me to be some contradictions in his position. As David Bidney has summed up the position in his sharply critical essay in the symposium already referred to : "Man's metabiological impulse to identify himself with, and participate in, the life of nature as a whole leads him to express himself directly in symbolic rites of a religious-magical character in order to ensure his survival and well-being. In myth these acts are 'explained' and validated." Such an approach is more helpful to the literary historian than to the literary critic. From Gilbert Murray's lecture on "Hamlet and the Orestes", originally delivered in 1914, to Herbert Weisinger's *Tragedy and the Paradox of the Fortunate Fall*, published in 1953, there have been fruitful attempts to link up the origins of drama with ritual and myth. But to explain origins is not necessarily to explain present significance. What the literary critic, as distinct from the literary historian, wants to ask is : Does myth represent a way of apprehending or interpreting reality, and a related use of the imagination and method of handling language, which is identical with or significantly analagous to the way in which the literary artist functions? Whether, as Lord Raglan argues in his book *The Hero*, there is in the development of literature a regular progression from ritual to drama to ballad to tale, is for my purposes as a literary critic beside the point. Is there a necessary element of ritual in all great drama? Is there necessarily an element of myth in all great works of imaginative literature? If so, how can we define that element and how will our definition give us a greater insight into the nature of poetry? (And by "poetry" I mean imaginative literature in general.) I said earlier that the identification or association of poetry, myth, and religion was a teasing metaphor. But what are the implications of the metaphor? In what direction does its teasing suggestiveness lead us?

Among the bewildering number of modern writers on myth, from

[2] *The Labyrinth*, ed. S. H. Hooke, London, 1955.

Malinowsky to Gertrude Levy—or, to take a wider perspective, from Max Müller and Andrew Lang to Ernst Cassirer and Philip Wheelwright—is the recurring view, expressed in different contexts and in different ways, that myth represents a symbolic mode of discourse, either pointing to and imposing meaning on a non-symbolic reality or, as Cassirer would argue, directly embodying reality, which according to him is always symbolic. Symbolic discourse is necessary if we are to tell an *implicated* truth about reality. This phrase "implicated truth" I have coined for lack of a better : by it I mean a truth which reflects human hopes, fears, yearnings, aspirations, intuitions—one could extend the list indefinitely. If I remarked that it is 6 a.m. and the earth, turning on its axis, is moving this part of its surface towards the sun again, I am making an unimplicated statement. If I say "the sun is rising", I am making a partially implicated statement. The implication arises from the fact that I am speaking metaphorically, in terms of our human feelings about the phenomenon in question : the sun is not really rising, it is the earth that is moving. But our relation to the sun is based on a whole complex of feeling about the source of light and heat and growth. The sun appears even to the most sophisticated human consciousness as in some degree godlike, moving up from the horizon to warm and bless the earth. We retain an antiquated and scientifically inaccurate phrase such as "the sun is rising" not merely out of linguistic inertia, but also because that semi-mythical formulation represents in some degree our implication as human beings in that phenomenon. Yet the phrase represents only a partial implication, because it is a conventional phrase used thoughtlessly and more or less mechanically ; it is not specially created to suggest implication ; it is a traditional formulation representing an implication of which we are not fully conscious. But suppose we describe the sunrise this way :

> But look, the morn, in russet mantle clad,
> Walks o'er the dew of yon high eastward hill.

In the first place, there is a difference in tone here. We are arrested at once by a gesture. The gesture beckons us to watch a scene in our mind's eye—almost, it might be said, to participate in a ritual. The morning is implicitly personified as a goddess, who "walks o'er the dew of yon high eastward hill". She does not walk over the grass, but over the dew ; and the human imagination has for long been committed to the dew as a magic liquid, mysteriously falling from heaven (which it does not in fact do, of course) and having regenerative qualities so that in the folk-lore of many countries young girls who want to be beautiful must wash their faces in the dew on May Day. Grass is the lowest common denominator of growth ; to say that the morn walked over the grass would be to suggest an association between the dawn and routine vegetable growth : but to make her walk over the dew is to suggest the mysteriously regenerative effects of the coming of a new day. And of course it *is* mysterious, this perpetual and regular recurrence of day after night, as mysterious as the regular procession of the seasons which God promised Noah after the flood, in one of the most haunting passages of the Bible, should never be interrupted again. It is a quiet and sober goddess who walks in russet mantle, across the dew. This is the quiet colouring of early dawn. She wears a mantle, a word which suggests a poetic or a prophetic robe : this is not the rosy-fingered dawn of Homer—and Homer's dawn is, after all, rather pretty-pretty—but a dawn which suggests a Life Force quietly setting about the profound business of keeping life going. But the phrase most suggestive of all what I call human implication is "yon high eastward hill". It was not necessary for Shakespeare, in putting this description of the dawn into Horatio's mouth, to specify a hill. But "high eastward hill" is a profoundly evocative phrase for anyone familiar with the symbols of western civilisation. The east is not the orient, but the biblical east, where Christianity was born, and a high eastward hill inevitably conveys echoes of Sinai, Carmel, Calvary, among others. The hill is in the east, where revelation comes from. It is to the hills that the Psalmist lifts up his eyes when he seeks divine aid. So the morning walking over the dew of yon high eastward hill is a symbolic image full of blending suggestions of hope and regeneration. The dawn goddess (an implied, not an explicit figure) walks over the dew on a high hill in the east, symbolising not only the hopeful dependability of diurnal movement and not only the banishing of nightmare by day-light but also a ritual of renewal.

This is only to skim the surface of poetic meaning. Why the monosyllabic word "morn" rather than "morning" or another monosyllable such as "dawn"? Why the precise adjective, "russet", with its suggestion of what Milton called "the homely slighted shepherd's trade"? Why the pedestrian verb "walks"? Every

sensitive reader will find his own answer to these questions. I will
pause only to say a word about "walks". The morn walks over the
dew. There is a suggestion of a ritual act here. (In Latin, I feel, the
verb would have to be *spatiatur*, not *ambulat*; *spatior*, as Yeats saw
in his cunning rendering of the word in some lines from Propertius,
has a sense of grave and deliberate movement.) "Walks" has the
simple, elemental suggestion that is required. The morning is treading
a daily round, going on a daily journey. One can emphasise either
the dailiness, as it were, of the journey, or the fact that it is a journey,
a way to be trodden, and the journey, of course, is one of the most
elemental symbols of life :

> Nel mezzo del cammin di nostra vita . . .

Life as a journey and life as a progress through the seasons are intimately connected notions. When Macbeth says

> My way of life is fallen
> Into the sere, the yellow leaf

Shakespeare is deliberately combining these two elemental suggestions ;
and the efforts of earlier editors to emend the phrase into "my *May*
of life", to preserve the logic of the seasonal imagery, showed a lack
of appreciation of the way in which the poetic mind works. In terms
of poetic suggestiveness the movement from life as a journey along
a road to life as a journey through the seasons—or perhaps it is not
so much a movement from one to the other as the identification of
one with the other—is profoundly right. Human commitment is
achieved by metaphor, and multiple metaphor, if properly used,
increases the degree of commitment. We are drawn into the situation
Macbeth describes, trapped and involved by the echoing meanings of
the twin metaphors, each so elemental and, in the phrase which Maud
Bodkin has made so popular among critics, "archetypal". We are
implicated, we are involved ; this man is living in our world and his
fate is a human fate—not just related to *us*, but related to the human
condition as the poetic records of our civilisation have preserved and
rendered it.

I have said nothing of the *pattern* of the words in the quotation from
Hamlet, of the way the rhythm operates on our sensibilities and both
co-operates with and pulls against the meaning achieved by the words
themselves to achieve a rich complex of meaning and suggestion. The

word "walks", on which I have commented, wrenches the initial stress
of the iambic line : though the formal rhythmic pattern says

> Walks o'er the dew of yon high eastward hill

the pattern demanded by the words in their context is

> Walks o'er the dew of yon high eastward hill,

the high eastward hill shining out with mysterious emphasis to add a
comment, or a qualification, or a series of suggestions that take us to
all sorts of magic mountains, castles in Spain, haunts of gods and
symbolic towers, so that the literate reader finds echoing somewhere
in the penumbra of his consciousness lines such as

> Le Prince d'Aquitaine à la tour abolie

and

> Where the great Vision of the guarded mount
> Looks towards Namancos and Bayona's hold

and

> I declare this tower is my symbol ; I declare
> The winding, gyring, spring treadmill of a stair is
>   my ancestral stair ; . . .

Once true contact is made, once human commitment and implication
are achieved, we are well away ; the imagination cannot rest but
echoes off into infinitely reverberating suggestions, reminiscences,
glimpses of new meanings within meanings

> Those images that yet
> Fresh images beget,
> That dolphin-torn, that gong-tormented sea.

What has all this to do with myth? Can we perhaps say that myth
(whatever else it may be) is symbolic discourse aimed at achieving
human involvement in a neutral universe? It aims at *implication* in
the sense in which I am using the word, at implicating man in nature
and nature in man—and, but only indirectly, implicating man in man
through a common implication in nature. If we can accept this,
perhaps we can go on to say that poetry is symbolic discourse, of a
much more complex and flexible kind, which aims at achieving

B

maximum human implication in a given situation and is involved in committing man to man, not indirectly through a common commitment to nature, as in myth, but directly, by releasing images of a common fate. Both myth and poetry have for their function *de-neutralisation*, but myth does so, originally at least, in order to enable man to come to terms with the terrifyingly impersonal forces of nature, while poetry does so, in a somewhat different way, in order to maximise the human meanings that can be found in any situation that involves a human experience.

I have used the term "symbol" and "symbolic discourse", and perhaps a definition is called for. But I think the nature of symbolic discourse is made clearer by example than by attempted definition. The opening chapter of William Y. Tindall's book, *The Literary Symbol*, wrestles nobly but not wholly satisfactorily with the problem of saying what a symbol is ; his examples are more illuminating than the definitions he frames or quotes. Yet, his own definition of the literary symbol is of some help : it is "an analogy for something unstated, consists of an articulation of verbal elements that, going beyond reference and the limits of discourse, embodies and offers a complex of feeling and thought". The term "analogy" in this definition seems to me too limited, but the phrase "going beyond reference and the limits of discourse" perhaps remedies that—except that there is a paradox, perhaps intended, in describing a kind of discourse as going beyond the limits of discourse ; going beyond the limits of *other* kinds of discourse is presumably what is meant. Perhaps all that need be said is that a literary symbol is a way of directing the reader's intellectual and emotional attention (the two running together), by means of an image, a statement, or a verbally expressed situation, to an area of experience that cannot be directly described in any other way without loss of meaning. Thus one could only adequately define a symbol symbolically. It seems to me less important to define a symbol, a term which most educated readers of literature understand, than to distinguish between two kinds of literary symbol—the intrinsic symbol, whose meaning depends either on human history or on the nature of the human mind, and the positional symbol, which achieves symbolic meaning in virtue of its position within a pattern of expression. When one has both, as happens, for example, in the greatest poems of Yeats, you have a symbol of peculiar power. A great poet can force a symbolic meaning on an image or a situation by the context with which he surrounds it. The rhythm, the pattern, the choosing of this word rather than that, the placing of it here rather than there, can help to give a mythic dimension to an image which, if expressed in any other way, has no mythic overtones at all.

A myth proper, in what might be called the anthropological sense, is independent of the particular form of expression given it. The symbolic element in myth derives from the elements in the story or the situation rather than from the way in which language is used to tell the story or describe the situation. If, then, one difference between myth and poetry is, as I have suggested, that myth aims at mutual implication between man and nature while poetry aims at implicating man in the history of human experience, another difference would lie in the fact that myth is determined by its content while in poetry form and content are inextricably bound up with one another. Even those poets who, like Yeats, believed in the "Great Memory" in which live images of symbolic value which always have meaning, and the same meaning, for men, never in their poetry trusted to the image itself to communicate its area of suggestion, but placed it in a poetic context. And where Yeats's symbols were derived from his private myth-making or from what has been called the "heterodox mystical tradition" he similarly gave them meaning by their poetic context, so that the full poetic impact from, say, *Byzantium* or *The Second Coming* is more likely to be achieved by the experienced and sensitive reader, who listens to the poems properly, than to the reader who thinks he can find all the clues by reading Yeats's prose exposition of his system in *A Vision*, or studying the works of Mr F. C. C. Wilson, immensely helpful though these activities can be. In this connexion I can commend to literary critics Richard Blackmur's comment on these strange and terrible lines from Part V of *The Waste Land* :[3]

> A woman drew her long black hair out tight
> And fiddled whisper music on those strings
> And bats with baby faces in the violet light
> Whistled, and beat their wings
> And crawled head downward down a blackened wall
> And upside down in air were towers
> Tolling reminiscent bells, that kept the hours
> And voices singing out of empty cisterns and exhausted wells.

[3] R. P. Blackmur, *Anni Mirabiles 1921-5.* The Library of Congress, Washington, 1956, p. 39.

Mr Blackmur comments : "The exegetes tell us, and it is true, that we
are in the Chapel Perilous and the Perilous Cemetery is no doubt near
at hand, and it may be as one of the exegetes says that we hear something like the voice of John the Baptist in the last line. But for myself,
I muse and merge and ache and find myself feeling with the very senses
of my thought and greetings and cries from all the senses that are."
Is not that how it is? And do we not hear, besides "greetings and
cries from all the senses that are", greetings and cries from our own
emotional past, from the depths of our imagination, from the whole
past of human experience? And this is not only true of poems with
obvious symbolic elements and mythic references like *The Waste Land*
or *Byzantium* ; it can be true of poems where the images are realistic
and everyday, but they are forced into a pattern of symbolic meaning
by the interweaving of sound, sense, and suggestion which the poet
has created.

The search for archetypal images, for the contents of Yeats's Great
Memory or Jung's collective unconscious, is not always the surest
way of accounting for the suggestion of myth, the symbolic expansion
of meaning to something that brings "greetings and cries from all the
senses that are" and from the very depths of human awareness. One
could use all the symbols in the book and still achieve no adequate
poetic expression. Myth may have originally been magical speech
intended to give the proper implication to a pre-existing ritual, and
poetry is still in some sense magical speech—but it is not table-rapping,
though such a great poet as Yeats sometimes talked as though he
believed it was. But Yeats knew better ; and the literary critic should
know better, too—he should know that the mere assimilation of
poetry to myth or to the utterance of symbolic words or archetypal
images cannot explain what poetry is. The curse imposed on fallen
man in Genesis was that he should work for a living instead of living
in ideal bliss in a garden where it was always perpetual spring. So
says the myth, and a powerful and searching myth it is. But Milton,
in weaving the complex pattern of *Paradise Lost*, and while drawing
on this and other myths, continually uses images of rustic labour as
symbols of human dignity and achievement and seasonal imagery to
suggest hope and purpose and order ; he crosses the myth with an
implied counter-statement and uses the archetypal images in two
opposing senses at once, so that at every turn the paradox of the
human situation is evoked and suggested and the sensitive reader

achieves a combination of new awareness and old recollection, a sense both of the familiar and the strange, of recognition and surprise, which only poetry can give. Thus poetic order, while making use of myth, can give it a new dimension by conscious literary devices.

I remarked earlier, in trying to show what myth and poetry have in common and how they differ, that poetry is a de-neutralising force seeking to maximise the human meanings that can be found in any situation that involved a human experience. This implies that human experience is at least in some degree uniform. Are we then prepared to agree with Dr Johnson when he declared that "nothing can please many, and please long, but just representations of general nature"? I do not think so. What we would boggle at here—apart from wanting a more precise definition of the word "please" in this context—is the word "representations". The poetic use of language involves a way of reaching out into the depths and the hinterland of human awareness, a special way of handling words dependent on a special way of knowing and apprehending, that it makes impossibly naïve for us to talk about it in simple mimetic terms. Dr Johnson, great critic though he was in his own way, lacked, as his age lacked, all sense of the uniqueness of the poetic mode of apprehending as well as expressing. Yet, in a sense, if we interpret his terms in our own way, Dr Johnson is right. Can we perhaps paraphrase his statement like this? Nothing can achieve the kind of response described by Mr Blackmur, in commenting on the passage from *The Waste Land*, except a way of handling language that shows a humanly committed pattern of truths about an aspect of reality. My whole concept of implication or commitment would seem to imply some belief in what Johnson called "general human nature". Yet it is the differences between cultures, often so profound as to make us despair of finding any common terms in human experience, that makes great poetry possible. If there were no differences it would not require poetry to achieve implication. The poet works down from the top of the pyramid, which represents the differentiating features of his own civilisation, to the base, which represents the elemental hopes, fears, aspirations of mankind. If we formulate these elemental hopes and fears, we shall have a crude enough common human denominator. The poet's task, however, is not to formulate them, but to counterpoint the patterns of his own culture with those primitive elements in such a way as to give those

primitive elements new life, new modernity. We do not, and Shakespeare did not, believe in a Dawn goddess ; but by describing sunrise
in terms suggestive of a walking goddess Shakespeare reminds us
both that the dawn is *not* a goddess and that many of our responses
to the notion of dawn can be more significantly organised if we
describe the dawn in real or implied metaphors suggestive of that
earlier belief. Shakespeare's dawn goddess, in the passage from
Hamlet that I quoted, is less literal and far more suggestive than
Homer's "rosy fingered Dawn", who is a nonchalant cliché (and, I
should add, meant to be). We make poetic contact with our human
past by metaphor ; a myth used metaphorically is, if it is properly
handled, a myth used after its literal belief has passed away in order to
explore areas of feeling and awareness to which that myth can still be
made relevant. And the relevance is not simple ; it is complex and
suggestive, revealing that there both is and is not a "general nature",
that the primitive mind is still with us but so changed, or so hidden,
that a revelation of it, and the relating of it to our present ways of
thinking and feeling, startles us into a new awareness of the human
dimension. And this also must be said : if the human dimension is
wholly unpredictable and basically different from one generation to
another, then there is no great literature, and the idea of it is a delusion.
To that extent I would have to agree with Dr Johnson.

Metaphor is the time- and the space-binder. It represents the
earliest impulse to poetry and enables the poet to make usable the
faded beliefs of other times and places. Keats's nightingale is the
prime symbol of such a time- and space-binder ; like the Grecian urn
it binds the generations in a common awareness of timeless beauty,
and it also binds "emperor and clown".

Professor Reidar Christiansen, of the Norwegian Folklore Institute
at Oslo, has tried to show the relation between myth and metaphor by
discussing the riddle of folk-lore.[4] He mentions the rainbow riddles,
for example, quoting several Norwegian versions, such as this :
"There is a bridge across a river. / It is neither rotten nor raw. / No one
can walk across it / And nobody can cut bits from it." And I think
of dozens from my childhood in Scotland. Here is one :

> Come a riddle, come a riddle,
> Come a rot-tot-tot ;

[4] "Myth, Metaphor, and Simile", in *Myth : A Symposium*, ed. Thos. A. Sebeok,
Philadelphia, American Folklore Society, 1955, p. 43.

A wee, wee man in a red, red coat ;
A staff in his hand and a bane in his throat :
Come a riddle, come a riddle,
Come a rot-tot-tot.

The answer is "a cherry". Or this one, to which the answer is "an egg" :

There's a wee, wee hoose,
An' it's fu' o' meat ;
But neither door nor window
Will let you in tae eat.

There is a crude enough poetic impulse at work here, but it is the true one. To see one thing as another, is to say that the two things are both the same and different ; this dual awareness is poetic in kind. If this does not sound altogether too trivial an example, I might say that to compare an egg to a house is to increase awareness of the place in human experience of both eggs and houses. In metaphor we both believe and don't believe ; or perhaps it is better to say that in pro- ducing a metaphor a poet is drawing attention to ways of knowing that are not dependent on literal belief. That is why poets have always found it hard to come to terms with the surface realities of their own civilisation as a source of poetic imagery. The poet needs the tension between what he believes, because it is in front of his nose, and what he believes not because it is literally and physically true, but because by supposing it to be true he finds he achieves a new dimension for the literal truth. Classical mythology haunted the Christian imagination for centuries ; it could not be true, yet if you talk about the Garden of Eden in terms of the Garden of the Hesperides, as Milton does, you get a deeper awareness of what the Garden of Eden means or might mean —you increase its area of human implication. It is fascinating to watch Milton, in *Paradise Lost,* manipulating biblical story into classical terms and back again and to see the effects he achieves by this. In describing the early activities of Satan and his crew he pauses, when he comes to the fallen angel whom the Greeks were to worship as Hephaestus and the Romans as Vulcan, to tell the Greek story of his being thrown out of heaven by Zeus. The whole tone of the narrative suddenly projects the reader into a fabled summer eve in the ancient Greek world :

> and in Ausonian land
> Men calld him *Mulciber* and how he fell
> From Heav'n, they fabl'd, thrown by angry *Jove*
> Sheer ore the Crystal battlements : from Morn
> To Noon he fell, from Noon to dewy Eve,
> A Summers day; and with the setting Sun
> Dropd from the Zenith like a falling Star
> On Lemnos th' *Aegean* Ile.

Or consider Milton's description of unfallen Eve, naked and innocent, ministering to the angel Raphael :

> but *Eve*
> Undeckt, save with her self, more lovely fair
> Than Wood-Nymph, or the fairest Goddess feigned
> Of three that in Mount *Ida* naked strove,
> Stood to entertain her guest from Heav'n ; . . .

There is a counterpointing of levels of reality here—at least they were different levels of reality to Milton—a deliberate playing with different kinds of meaning and of reference, which would repay the closest analysis.

Metaphor is often the more obvious means by which poetry makes contact with myth and straddles different kinds of meaning and of reference. But sometimes a great writer can incorporate elements from myth or folk-lore more directly, in a deliberate attempt to impose a new level of meaning on a literal situation. This, it seems to me, is what Shakespeare did with his use of Bassanio, Portia, and the casket plot in *The Merchant of Venice*. Bassanio is clearly related to the lucky youngest son of folk-lore. A fortune hunter and a moral light-weight in any realistic context, he represents the corrective wisdom with which an anonymous folk literature often counters the neat moral patterns of the formal religious teachers of a people. Some people, like Jack the Giant Killer and others who are consistently favoured by good luck, are simply born to be lucky, and their good luck has nothing to do with character. Bassanio chooses the right casket in Belmont not because he is the wisest of Portia's suitors, but simply because he is the luckiest. And this represents a truth : there are occasions when luck goes further than wisdom. But Belmont is a magic environment, where the moon is always at the full and the roses are always in bloom, and any predestined Lucky Jim who goes there can be sure that he will win the hand of the fair lady. One might think that an appropriate element in this mythic picture of predestinate good fortune in a magic city would be Shylock, the fairy-tale villain derived straight from medieval folk-lore : but in handling Shylock, Shakespeare is led to develop a kind of psychological realism which makes it very difficult, if not impossible, for us to accept Shylock as an inhabitant of Bassanio's world at all. Indeed, he almost destroys it, and Shakespeare has a hard time trying to patch things up again with music and moonlight and violets, using Jessica's marriage (which, in Shylock's world, is a savage business, though in Belmont it is right and inevitable) as an excuse for setting these overtones going. Perhaps it would have been better if Shakespeare had kept the two worlds going by poetic metaphor, as he does so richly and brilliantly in *Antony and Cleopatra*, where the hero and heroine are simultaneously both shoddy and magnificent. The court scene in *The Merchant of Venice* will not stay in the magic world of Belmont, but breaks right out of that atmosphere to reflect back on the world of Bassanio and the caskets in such a way that the two worlds are not counterpointed against each other but rather threaten each other. And Shylock's world, being the stronger, wins. This is not to say that Shylock is a romantic hero ; he is a conventional comic villain, a stage Jew, who ought to have been given no more individual reality than the stage Italian of the time or the stage Irishman of the nineteenth century. But he is treated as a given person in a given time and place, and when he or his creator uses metaphor it is not to counterpoint his world against that of Belmont but rather to commit him to mankind as we know it. *The Merchant of Venice* is a remarkable play, but I have always felt that the poetry in it—the metaphorical and other devices— is turned in the wrong direction, relating each of the two worlds independently to us rather than relating them first to each other before presenting to us a complex and richly suggestive patterning of ex- perience. It is an interesting example of a great dramatic poet not wholly coming to terms with the mythic elements in his plot, and failing to use metaphor as a binder in the proper sense.

I have not tried to present a theory of myth, or of metaphor, or of poetry. My task has rather been to reflect aloud on some of the mean- ings of these terms and on some of the ways in which they can helpfully be looked at by someone who is concerned to account for the kinds of excitement and illumination we get from poetry. One exaggerates or oversimplifies here, strains an analogy there, hews out a pattern somewhere else, in an endeavour to point towards a truth too complex or too elusive for complete schematic expression. I have tried simply to suggest some fruitful ways of thinking about the subject.

2

Misunderstanding as Humour: An Aspect of the English Comic Tradition[1]

One of the most frequently discussed themes in modern literature throughout the whole western world is alienation. Not only does the artist often feel himself alienated in our society: every individual, in virtue of his individuality, is seen as locked in his private consciousness and so unable to communicate adequately with his fellows. This is felt as a dilemma, often a tragic dilemma. Eliot's J. Alfred Prufrock is afraid of saying what he means lest someone

> Should say : "That is not what I meant at all.
> That is not it, at all."

The most extreme form of this dilemma is presented by Conrad in *Under Western Eyes* where the hero is forced by circumstances to act out a wholly false role, and to engage in gestures of communication that are diametrically opposed to his real situation. Virginia Woolf's Mrs Dalloway is concerned to make real contact with people and is continually driven back on to her sense of her own lonely individuality. Joyce's Leopold Bloom, wandering around Dublin with his consciousness continuously charged with thoughts and feelings from his own private history, never achieves real communication with anybody. Yet in Joyce there is also a comic element in this predicament. In the fifth section of *Ulysses* ("The Lotus Eaters") Bloom presents Bantam Lyons with his newspaper, remarking "I was just going to throw it away", and then, on Lyons expressing surprise and interest he repeats : "I was just going to throw it away that moment." Lyons, whose mind is occupied entirely with horse-racing, imagines

[1] Delivered at the Fifth Congress of the Société des Anglicistes de l'Enseignement Supérieur, Lille, March 1965.

19

that this is Bloom's cryptic way of telling him to bet on a horse called "Throwaway" in a race to be run that day. The horse in fact wins the race, and much later in the novel, in the "Cyclops" episode, Bloom enters a public house with the charitable intention of raising money to help Paddy Dignam's widow only to find that everybody there, having been told by Lyons that Bloom had bet on "Throwaway", thinks he must have made a lot on money on the race and expects him therefore to stand drinks all round. Bloom is of course totally unaware of this false view and this expectation, and the resulting situation is comic. But it is not entirely comic. Bloom and the frequenters of the pub talk at cross purposes, with Bloom becoming more and more isolated from the others, until at last he becomes the object of anti-semitic and xenophobic feeling. His humane and sensible remarks are met by jeers and finally by threats of violence, and he escapes only in the nick of time.

Joyce here shows himself aware of both the comic and the tragic possibilities of misunderstanding. The characteristic modern attitude to the phenomenon is tragic. The lessons taught by modern psychology about the significance of the individual's private consciousness (and of the subconscious too), and the importance of the whole previous history of that consciousness for an understanding of the individual at any given moment of time, have been learnt all too well. The signals we send out from our personal centres of thought and feeling are inevitably misunderstood by the recipient, who reads them in the light of his own thoughts and feelings and so adapts them to his own needs, getting them wrong. On this view, loneliness is a part of the human condition, and the possibilities of true communication are few and precious. The relationships which man's social nature imposes on him are for the most part mechanical and unsatisfactory ; writers like E. M. Forster and D. H. Lawerence explored ways in which more genuine relationships could—precariously and with difficulty—be established.

If Joyce is a rare example among modern writers to see this pre-dicament as capable of yielding comedy, this does not mean that its comic aspects have not been widely explored in earlier literature. Indeed, modern psychology is not unique in emphasising the special nature of the individual consciousness. In the seventeenth century John Locke produced an immensely popular theory of consciousness based on the individual chain of association which he saw as the result of the particular experiences and sensations which the accidents of each individual life produced. The association of ideas produced habits of mind and thus formed character. The same words would have different associations for different people, so that people might imagine they were communicating by employing a common vocabulary when in fact each was talking about something quite different. The classic example of this is the relationship between Walter and Toby Shandy in Sterne's *Tristram Shandy*. Sterne inferred from Locke's psychology and epistomology a doctrine of the isolation of the individual consciousness very similar to that which modern writers learned from Freud and other modern psychologists. But, as this inference was not in Sterne's case linked with any more general feeling of the decline of a civilisation or the disintegration of the norms that held society together, as it was for so many modern writers, he felt it natural to use it comically, not tragically. And long before Sterne, an even earlier psychological theory—the theory of humours—had produced an awareness of the ways in which an individual can be obsessed with one set of ideas and responses, so that in talking to others he misinterprets their remarks entirely in the light of his own obsessions. A dialogue between two such obsessed persons, each dominated by a different "humour", could produce a richly comic situation. That is after all how we got the English word "humour". Humour, in the sense of individual psychological and mental make-up, produces oddity ; and oddity is, or can be, funny. It was as natural for Ben Jonson to think of a Comedy of Humours as it is for so many modern writers to think of a tragedy (or at least a *black* comedy) of humours.

My point is, then, that for a long period in the history of English literature misunderstanding, deriving from the clash of opposing idiosyncrasies, has been a fruitful source of comedy, and only in fairly modern times, as a result of changes in what might be called the general texture of civilisation, has it been seen as a tragic theme. I have mentioned Sterne as an example of the older treatment. He is perhaps an extreme case, for the whole of *Tristram Shandy* is, from one point of view, an illustration of the meaning in terms of human behaviour, human relationships, and human feelings, of aspects of Locke's *Essay Concerning Human Understanding*, from the opening joke about the winding of the clock to Uncle Toby's misunderstanding of the nature of Mrs Wadman's concern for his wound. The initial

sentences of the novel emphasise the significance of individual temperament :

> I wish either my father or my mother, or indeed both of them, as
> they were in duty both equally bound to it, had minded what they
> were about when they begot me ; had they duly consider'd how much
> depended upon what they were then doing ;—that not only the pro-
> duction of a rational Being was concern'd in it, but that possibly the
> happy formation and temperature of his body, perhaps his genius and
> the very cast of his mind ;—and, for aught they knew to the contrary,
> even the fortunes of his whole house might take their turn from the
> humours and dispositions which were then uppermost :—

"Perhaps his genius and the very cast of his mind" ; "the humours
and dispositions which were then uppermost" ;—thus Sterne gives
notice at once that he is going to make capital out of individual
temperament, though as it turns out it is not the temperament of the
narrator, Tristram Shandy, but that of his father, his uncle, and others.
When Mrs Shandy asked her husband whether he had remembered to
wind up the clock, at a delicate moment in the history of Tristram's
begetting, with consequences for Tristram's physical and psychological
make-up, it was because

> from an unhappy association of ideas which have no connection in
> nature, it so fell out at length, that my poor mother could never hear
> the said clock wound up,—but the thoughts of some other things
> unavoidably popp'd into her head, —and *vice versa:*—which strange
> combination of ideas, the sagacious *Locke,* who certainly understood
> the nature of these things better than most men, affirms to have pro-
> duced more wry actions than all other sources of prejudice whatsoever.

Sterne here is absolutely frank about the source of his humour ;
the individual association of ideas, Locke maintained and Sterne
agreed, have "produced more wry actions" than anything else. It is
the "wry" behaviour of his characters (and the basic meaning of the
word is "twisted" or "distorted") that results in comic situations and
more especially in comic encounters that produce nothing but mutual
misunderstanding.

> *For if you will turn your eyes inwards upon your mind,* continued my
> father, *and observe attentively, you will perceive, brother, that whilst you and
> I are talking together, and thinking and smoking our pipes : or whilst
> we receive successively ideas in our minds, we know that we do exist, and
> so we estimate the existence, or the continuation of the existence of our-*

selves, or any thing else commensurate to the succession of any ideas in *our minds, the duration of ourselves, or any such other thing co existing* *with our thinking,—and so according to that preconceived*—You puzzle me to death, cried my uncle *Toby.*—

—'Tis owing to this, replied my father, that in our computations of *time*, we are so used to minutes, hours, weeks and months,—and of clocks (I wish there was not a clock in the kingdom) to measure out their several portions to us, and to those who belong to us,—that 'twill be well, if in time to come, the *succession of our ideas* be of any use or service to us at all.

Now, whether we observe it or no, continued my father, in every sound man's head, there is a regular succession of ideas of one sort or other, which follow each other in train just like—A train of artillery? said my uncle *Toby.*—A train of a fiddle stick!—quoth my father,— which follow and succeed one another in our minds at certain distances, just like the images in the inside of a lanthorn turned round by the heat of a candle.—I declare, quoth my uncle *Toby*, mine are like a smoak-jack.—Then, brother *Toby*, I have nothing more to say to you upon the subject, said my father.

Toby is obsessed with military matters and his theory of sieges and fortifications, so that when his brother Walter talks of ideas "following each other in train" the only train he can think of is a train of artillery. This kind of situation occurs again and again in the novel, with each brother misunderstanding the other because each interprets the other's words in the light of his own obsessions. Sometimes the misunderstanding is purely verbal, like that which resulted in Tristram's name ; he was meant by his father (who was obsessed with a theory of names) to be called Trismegistus. When the maid Susannah delivered to the curate the message that the the infant was to be baptised "Tristramgistus" the curate replied : "There is no *gistus* to it, noodle !—'tis my own name." And he christened the child "Tristram", a name to which Mr Shandy had a particular aversion. This is in a way a microcosm of the whole book. " 'Tis my own name." The curate interpreted the slightly garbled message in the light of his own interests and knowledge. "Trismegistus", having become "Tristramgistus" through ignorance, now becomes "Tristram" through irrelevant knowledge.

Or consider this little passage :

'Tis a pity, said my father, that truth can only be on one side, brother *Toby*,—considering what ingenuity these learned men have all shewn in their solutions of noses.—Can noses be dissolved! replied my uncle *Toby*.—

A common source of humour is the taking literally of a metaphor. Walter Shandy is complaining of the lashes he has received from Fate, and his brother Toby takes him literally :

> Did ever man, brother Toby, cried my father, raising himself up upon his elbow, and turning himself round to the opposite side of the bed where my uncle *Toby* was sitting in his old fringed chair, with his chin resting upon his crutch—did ever a poor unfortunate man, brother *Toby*, cried my father, receive so many lashes?—The most I ever saw given, quoth my uncle *Toby*, (ringing the bell at the bed's head for *Trim*) was to a grenadier, I think in *Mekay's* regiment.
>
> —Had my uncle *Toby* shot a bullet thro' my father's heart, he could not have fallen down with his nose upon the quilt more suddenly.
>
> Bless me! said my uncle *Toby*.

Tristram's nose was crushed by the doctor's forceps as he was being delivered, and the doctor proceeds to make a false bridge out of cotton and whalebone.

> When *Trim* came in and told my father, that Dr *Slop* was in the kitchen, and busy in making a bridge,—my uncle *Toby*,—the affair of the jack-boots having just then raised a train of military ideas in his brain,— took it instantly for granted that Dr *Slop* was making a model of the marquis *d'Hôpital's* bridge.—'Tis very obliging in him, quoth my uncle *Toby* ;—pray give my humble service to Dr *Slop*, *Trim*, and tell him I thank him heartily.

Walter Shandy, on hearing of the death of his son (Tristram's elder brother), consoles himself by quoting from Cicero's *Epistolae ad Familiores*, with odd consequences :

> "Returning out of Asia, when I sailed from *Ægina* towards *Megara*," (*when can this have been? thought my uncle Toby*) "I began to view the country round about. *Ægina* was behind me, *Megara* was before, *Pyraeus* on the right hand, *Corinth* on the left.—What flourishing towns now prostrate upon the earth! Alas! alas! said I to myself, that man should disturb his soul for the loss of a child, when so much as this lies awfully buried in his presence—Remember, said I to myself again—remember thou art a man."—
>
> Now my uncle *Toby* knew not that this last paragraph was an extract of *Servius Sulpicius's* consolatory letter to *Tully*.—He had as little

skill, honest man, in the fragments, as he had in the whole pieces of antiquity.—And as my father, whilst he was concerned in the *Turky* trade, had been three or four different times in the *Levant*, in one of which he had staid a whole year and an half at Zant, my uncle *Toby* naturally concluded, that in some one of these periods he had taken a trip across the *Archipelago* into *Asia*; and that all this sailing affair with *Ægina* behind, and *Megara* before, and *Pyraeus* on the right hand, etc. etc. was nothing more than the true course of my father's voyage and reflections.—'Twas certainly in his *manner*, and many an undertaking critick would have built two stories higher upon worse foundations.—And pray, brother, quoth my uncle *Toby*, laying the end of his pipe upon my father's hand in a kindly way of interruption— but waiting till he finished the account—what year of our Lord was this?—'Twas no year of our Lord, replied my father.—That's impossible, cried my uncle *Toby*.—Simpleton! said my father,—'twas forty years before Christ was born.

My uncle *Toby* had but two things for it; either to suppose his brother to be the wandering *Jew*, or that his misfortunes had disordered his brain.—"May the Lord God of heaven and earth protect him and restore him," said my uncle *Toby*, praying silently for my father, and with tears in his eyes.

The Sternian hobby-horse is of course the Jonsonian humour; each results in comedy, satirical in Jonson and sentimental in Sterne. Sterne's is sentimental in the sense that while he recognises that individual hobby-horses make true communication impossible, he sees this as overcome by affectionate *feeling*. Again and again we find that after the two brothers Shandy have endeavoured in vain to communicate, and each has become bogged down in his private misinterpretation of the other's words, one brother or the other is overcome with a rush of affection and breaks the deadlock by a loving look or touch. Unlike Ben Jonson and unlike the moderns, Sterne believed that while egotism can prevent adequate communication it is not incompatible with love. From one point of view it could be said to be sentimental to hold that solipsism and love can co-exist. Sterne's sentimentalism is necessary in order to enable him to get out of a solipsistic world. Uncle Toby lives in an obsessive world of his own, yet he has a tender and a loving heart, without which he would be totally cut off from his fellows. Ben Jonson regarded the obsessed man as the exception, to be mocked out of his obsessions by satire back into a right frame of mind and into a right relationship with society. But Sterne regarded the

C

obsessed man as the norm—we *all* have our hobby-horses—so that satire cannot help. The only available reactions to this are sentimentality or despair, and civilisation was not felt to be precarious enough in Sterne's time to warrant the latter alternative. The sentimental solution leaves it open to us to see oddity as *comic*, since we do not have to regard it as making human communion impossible. Of course oddity is comic in Ben Jonson too, but there it is satirically comic. In Sterne (as often though not always in Dickens) oddity is affectionately comic.

A simpler kind of misunderstanding, which has been the source of humour in many different areas of English literature, is the purely verbal misunderstanding resulting not from an inner obsession but from sheer ignorance. This is related to the kind of humour that, as I have already noted, can be derived from making one character take literally what another intends metaphorically. Shakespeare, particularly in his earlier plays, is not above the sort of verbal humour which is based on differences in education. When in *Love's Labour's Lost*, Armado gives Costard a tip saying "There is remuneration", Costard looks at the money :

> Now will I look to his remuneration. Remuneration! O that's the Latin word for three farthings : three farthings, remuneration. "What's the price of this inkle?" "One penny" : "No, I'll give you a remuneration" : why, it carries it. Remuneration! why it is a fairer name than French crown. I will never buy and sell out of this word.

Later, when he gets a shilling from Berowne with the remark "There's thy guerdon", Costard exclaims :

> Gardon, O sweet gardon! better than remuneration ; a 'leven-pence farthing better. Most sweet gardon!

One can make a pretentious generalisation about this kind of humour, and say that it arises when someone hears for the first time a word which denotes a class of things and takes it to refer only to the particular member of that class which is involved at that moment—as though a one-eyed Siamese cat were referred to as an animal in the presence of someone who had never heard the word "animal" and who therefore wrongly inferred that "animal" meant "one-eyed Siamese cat". But what is more interesting about this kind of humour in English literature is the class feeling which nearly always surrounds it. In this respect it is closely related to the humour of Malapropisms, which arise when someone tries to use a speech too elaborate for his education. The misuse by the uneducated of the language of the educated is of course common in Shakespeare as it is in English fiction particularly of the nineteenth century. The classic, and indeed the seminal, example is the case of Dogberry and Verges in *Much Ado About Nothing* :

DOGBERRY.   Are you good men and true?

VERGES.   Yea, or else it were pity but they should suffer salvation body and soul.

DOGBERRY.   Nay, that were a punishment too good for them, if they have any allegiance in them, being chosen for the Prince's watch.

VERGES.   Well, give them their charge, neighbour Dogberry.

DOGBERRY.   First, who think you the most desartless man to be constable?

Later, Dogberry tells his colleague, "You are thought here to be the most senseless and fit man for the constable of the watch."

Or consider this, from a later scene :

DOGBERRY.   Comparisons are odorous—palabras, neighbour Verges.

LEONATO.   Neighbours, you are tedious.

DOGBERRY.   It pleases your worship to say so, but we are the poor Duke's officers. But truly for mine own part if I were as tedious as a king, I could find in my heart to bestow it all of your worship.

LEONATO.   All thy tediousness on me, ah?

DOGBERRY.   Yea, an 'twere a thousand pound more than 'tis, for I hear as good exclamation on your worship as of any man in the city ; and though I be a poor man, I am glad to hear it.

There are all kinds of variations to be found in this kind of verbal humour. Bottom's mis-punctuation in his reading of the prologue to his play in Act V of *A Midsummer Night's Dream* is an obvious kind of variation. He had already shown himself a master-Malapropist. ("There we may rehearse most obscenely and courageously".) There is a relationship between the humour of verbal misunderstanding, and the humour of the pun. Consider, for example, how in this passage

from *Twelfth Night* Sir Toby's misunderstandings of Maria's words
are partly wilful; and, in so far as they are wilful, they involve
deliberate punning :

> MARIA.   By my troth, Sir Toby, you must come in earlier o'
>   nights. Your cousin, my lady, takes great exception to
>   your ill hours.
>
> SIR TOBY.   Why, let her except before excepted.
>
> MARIA.   Ay, but you must confine yourself within the modest
>   limits of order.
>
> SIR TOBY.   Confine? I'll confine myself no finer than I am. These
>   clothes are good enough to drink in, and so be these boots
>   too ; an they be not, let them hang themselves in their
>   own straps.

As between Maria and Sir Toby, the misunderstandings are generally
mischievous and wilful ; as between Sir Toby and Sir Andrew they
are more often the result of pure stupidity on Sir Andrew's part, a
stupidity relished and encouraged by his friend. Shakespeare con-
structs a delicate spectrum which ranges all the way from wholly
wilful to wholly ignorant misapprehension. The comedy of verbal
misunderstanding is here indulged in with great artistry and great
zest.

It is interesting that in *Twelfth Night* the humour of verbal misunderstanding is not based on class feeling, as in some degree it is
with Dogberry and Verges. Normally the class element in this kind
of humour is clearly perceptible. This element can be even more
clearly seen when the situation involves not just the language but the
whole action, as in Goldsmith's *She Stoops to Conquer*. Here is a most
clear case of comedy based on misunderstanding : the whole plot
depends on two gentlemen imagining that a private house is an inn
and treating the daughter of the house as though she were an inn
servant. I don't suppose it ever occurred to Goldsmith that a time
would come when the idea that you treated a girl differently, according
to whether she was a gentleman's daughter or an innkeeper's daughter,
would be regarded as monstrous, though it is not at all long ago since
the authorities of some colleges at England's two older universities
imposed quite different standards governing the behaviour of under-
graduates with respect to "ladies" and to "women". This kind of
class comedy dies hard. The nineteenth-century novel was full of

characters who after successfully masquerading as a "lady" or a "gentleman" for a certain period, were finally unmasked as the bounders they really were. Thackeray's Becky Sharp is only the best known of many of her kind, both male and female. The Victorians tended to make melodrama or at least high social fiction out of such situations, rather than comedy. There is nothing comic about poor Ferdinand Lopez in Trollope's *The Prime Minister*; though he is intelligent and personable, he is not a gentleman, and he is of Portuguese (perhaps even Jewish) origin to boot. It is not therefore surprising that he ends by committing suicide. The comedy of social misunderstanding—where one character mistakes another's true social status and addresses him in the language appropriate to the wrongly supposed status—is mostly pre-Victorian. *Verbal* humour based on class distinctions continues, however, throughout the nineteenth century.

In Goldsmith's play the irony is minimal and the misunderstanding is accidental in origin, even though encouraged by the heroine for her own purposes once it has developed. Maliciously induced misunderstanding can yield a much grimmer kind of comedy, as in Ben Jonson's *Volpone*. *Gulling* is misunderstanding deliberately created to serve the ends of the guller, and is related to the deceptions of the pseudo-gentleman adventurer in Victorian fiction. Gulling can be enjoyed as comedy only if the reader or spectator identifies himself in considerable degree with the guller so that he can watch with pleasure the deluded responses of the gulled. One of the difficulties about *Volpone* is that we are invited to admire the artfulness of Volpone and Mosca, and though we are at the same time invited to condemn them morally, this invitation is less than overwhelming in view of the fact that their wiles are exerted on people at least as reprehensible as they. Gulled and guller are alike immoral (we find the same pattern in *The Alchemist*), and this gives us a sort of moral excuse for admiring the guller. When one guller is over-reached by his co-guller we can feel moral satisfaction that *somebody's* evil practices are coming home to roost while still admiring the virtuosity of the remaining guller. But the basis of the ironic humour is misunderstanding, wilfully induced and wickedly enjoyed by the inducers. This is what happens in that great scene at the beginning of *Volpone* where Volpone feigns to be dying and Mosca his servant gets Volpone's alleged friends to visit him with expensive presents on the grounds that Mosca will persuade Volpone

to leave his immense wealth to the most generous of his friends. Mosca
has persuaded Corvino that he is Volpone's heir.

CORVINO. He is not dead?

MOSCA.   Not dead, sir, but as good ;
He knows no man.

CORVINO.   How shall I do, then?

MOSCA.   Why, sir?

CORVINO. I have brought him here a pearl.

MOSCA.   Perhaps he has
So much remembrance left as to know you, sir :
He still calls on you ; nothing but your name
Is in his mouth.   Is your pearl orient, sir?

CORVINO. Venice was never owner of the like.

VOLPONE. Signior Corvino!

MOSCA.   Hark!

VOLPONE.   Signior Corvino!

MOSCA. He calls you.   Step and give it him.
[To VOLPONE] He's here, sir,
And he has brought you a rich pearl.

CORVINO.   How do you, sir?
Tell him it doubles the twelfth carat.

MOSCA.   Sir,
He cannot understand : his hearing's gone ;
And yet it comforts him to see you—

CORVINO.   Say
I have a diamond for him too.

MOSCA.   Best show it, sir ;
Put it into his hand : 'tis only there
He apprehends.   He has his feeling yet.
See how he grasps it!

CORVINO.   Alas, good gentleman!
How pitiful the sight is!

MOSCA.   Tut, forget, sir.
The weeping of an heir should still be laughter
Under a visor.

CORVINO.   Why, am I his heir?

MOSCA. Sir, I am sworn : I may not show the will
Till he be dead ; but here has been Corbaccio,
Here has been Voltore, here were others too—

I cannot number 'em, they were so many—
All gaping here for legacies ; but I,
Taking the vantage of his naming you,
"Signor Corvino, Signor Corvino," took
Paper, and pen, and ink, and there I asked him
Whom he would have his heir! "Corvino." Who
Should be executor? "Corvino." And
To any question he was silent to,
I still interpreted the nods he made,
Through weakness, for consent ; and sent home the
    others,
Nothing bequeathed them but to cry and curse.

CORVINO.   O, my dear Mosca. [*They embrace*]. Does he not
    perceive us?

MOSCA.   No more than a blind harper. He knows no man,
No face of friend, nor name of any servant,
Who 'twas that fed him last, or gave him drink ;
Not those he hath begotten, or brought up,
Can he remember.

CORVINO.   Has he children?

MOSCA.   Bastards,
Some dozen or more that he begot on beggars,
Gypsies, and Jews, and black-moors, when he was drunk.
Knew you not that, sir? 'Tis the common fable
The dwarf, the fool, the eunuch, are all his ;
He's the true father of his family,
In all save me—but he has given them nothing.

CORVINO.   That's well, that's well! Art sure he does not hear us?

MOSCA.   Sure, sir? Why, look you, credit your own sense.
[*Shouting in* VOLPONE's *ear :*] The pox approach and add
    to your diseases,
If it would send you hence the sooner, sir.
For your incontinence, it hath deserved it
Throughly and throughly, and the plague to boot!
[*To* CORVINO] You may come near, sir.
[*To* VOLPONE] Would you would once close
Those filthy eyes of yours, that flow with slime
Like two frog-pits ; and those same hanging cheeks,
Covered with hide instead of skin—
    [*To* CORVINO] Nay, help, sir—
That look like frozen dish-clouts set on end!

CORVINO. Or like an old smoked wall, on which the rain
Ran down in streaks!

MOSCA. Excellent, sir, speak out;
You may be louder yet: a culverin
Discharged in his ear would hardly bore it.

CORVINO. His nose is like a common sewer, still running.

MOSCA. 'Tis good! And what his mouth?

CORVINO. A very draught.

MOSCA. O, stop it up—

CORVINO. By no means.

MOSCA. Pray you, let me.
Faith, I could stifle him rarely with a pillow
As well as any woman that should keep him.

CORVINO. Do as you will, but I'll begone.

MOSCA. Be so;
It is your presence makes him last so long.

CORVINO. I pray you use no violence.

MOSCA. No, sir? Why?
Why should you be thus scrupulous, pray you, sir?

CORVINO. Nay, at your discretion.

MOSCA. Well, good sir, be gone.

CORVINO. I will not trouble him now to take my pearl.

MOSCA. Pooh! Nor your diamond. What a needless care
Is this afflicts you? Is not all here yours?
Am not I here, whom you have made your creature?
That own my being to you?

CORVINO. Grateful Mosca!
Thou art my friend, my fellow, my companion,
My partner, and shalt share in all my fortunes.

This is a very sophisticated use of misunderstanding in ironic comedy. First, there is Corvino's misunderstanding of Volpone's true condition. Volpone is only feigning illness. Then there is the misunderstandings induced by Mosca, about Volpone's intentions towards Corvino. Finally there is that peculiarly savage kind of humour that arises from Corvino's belief in Volpone's insensibility and his shouting insults at him under the impression that he cannot hear or understand. This last kind of humour is common in recent times in certain kinds of film comedies where an English or American character, imagining a foreigner to be ignorant of English, talks the most abusive nonsense to the foreigner with a smiling expression as though paying compliments, only to find in the end that the foreigner has a perfect knowledge of English. Jonson doesn't do this double-take at the end, because he has grimmer double-takes to produce in the play—Mosca's own double-crossing of Volpone and the final over-reaching themselves of both characters.

What is going on in *Volpone* is different from what goes on in the earlier Jonsonian comedy of humours. There, the obsessive behaviour of individuals is noted with ironic relish. But here, as in *The Alchemist*, everyone is obsessed with the same passion—greed—and as a result of this not only can they not communicate genuinely with each other— they do not wish to communicate. It is not a question of exposing your true self and being misunderstood, as it is in Sterne. It is a question of never daring or wanting to expose your true self. Greed induces selfishness, which makes men incapable of seeking, let alone of enjoying, community. Corvino in the end wants to prostitute his wife to Volpone in order to do him the final favour and secure his position as Volpone's heir. Similarly, Corbaccio disinherits his son in Volpone's favour. All human relationships are destroyed. But one is not even left with the individual in his solipsistic world, for the mass of pretences which greed has forced on each character's behaviour has resulted in all reality disappearing from their personalities. They have no real character any more. Everybody has been so busy trying to gull everybody else, concealing his own true situation and motives and endeavouring to pull the wool over others' eyes, that misunder-standing has reached a point of absurdity : everything and everyone is misunderstood, and people misunderstand themselves. What begins with deliberately induced misunderstanding which we can watch as comedy with some reluctant admiration for the deceivers and con-tempt for the deceived, ends as a frightening chaos with deception of others and self-deception prevailing everywhere and the truth of human personality savaged into nothingness. If you spend your life misleading others you end by not being able to understand even your-self, for there will be no real self left to understand. The hero of Conrad's *Under Western Eyes* has enough integrity of personality left to get himself out of this sort of situation by an act of deliberate self-sacrifice. Volpone and Mosca, the fox and the fly, have no such resources available to them ; they have reduced themselves to the

level of the animals signified by their names. Once misunderstanding
has been unleashed as a policy, its destructive force is overwhelming.
This is a very special kind of comedy of misunderstanding, a grimly
ironic comedy equally far from the worlds of hobby-horses, malapropisms and social masquerading.

   The comedy of Jonson's *Volpone* thus stands apart from most other
kinds of comedy based on misunderstanding, though we can find in
English fiction more gently satirical varieties of misunderstanding
which show kinship with some of those employed by Jonson in this
play. A misapprehension of the situation leading to a speaker's utter
lack of awareness of the real impact of what he is saying, such as we
find when Corvino abuses the supposedly dying Volpone, has points
of similarity (as well as points of great difference) with the kind of
thing we find, for example, in Jane Austen's *Pride and Prejudice* when
Mr Collins proposes to Elizabeth Bennet and is so completely unaware
of how ridiculous he is making himself that he takes Elizabeth's strong
and almost contemptuous refusal as a maidenly kind of acceptance :

> "I am not now to learn," replied Mr Collins, with a formal wave of
> the hand, "that it is usual with young ladies to reject the addresses of
> the man whom they secretly mean to accept, when he first applies for
> their favour ; and that sometimes the refusal is repeated a second or
> even a third time. . I am therefore by no means discouraged by what
> you have just said, and shall hope to lead you to the altar ere long."

The humour of this situation is clearly based on misunderstanding,
and Elizabeth's increasing bewilderment and finally anger at Mr
Collins' inability to see that she is rejecting him as firmly as can be
done in the English language puts her in a comic predicament as well
as Mr Collins. Mr Collins' inability to understand what Elizabeth
means is the result of his own preposterous self-importance, and this
point is linked to the most central areas of Jane Austen's moral
imagination. Self-importance and preoccupation with one's social
status can make it impossible for a person to achieve true communion
with anyone else. Mr Collins' patroness, Lady Catherine, suffers from
a similar fault with similar consequences for her character, and in Jane
Austen's *Emma* Mr Elton's fatuous proposal to the heroine is the
result of a similar kind of self-importance, a fault of both the Eltons,
which renders them insensitive and at the same time comic in their
blithe unawareness of their insensitivity.

Jane Austen constantly uses misunderstanding as a means of revealing, chastening, and educating her characters, though it is only the good characters who are chastened and educated—the bad are only exposed and mocked. *Emma*, of course, is a novel based on the misunderstandings that derive from a lack of self-knowledge and proper humility on the part of the heroine ; so far as the heroine herself goes, these misunderstandings are educative. Emma deludes herself into thinking that Mr Elton wants to marry Harriet while he really wants to marry herself ; that Frank Churchill is interested in her whereas he is really engaged to Jane Fairfax ; that Harriet's affections have transferred themselves to Frank Churchill whereas they have really been transferred to Mr Knightley ; and so on. All these misunderstandings derive from Emma's misreading of the evidence because she reads it in the light of her own opinions and desires and not of the objective situation. But the situation is more complicated than this, for Emma misreads her own desires : it is only when she discovers that Harriet is thinking of the possibility of marriage with Mr Knightley, and when she believes that Mr Knightley may be in love with Harriet, that she realises that she has been in love with him herself all along. The comic irony of the whole situation involves the fact that Emma's lack of self-knowledge makes her misinterpret the actions and speeches of others because she is deluded by what she wrongly believes to be her own desires. This is a much more complex —and a more seriously moral—use of misunderstanding than, say, Mrs Bardell's misunderstanding of Mr Pickwick's telling her that he had engaged a personal servant to live with him in *The Pickwick Papers*. Dickens is ingenious enough to construct the dialogue in such a way so that while Mr Pickwick is making the perfectly innocent suggestion about his servant, Mrs Bardell plausibly misunderstands him as proposing marriage. The result is very funny, and the consequences important in the latter part of the novel ; but the basic situation represents a very simple formula which has long been popular in music-hall sketches and in vulgar anecdote.

I have talked earlier of the kind of comedy which results from the confrontation of two equally but very differently obsessed characters, and traced this at least as far back as the Jonsonian Comedy of Humours. There is a rather special use of this kind of comedy in a remarkable scene in Scott's *Redgauntlet*, which is worth separate discussion because the comedy serves a very special *critical* purpose. The character called Redgauntlet is a fanatical Jacobite some twenty years after the final collapse of the Jacobite rebellion at the battle of Culloden. His brother, the head of the Redgauntlet family, had been executed at Carlisle in 1746 as one of the leaders of the rebellion. He himself has ever since nursed high romantic hopes of leading a new successful Jacobite rebellion. He has come to associate the Jacobite movement with the lost national independence of Scotland and all the former (highly romanticised) glories of the old kingdom of Scotland. He sees Prince Charlie (now middle-aged and debauched) as Robert the Bruce. He is in fact living in a world that no longer exists, and the pathetic meaninglessness of his dreams is movingly illustrated by Scott when the little band of belated Jacobites is surprised by the loyalist general, who, though he has an army at his back, simply laughs at the rebels and tells them to run away and play. This kind of nonsense is not to be taken seriously in the 1760s and the Jacobites are not now significant enough to warrant persecuting or to merit martyrdom. Now, side by side with his building up of the character of the fanatical Redgauntlet, Scott has been building up in the novel the character of a very different kind of fanatic. This is Peter Peebles, a man who has lost his fortune and his reason in a protracted lawsuit and is now capable of talking only about his own case in technical terms derived from Scots law. The Scottish legal system was one of the two national institutions (the other was the Church) left untouched after the Union of England and Scotland in 1707, so that Scots law became a focus for certain kinds of national feeling in the eighteenth century. But just as the anachronistic dreams of a Stuart restoration destroy Redgauntlet, so Peter Peebles has been destroyed by his clinging all his adult life to Scots law. In the one case a dream of nationhood, in the other a genuine national institution, has proved fatal.

Scott brings the two characters together at the very moment when the reader is most fully aware of Redgauntlet's grandiose ambitions for Jacobitism and for Scotland. Peebles had known Redgauntlet earlier, when he went under the assumed name of Herries of Birrenswork to avoid arrest after the rebellion of 1745. But Redgauntlet is now anxious to disclaim the earlier name and play the part not of a pseudonymous fugitive but of a national hero. He is disconcerted when Peebles addresses him by the old name and totally ignores the histrionic posture which Redgauntlet now habitually assumes. The two obsessions, the legal and the national, confront each other, and in the confrontation is the revelation of the ultimate meaninglessness of Redgauntlet's histrionics about Jacobitism as well as of Peebles' trust in the law :

"Ay, ay, Mr Herries of Birrenswork, is this your ainsell in blood and bane? I thought ye had been hanged at Kennington Common, or Hairiebie, or some of these places, after the bonny ploy ye made in the forty-five."

"I believe you are mistaken, friend," said Herries, sternly, with whose name and designation I was thus made unexpectedly acquainted.

"The deil a bit," answered the undaunted Peter Peebles ; "I mind ye weel, for ye lodged in my house the great year of forty-five, for a great year it was ; the Grand Rebellion broke out, and my cause—the great cause— Peebles against Plainstanes, *et per contra*—was called in the beginning of the winter Session, and would have been heard, but that there was a surcease of justice, with your plaids, and your piping, and your nonsense."

"I tell you fellow," said Herries, yet more fiercely, "you have confused me with some of the other furniture of your crazy pate."

" Speak like a gentleman, sir," answered Peebles ; "these are not legal phrases, Mr Herries of Birrenswork. Speak in form of law, or I shall bid ye gude-day, sir. I have nae pleasure in speaking to proud folk, though I am willing to answer ony thing in a legal way ; so if you are for a crack about auld langsyne, and the splores that you and Captain Redgimlet used to breed in my house, and the girded cask of brandy that ye drank and ne'er thought of paying for it (not that I minded it muckle in thae days, though I have felt a lack of it sinsyne), why I will waste an hour on ye at ony time.—And where is Captain Redgimlet now? he was a wild chap, like yoursell, though they are nae sae keen after you poor bodies for these some years bygane ; the heading and hanging is weel ower now—awful job—awful job—will ye try my sneeshing?"

He concluded his desultory speech by thrusting out his large bony paw, filled with a Scottish mull of huge dimensions, which Herries, who had been standing like one petrified by the assurance of this unexpected address, rejected with a contemptuous motion of his hand, which spilled some of the contents of the box.

"Aweel, aweel," said Peter Peebles, totally unabashed by the repulse, "e'en as ye like, a wilful man maun hae his way ; but," he added, stooping down, and endeavouring to gather the spilt snuff from the polished floor, "I canna afford to lose my sneeshing for a' that ye are gumple-foisted wi' me."

This is Scott criticising his own romanticism, by means of a dialogue which is both comic and diagnostic. It reminds us of Jeanie Deans in *The Heart of Midlothian* saying to the Duke of Argyll "Does your honour like cheese?", or of the confrontation between the melo-dramatic Helen Macgregor and the shrewdly realistic Bailie Nicol Jarvie in *Rob Roy*. But the main point I wish to make here is that in the dialogue between Peter Peebles and Redgauntlet, Scott uses the mutual misunderstanding of obsessed characters in order to expose both the fatuity of living in a romantic dream of the past, and the folly of committing oneself totally and naïvely to an institution of the present. Military glory and legal action are two opposite ways of getting things done ; Scott frequently uses them in deliberate opposi-tion ; here each exposes the other. It is tempting, in an age which wrongly rejects Scott and rightly elevates Dickens, to contrast the characteristically Dickensian kind of confrontation of obsessed characters, which generally serves no large moral or critical purpose but simply adds to the colour and intensity of the narrative at that point, with Scott's critical use of the comedy of obsession in *Redgauntlet*.

The tendency to see mutual misunderstanding as humorous seems to be so built in to human nature that even when a situation involving such misunderstanding is presented with a wholly serious intention the result is often taken to be comic. Nothing could be more seriously intended than Wordsworth's "We Are Seven", and indeed it is not difficult to put oneself when reading it into a frame of mind in which one recognises and appreciates that intention. The fact remains that most readers, in the English-speaking world at least, have always found the poem rather comic. I can certainly vouch for this reaction on the part of generations of students in both Britain and America. The two speakers in the poem are completely at cross purposes :

> "Sisters and brothers, little maid,
> How many may you be?"
> "How many? Seven in all," she said,
> And wondering looked at me.

> "And where are they? I pray you tell."
> She answered, "Seven are we ;
> And two of us at Conway dwell,
> And two are gone to sea.

"Two of us in the church-yard lie,
My sister and my brother;
And, in the church-yard cottage, I
Dwell near them with my mother."

"You say that two at Conway dwell,
And two are gone to sea,
Yet ye are seven! I pray you tell,
Sweet Maid, how this may be."

Then did the little Maid reply,
"Seven boys and girls are we;
Two of us in the church-yard lie,
Beneath the church-yard tree."

"You run about, my little Maid,
Your limbs they are alive;
If two are in the church-yard laid,
Then ye are only five."

But the little maid won't have the poet's arithmetic: "We are seven",
she insists. The poet goes on and on trying to explain to the girl that
she mustn't count the two dead ones, but she remains obstinate:

"But they are dead; those two are dead!
Their spirits are in heaven!"
'Twas throwing words away; for still
The little Maid would have her will,
And said, "Nay, we are seven!"

The humour of the situation lies in the fact that it is the poet and not
the little girl who is obtuse: he fails to realise the way in which the
two dead children play a living part in her imagination. Of course,
Wordsworth is making the point that a child's mind works that way,
and there is the implication that there is something fine about this;
nevertheless, the poet's obstinate questioning creates an unintended
atmosphere of comedy.

Speech developed as an instrument of human communication, but
its existence also implies the possibility of misunderstanding. "You
taught me language; and my profit on't / Is, I know how to curse",
says Caliban to Prospero, emphasising the dangerous as well as the
profitable uses of this ambiguous instrument. Similarly, we might
say that when a man has acquired language he has acquired a powerful

means of deceiving his neighbour. And where there is language there is always liable to be misunderstanding. With language, *Homo sapiens* has developed a permanent source of misunderstanding—and of humour. The conditions under which misunderstanding, engendered by mutually misunderstood speech, can produce comedy rather than frustration, or even tragedy, demand much fuller examination than anybody has yet given to the subject. There is a complete spectrum here, from the simple music-hall humour that arises when one character takes a word or phrase in a different sense from that intended, through the more sophisticated humour provided by the encounter between two different obsessions, to the grimmer comedy of deliberate deception and its moral and pyschological consequences, right on to the tragedy of the isolated individual trapped by the uniqueness of his own consciousness into an inescapable loneliness. And, at each point in the spectrum, different kinds of comedy or of irony or of comment on the human situation can arise.

Many years ago, when I was a junior fellow of Balliol College, Oxford, I had dinner with the young king of Egypt under circumstances which led me to hold the absurdly erroneous notion that he was in fact a country cousin of the Master of Balliol. The result was socially disastrous, but when I wrote it up long afterwards as my first prose contribution to *The New Yorker* it was accepted as a richly comic story. Situations which may not be comic to the participants may be comic to the observer or even to the participants in retrospect. Misunderstanding is part of the human condition. That man has found ways of treating it comically is a tribute to human resilience. Some day, perhaps, the series of mutual misapprehensions and misinterpretations that form part of the Cold War between East and West may be seen as comic. It seems to me that one needs to live in a pretty stable period of civilisation before one can afford to view misunderstanding as possessing real comic potential. In periods of lesser stability misunderstanding ceases to be comic, and the humour of mutually misunderstood speech gives way to the more twisted humour of speech which seeks to avoid all commitment by deliberate ambiguities and even multiple punning. The humour of *Finnegans Wake* is at the opposite pole from the kind of humour which Sterne evoked from the verbal encounters between Walter and Toby Shandy. The mutiple pun is the last refuge of relativism ; it implies that everything might be true and, indeed, that everything can really be con-

sidered as everything else. Far from being obsessive the mutiple pun
is the last word in sceptical tolerance. To the conflict of hobby-horses
the agnostic can say either "A plague on both your horses!" or he can
try to subsume both creatures in a single multiple animal. This aspect
of the matter was put very well by Lewis Carroll in the final paragraph
of his introduction to "The Hunting of the Snark", which can be
taken as an introduction to a whole area of modern literature :

> Supposing that, when Pistol uttered the well-known words—
> "Under which king, Bezonian? Speak or die!"
> Justice Shallow had felt certain that it was either William or Richard,
> but had not been able to settle which, so that he could not possibly
> say either name before the other, can it be doubted that, rather than
> die, he would have gasped out "Rilchiam!"

And so the humour of misunderstanding is replaced by the humour
of the "portmanteau word". But that begins another story.

D

3

Language and Action in
Marlowe's *Tamburlaine*[1]

The greatest drama demands poetry rather than prose, and the reason is not far to seek. In drama the total meaning must be carried by the speech of the characters; the author cannot, as he can in the more discursive form of the novel, allow himself to comment or explain or moralise or in any other way to comment on or interpret the action. The author disappears behind his characters, whose speech and action constitute the play. The novel, which allows of every variety of author's direct and indirect comment and manipulation, does not require a language rich enough to be capable of satisfying simultaneously both the needs of the plot and the full range of awareness of the author's imaginative understanding of all its implications and suggestions. There the author can always speak in his own person. But the drama needs poetry because it needs an extra dimension of meaning built in to the speech of the characters. Modern dramatists of any stature who have used prose have tended to insert bits of novels under the guise of stage directions, as Bernard Shaw did, giving detailed biographical and psychological information in explanatory prose before allowing any character to come on to the stage. But we could hardly imagine Shakespeare inserting a long stage direction before Hamlet's first appearance telling us that he was a sensitive young man who had recently had a severe shock and discussing the implications of his childhood relations with his dead father, his adored mother, and his smooth and resourceful uncle. In *Hamlet* all this comes out in the speech of the characters, in the language they use, in the overtones, associations, suggestions, and explorations achieved by poetic dialogue and soliloquy.

[1] Delivered at the Sorbonne, November 1961.

42

If, then, drama always tends towards poetic speech—even when, as often in Ibsen, it is formally written in prose—because it is only through poetic speech that the dramatist can make us aware of the full implications of the action, we surely do right to seek for the dramatist's meaning, his personal sense of the significance of the action he is showing us, in patterns of imagery and other characteristically poetical aspects of his use of language. To put it crudely, one might say that it is the way in which the characters talk about the actions in which they are involved that shows us what those actions mean both to the characters and to the author. In Shakespeare we often find a most suggestive counterpointing between those aspects of the language which suggest a character's own view of the significance of his actions and those which suggest if not the author's then at least some more objective or inclusive vision. In Marlowe, especially in the early Marlowe (and though the chronology of Marlowe's plays is largely a matter of inference, there can be little real doubt as to which are the earlier plays), the situation is rather different : the poetry is used not so much to interpret the action as to embody it. In *Tamburlaine* particularly there is a kind of relationship between language and action which is not easily parallelled in other poetic drama and which clearly reflects something of Marlowe's own temperament and approach to the subject. Before developing this point, let me try and illustrate it by some examples.

The Prologue, as has often been noted, shows Marlowe repudiating the more popular modes of drama of his time : he announces that he will eschew equally the "jigging veins of riming mother wits" and "such conceits as clownage keeps in pay"—that is, jog-trot rhyming verse and rough-and-tumble comic scenes. Instead

> We'll lead you to the stately tent of war
> Where you shall hear the Scythian Tamburlaine
> Threatening the world with high astounding terms
> And scourging kingdoms with his conquering sword.

We are going to see Tamburlaine in action, and that action involves, first, his "threatening the world in high astounding terms" and then "scourging kingdoms with his conquering sword". His action, that is, involves his way of talking, and indeed we might almost say that in view of the way it is put here language and action are actually equated : threatening with words and scourging with swords are

parallel and even equivalent activities. The high imagination that
leads to the desire for great actions must always first prove itself in
rhetoric. Rhetoric, indeed, is shown in this play to be itself a form of
action. We move immediately from the Prologue to the opening
scene, where we find the weak Persian king Mycetes expressing to his
brother his incapacity to express in words what the occasion demands :

> Brother Cosroe, I find myself agriev'd ;
> Yet insufficient to express the same,
> For it requires a great and thundering speech :
> Good brother, tell the cause unto my lords ;
> I know you have a better wit than I.

It seems clear from these few lines that Marlowe is implying that the
ability to take appropriate action is bound up with the ability to express
forcibly in "a great and thundering speech" the nature of the action
proposed and of the situation which provokes it. Cosroe, the
stronger brother, replies to the weaker in a speech which attempts to
recover in language something of the lost might and glory of Persia :

> Unhappy Persia, that in former age
> Hast been the seat of mighty conquerors,
> That, in their prowess and their policies,
> Have triumphed over Afric, and the bounds
> Of Europe where the sun dares scarce appear
> For freezing meteors and congealed cold.

This is Marlowe's first introduction of the vocabulary of power which
so dominates the play. "Might", "conquerors", "prowess", "tri-
umphed", "dares"—these potent words rise in the beat of the blank
verse with a martial clang. Their force is feeble compared to the
force of Tamburlaine's own speeches, but at this opening moment in
the play they sufficiently express the difference between the two
brothers—just as Tamburlaine's even more soaring speech will
express *his* martial superiority to Cosroe.

Now this is not simply a question of Marlowe's realising the
limitations of the stage, as Professor Harry Levin suggests. "Driven
by an impetus towards infinity and faced with the limitations of the
stage", Professor Levin writes, "the basic convention of the Marlovian
drama is to take the word for the deed". This is true, and the point
is acutely made, yet is seems to me wrong to suggest that "the limitations of the stage" represent a significant cause of this characteristic

of Marlovian drama. It is not as though Marlowe were saying, "I cannot show you their actions, the limitations of the stage being what they are; I shall therefore have to content myself by letting you listen to them talking about their actions". It is made clear in innumerable ways that for Marlowe the proper kind of talk is both the precondition for and in a sense the equivalent of action. Soaring talk is the sign of the soaring mind, and only the soaring mind can achieve spectacularly successful action. I am not altogether happy, either, about the other cause which Professor Levin gives for Marlowe's characters taking the word for the deed—"an impetus towards infinity". One needs to be more specific about what is involved here. The infinite ambitions which spur on the Marlovian hero represent the impulse to do something more than can ever be achieved or even defined, but which at best can only be suggested by a particular kind of poetic imagery and rhetorical splendour. There is never an objective correlative in action to the ambitions of such a hero. When Dr Faustus exclaims

> O what a world of profit and delight,
> Of power, of honour, of omnipotence
> Is promised to the studious artisan!

he is not merely giving expression to the Baconian concept of knowledge as power, as control over one's environment; both the abstractness and the variety of the words he chooses—"profit", "delight", "power", "honour", "omnipotence"—suggests that he seeks something greater than could be represented by any practical example. True, Faustus' trivial use of the power which he gets—playing practical jokes on the Pope and similar pranks—suggests the fatuity which overcomes man once he has achieved power through infernal help, and this is an important moral point: but it is also true that any given example of power in action must be trivial beside the exalted human imagination that aspires after it. The disparity between desire and achievement is for Marlowe part of the human condition, and, this being so, it is in the expression of the desire rather than in accomplishing the achievement that man reveals his most striking qualities.

To return to the opening scene of *Tamburlaine*. The first mention of the hero's name is deliberately reductive: the Persians are trying to diminish him by reducing his stature verbally, by denying his claims to a grand description. The initial description of him is as a highway robber, compared to a fox in harvest time :

> ... that Tamburlaine,
> That, like a fox in midst of harvest-time,
> Doth prey upon my flocks of passengers, ...

And Meander follows this up by describing him as

> that sturdy Scythian thief,
> That robs your merchants of Persepolis
> Trading by land unto the Western Isles,
> And in your confines with his lawless train
> Daily commits incivil outrages, ...

Marlowe wants to give Tamburlaine a chance to build himself up from the lowest possible position. What could be more lowering than "sturdy Scythian thief" and "lawless train", and what a contemptuous and reductive phrase we have in "incivil outrages" when applied to Tamburlaine's deeds! When we first see Tamburlaine in the following scene, he does not immediately proceed to build himself up by magnificent rhetoric. When the Medean lords tell him that

> Besides rich presents from the puissant Cham
> We have his highness' letters to command
> Aid and assistance, if we stand in need,

he vaults over all intermediate ranks in a single quiet sentence :

> But now you see these letters and commands
> Are countermanded by a greater man.

Tamburlaine excels in the expression of the consciousness of superiority, and this is in fact one important reason why he *is* superior.

Consciousness and acceptance of mortality limits both speech and action. The weak Mycetes charges his captain Theridamas to destroy Tamburlaine and return swiftly :

> Return with speed, time passeth swift away,
> Our life is frail, and we may die to-day.

Like Tamburlaine, he can imagine destruction, but not with the intoxicating sense of being the "scourge of God" and acting in the spirit of divine wrath, rather merely as a more passive observer of his dead enemies :

> I long to see thee back return from thence,
> That I may view these milk-white steeds of mine
> All loaden with the heads of killed men, . . .

No sooner is Mycetes off the stage than his brother Cosroe asserts his power and is crowned king by Ortygius and Ceneus. The rhetoric begins to rise :

> Magnificent and mighty prince Cosroe,
> We, in the name of other Persian states
> And commons of this mighty monarchy,
> Present thee with th' imperial diadem.

This is followed shortly afterwards by the first of many speeches in which exotic geographical names sound trumpet-like, proclaiming pomp and power :

> We here do crown thee monarch of the East,
> Emperor of Asia and of Persia,
> Great lord of Media and Armenia,
> Duke of Africa and Albania,
> Mesopotamia and of Parthia,
> East India and the late discovered isles,
> Chief lord of all the wide vast Euxine Sea,
> And of the ever raging Caspian Lake.
> Long live Cosroe, mighty emperor!

Eventually, of course, Tamburlaine's trumpets out-blow all others ; his rhetoric soars to heights unequalled by any other speaker in the play. But his first appearance, following immediately on Cosroe's magniloquence and Ortygius' cry, "Sound up the trumpets, then. God save the king!", shows him as relatively subdued. He is still merely the robber-shepherd, leading in his captured treasure and his fair captive Zenocrate, to whom he speaks at first rather as Comus speaks to the Lady in Milton's Masque :

> Come lady, let not this appal your thoughts ;
> The jewels and the treasure we have ta'en
> Shall be reserv'd, and you in better state
> Than if you were arriv'd in Syria.

Zenocrate addresses him as "shepherd". Then, after Tamburlaine's second speech to Zenocrate, in which, as I have noted, he quietly raises himself above the "puissant Cham", Zenocrate addresses him as "my lord", adding significantly "for so you do import". Tamburlaine accepts the title, adding the characteristically Marlovian remark that it is his deeds rather than his birth that will prove him so. (It should be noted, in passing, that Marlowe was a rebel against a hereditary social hierarchy, and though his imagination revelled in all the ritual of power and rank—he several times makes great play, for example, with subordinate kings receiving their crowns from the chief of them all—he accepted it only when it was the reward of achievement rather than merely of birth. Thus Faustus was born of "parents base of stock" and Tamburlaine vaunts rather than denies his humble origin. The poverty of the University Wits bred a special kind of pride, which in Marlowe's case merged with one current of Renaissance humanism to produce a non-hereditary view of aristocracy.) Zeno-crate's third address to Tamburlaine appeals to him as one who

> hop'st to be eternised
> By living Asia's mighty emperor.

It is an interesting and rapid progression—from "shepherd", to "my lord", to "mighty emperor"—and is produced entirely by Tam-burlaine's way of speech.

It is perhaps surprising that Tamburlaine's first appearance should show him less as the warrior than as the lover. After all, the chief interest of the play centres on his power, whether of language or of action, and falling in love is a kind of submission rather than an exercise of power. But it is significant that Tamburlaine regards Zenocrate as someone precious whose possession signifies power. As the daughter of the Soldan of Egypt she represents a high and ancient lineage, as the betrothed of the King of Arabia she represents a challenge, and as having supreme beauty she is, like a supremely precious stone, of inestimable *value*. Tamburlaine manifests his growing power by talking about and by achieving the conquest of inexpressibly rich treasures and of kingdoms. Competitive speeches promising wealth and pomp to your favourites or to those who come over to your side, represent one of the recurring features of the play, one of Marlowe's ways of establishing relative greatness of character. In his wooing of Zenocrate Tamburlaine is outbidding all other kings and princes in the wealth and glory he can promise her and at the same time he is winning for himself something infinitely precious. His first speech of courtship both expresses his sense of Zenocrate's enormous value and promises her the highest possible style of living. Rhetoric is the art of persuasion : in putting a blazing rhetoric into Tamburlaine's mouth Marlowe expressly recognises that one of the roads to power is the ability to *win people over*. Great speech is not only both the guarantor and even the equivalent of great action ; it is also in itself a means to power which takes precedence of naked physical aggression. On several occasions Tamburlaine is shown as using it first, as trying to seduce his enemies into his service or into unconditional surrender. Action, we are sometimes made to feel, is only to be resorted to when speech meets with stubbornness or deafness. Or rather, to make the point yet again, speech is presented as being the primary form of action, that form which corresponds most closely to man's actual ambitions.

We first hear the full sound of Tamburlaine's rhetoric when he encounters Theridamas, the Persian captain sent against him by Mycetes. Before Theridamas' arrival, Tamburlaine has his soldiers lay out in public view their captured gold treasure, "that their re-flexions may amaze the Persians". Surrounded by this spectacular wealth, he is found by Theridamas and greets him with a huge elemental dignity :

Whom seeks thou, Persian? I am Tamburlaine.

Theridamas is impressed by Tamburlaine's appearance, and takes fire from it to speak in Tamburlaine-like tones :

His looks do menace heaven and dare the gods,
His fiery eyes are fixed upon the earth,
As if he now devis'd some stratagem,
Or meant to pierce Avernas' darksome vaults
To pull the triple headed dog from hell.

Tamburlaine responds at once to this kind of rhetoric : this is his way of talking, and he appreciates it. We may wonder perhaps why he takes it as a sign that Theridamas is "noble and mild", but I should think that we are to regard these adjectives as a general sign of approval of his worthiness on the one hand and his capacity for being won over on the other. Tamburlaine then returns the compliment paid by Theridamas to his appearance :

With what majesty he rears his looks!

He then embarks on the greatest of all the several speeches of competitive promising in the play.   The increasing abstractness of
Tamburlaine's imagery in the opening lines is the measure of his
rapidly soaring imagination.   The difference between being "but
captain of a thousand horse" and triumphing "over all the world"
is more than a difference in degree ; it is the difference between the
paltriness of a realisable kind of power and the magnificence of an
ambition too tremendous to be capable of concrete definition.   The
contrast is immediate :

> Art thou but captain of a thousand horse,
> That by characters graven in thy brows,
> And by thy martial face and stout aspect,
> Deserv'st to have the leading of an host?
> Forsake thy king and do but join with me,
> And we will triumph over all the world.

From this point—as though he has intoxicated himself with the phrase
"And we will triumph over all the world"—Tamburlaine's speech
moves into its full grandiloquence :

> I hold the Fates bound fast in iron chains,
> And with my hand turn Fortune's wheel about,
> And sooner shall the sun fall from his sphere
> Than Tamburlaine be slain or overcome.
> Draw forth thy sword, thou mighty man at arms,
> Intending but to raze my charmed skin,
> And Jove himself will stretch his hand from heaven
> To ward the blow, and shield me safe from harm.
> See how he rains down heaps of gold in showers,
> As if he meant to give my soldiers pay,
> And as a sure and grounded argument
> That I shall be the monarch of the East,
> He sends this Soldan's daughter rich and brave,
> To be my queen and portly emperess.
> If thou wilt stay with me, renowned man,
> And lead thy thousand horse with my conduct,
> Besides thy share of this Egyptian prize,
> Those thousand horse shall sweat with martial spoil
> Of conquered kingdoms and of cities sacked.
> Both we will walk upon the lofty clifts,
> And Christian merchants, that with Russian stems

Plough up huge furrows in the Caspian Sea,
Shall vail to us as lords of all the lake.
Both we will reign as consuls of the earth,
And mighty kings shall be our senators ;
Jove sometimes masked in a shepherd's weed,
And by those steps that he hath scal'd the heavens,
May we become immortal like the gods.
Join with me now in this my mean estate,
(I call it mean, because, being yet obscure,
The nations far remov'd admire me not,)
And when my name and honour shall be spread,
As far as Boreas claps his brazen wings,
Or fair Bootes sends his cheerful light,
Then shalt thou be competitor with me,
And sit with Tamburlaine in all his majesty.

One has the feeling, here as elsewhere, that when Marlowe uses
classical mythology it is not for decorative purposes or to make
literary capital out of references to known legends, but in order to
give the myths new meaning by showing their usefulness in illustrating
the limitless nature of human ambition at its most magnificent :

Jove sometimes masked in a shepherd's weed,
And by those steps that he hath scal'd the heavens,
May we become immortal like the gods.

It is as though Marlowe is showing us for the first time what classical
mythology is all about, what it is *for* : it helps to provide symbols for
the undefinable ambitions of the unfettered human imagination.
Similarly, the monstrous extravagance of

I hold the Fates bound fast in iron chains,
And with my hand turn Fortune's wheel about,

is not to be glossed simply by reference to the medieval notion of
Fortune's wheel, though of course Marlowe depends here for his
shock effect on his readers' and hearers' realising that this is a frontal
attack on the common idea of the fickleness of fortune. That attack
is not, however, as it has sometimes been taken to be, a sign of an
almost blasphemous arrogance on Tamburlaine's or on Marlowe's
part ; it is a way of expressing what it feels like to have limitless
ambition and limitless self-confidence. Once again one might say
that the use of this kind of language is a kind of action : to be able

to talk that way is half the battle. Marlowe does not present this kind
of talk as *boasting*, and the actual boasting of lesser figures, such as
Bajazeth, is clearly differentiated from this particular kind of abstract
extravagance. Tamburlaine, when he speaks like this, has gone far
beyond boasting : he is in an almost trance-like condition of relishing
the significance of his own highest imaginings. Such talk carries its
own conviction : a man who can talk like that is the man on whose
side we want to be. Theridamas makes this quite clear :

> Not Hermes, prolocutor to the gods,
> Could use persuasions more pathetical.

This scene ends with Tamburlaine's creating around him an atmosphere of total loyalty and mutual trust. Here Tamburlaine is at his most
attractive. Service on the one hand and protection on the other are
subsumed in a common notion of soldierly friendship and faithfulness
which has its own simpler eloquence :

> THERIDAMAS.   But shall I prove a traitor to my king?
> TAMBURLAINE.   No, but the trusty friend of Tamburlaine.
> THERIDAMAS.   Won with thy words, and conquered with thy looks,
> I yield myself, my men, and horse to thee :
> To be partaker of thy good or ill,
> As long as life maintains Theridamas.
> TAMBURLAINE.   Theridamas, my friend, take here my hand.
> Which is as much as if I swore by heaven,
> And call'd the gods to witness of my vow,
> Thus shall my heart be still combined with thine,
> Until our bodies turn to elements,
> And both our souls aspire celestial thrones.
> Techelles, and Casane, welcome him.
> TECHELLES.   Welcome renowned Persian to us all.
> USUMCASANE.   Long may Theridamas remain with us.
> TAMBURLAINE.   These are my friends in whom I more rejoice,
> Than doth the king of Persia in his crown : . . .

The next scene shows us Cosroe being swung round to Tamburlaine
by Menaphon's description of his appearance. Like Shakespeare's
Cleopatra, whose beauty is symbolised by its ability to inspire eloquence
in hard-bitten military men when they describe it, so Tamburlaine's
greatness lies partly in its capacity for being eloquently talked about.

The language here has not Tamburlaine's passion of grandeur, his commitment through language to the genuineness of his own enormous ambitions, but it strikes effectively the note of compelled admiration :

Of stature tall, and straightly fashioned,
Like his desire, lift upwards and divine,
So large of limbs, his joints so strongly knot,
Such breadth of shoulders as might mainly bear
Old Atlas' burthen ; 'twixt his manly pitch,
A pearl more worth than all the world is placed,
Wherein by curious sovereignty of art
Are fixed his piercing instruments of sight,
Whose fiery circles bear encompassed
A heaven of heavenly bodies in their spheres,
That guides his steps and actions to the throne
Where honour sits invested royally :
Pale of complexion, wrought in him with passion,
Thirsting with sovereignty and love of arms,
His lofty brows in folds do figure death,
And in their smoothness amity and life :
About them hangs a knot of amber hair,
Wrapped in curls, as fierce Achilles' was,
On which the breath of heaven delights to play,
Making it dance with wanton majesty :
His arms and fingers long and sinewy,
Betokening valour and excess of strength :
In every part proportioned like the man
Should make the world subdued to Tamburlaine.

This mediated persuasion does not work as effectively as the words of Tamburlaine himself work directly on Theridamas. Cosroe does not yield to Tamburlaine as a preliminary to gaining his true friendship ; he tries to make the best of both worlds by asserting that Tamburlaine will be his regent in Persia. Where Cosroe goes wrong is made abundantly clear in a later scene, where he patronises Tamburlaine and indicates that he is using him to further his own ambitions. He addresses Tamburlaine jovially as 'worthy Tamburlaine' and asks, in the tone of a squire addressing a farm labourer,

What thinkst thou, man, shall come of our attempts?

In answer to Tamburlaine's speech of boundless confidence, Cosroe simply reiterates that he expects that the efforts of Tamburlaine and his friends

> Shall make me solely emperor of Asia,

and proceeds to dole out promises of advancement in language that sounds very tame beside that of Tamburlaine in his promising mood :

> Then shall your meeds and valours be advanced
> To rooms of honour and nobility.

Tamburlaine replies with an irony of which Cosroe is totally oblivious :

> Then haste, Cosroe, to be king alone, . . .

We are prepared for Cosroe's ultimate rejection and destruction by Tamburlaine : he has not made the right response to Tamburlaine's language.

The scene in which the timid Mycetes, caught by Tamburlaine in the act of trying to hide the crown, is contemptuously given back the crown by Tamburlaine and then runs away, will be misconstrued by the modern reader if he reads Mycetes' opening line

> Accursed be he that first invented war!

as a serious pacifist argument. Those critics who see Marlowe here as showing a humanitarian feeling and voicing a proper horror of war, or as adding some subtle touches to his portrait of Mycetes, are not reading the play that Marlowe wrote. The point about Mycetes—one is tempted to add, the only relevant point—is that he can find neither language nor gesture to correspond to his royal state, and therefore his royal state is forfeit. A crown is a symbol of human aspiration ; in great spirits it provokes to eloquence of speech and magnificence of action, or at least to some behaviour correlative to the symbol's significance. All that Mycetes can think of doing with it is to hide it, to prevent himself from being known as king :

> So shall not I be known ; or if I be,
> They cannot take away my crown from me.
> Here will I hide it in this simple hole.

This is anti-rhetoric, one might say. To say of a crown "Here will I hide it in this simple hole" is the ultimate lack of response to the challenge of the symbol. Tamburlaine's words, "The thirst of reign and sweetness of a crown", spoken later, show the approved response. Mycetes tends to speak in monosyllables, "For kings are clouts that every man shoots at", "And far from any man that is a fool", and when he encounters Tamburlaine he is quite incapable of rising to the occasion. Even Tamburlaine in his presence speaks with an unwonted and contemptuous simplicity :

> Well, I mean you shall have it again.
> Here, take it for a while ; I lend it thee,
> Till I may see thee hemm'd with armed men.
> Then shalt thou see me pull it from thy head;
> Thou are no match for mighty Tamburlaine.

And when Mycetes discovers that it was Tamburlaine himself speaking, he records the fact in the most deflating language possible :

> O gods, is this Tamburlaine the thief?
> I marvel much he stole it not away.

Everywhere it is language that provides the clue. Compare, for example, the Persian Meander cheering up his army, with Tamburlaine's speaking to *his* men. Here is Meander :

> Therefore cheer up your minds ; prepare to fight.
> He that can take or slaughter Tamburlaine,
> Shall rule the province of Albania.
> Who brings that traitor's head, Theridamas,
> Shall have a government in Media,
> Beside the spoil of him and all his train.

The province of Albania or a government in Media is tame indeed beside the vaguer but infinitely more eloquent

> We'll chase the stars from heaven and dim their eyes
> That stand and muse at our admired arms.

Again, we find that for Marlowe what is realisable in precise terms cannot be the product of a truly inspired imagination. The greatest ambitions are undefinable save in terms of abstraction, mythology, or cosmic metaphor. The best that Meander can promise his soldiers is that they shall

> Share equally the gold that bought their lives,
> And live like gentlemen in Persia.

Live like gentlemen indeed! Tamburlaine's soldiers will live like gods:

> For fates and oracles of heaven have sworn
> To royalise the deeds of Tamburlaine,
> And make them blest that share in his attempts.

That Tamburlaine cannot enjoy his power unless he is talking about it or indulging in a gesture symbolical of it is not to be explained simply by the limitations of the stage : it is a paradox inherent in Marlowe's conception of human ambition. It is only after he has crowned Cosroe as emperor that Tamburlaine allows his imagination to batten on the thought of kingship. Menaphon promises Cosroe that he will "ride in triumph through Persepolis", and after he and Cosroe have gone out, leaving Tamburlaine, Theridamas, Techelles, and Usumcasane on the stage—that is, Tamburlaine and his most faithful officers—Tamburlaine repeats and savours the words :

> And ride in triumph through Persepolis!
> Is it not brave to be a king, Techelles?
> Usumcasane and Theridamas,
> Is is not passing brave to be a king,
> And ride in triumph through Persepolis?

Here for the first time we hear the note of pure incantation in Tamburlaine's language. What is in fact involved in being a king? If we think of it, limited things—limited functions, limited powers, above all, limited length of life. The idea of kingship as it kindles the aspiring mind is more significant than a king's actual rights and duties. The word suggests power and glory—"for Thine is the kingdom, the power and the glory"—of a kind more absolute than any given example of human power and glory can be. Human beings have the power of responding to this suggestion, and in this lies their especial capacity for tragedy. Macbeth and Lady Macbeth, captivated by the magic of the idea of kingship, destroyed themselves in order to obtain it and learned at the very moment of obtaining it that their imagination of it had had nothing to do with the reality. *Tamburlaine* however is not a tragedy : Marlowe is not concerned with the disparity between the magic of names and the true nature of things, between the imagination and the reality, or with the corruption of noble minds to which this disparity can lead. To this extent the play lacks a moral pattern, lacks any real core of meaning. There is no sense of the pity of it or the waste of it or even of the ambiguity of it, though Marlowe does show some awareness of some of the paradoxes involved in the relation between words and actions. Tamburlaine is held up to our admiration in the literal Latin sense of *admirari*. His cruelty, which can be appalling, has no real moral significance one way or the other; it is simply a mode of action appropriate to a soaring ambition, and to Marlowe a soaring ambition is a mode of feeling appropriate to man's restless desire to break out of the limiting bounds within which any given actions of his must be confined. The slaughtering of the virgins and the other inhabitants of Damascus is a *gesture*, like the change of Tamburlaine's colours from white to red to black, and gestures are attempts to find actions which, though inevitably limited, are at least symbolic of something larger than themselves. I am not here concerned with Part II, which raises some different questions, but I would remark that Tamburlaine's insistence on courage to bear wounds and so on, in his discussion with his sons in Part II, and the somewhat confused picture of Calyphas as part coward, part sensualist, part realist, and part pacifist, lead us into other realms altogether. Part I is the original play, and complete in itself: in continuing it Marlowe had to modify the purity of his original conception and introduce elements which if examined closely take us far from the essential play as first conceived and written.

Tamburlaine, then, in repeating the phrase about riding in triumph through Persepolis and building up from it into an incantatory speech on the joys of kingship, is demonstrating his superiority to more mundane imaginations and his capacity for enjoying speech as a mode of action. What a king actually does, how a king actually employs and enjoys his power, is not inquired into. The idea of kingly power is itself intoxicating. When he sounds the names of his followers in a litany of invoked kingship, he is trying to carry them with him in his imaginative conception of the sweets of power. But they are not Tamburlaine. All that Techelles can say is

O, my lord, 'tis sweet and full of pomp!

Usumcasane tries to go one better with

To be a king, is half to be a god.

E

But Tamburlaine brushes these tame expressions away impatiently :

> A god is not so glorious as a king :
> I think the pleasure they enjoy in heaven,
> Cannot compare with kingly joys in earth ;
> To wear a crown enchas'd with pearl and gold,
> Whose virtues carry with it life and death ;
> To ask and have, command and be obeyed ;
> When looks breed love, with looks to gain the prize,
> Such power attractive shines in princes' eyes.

From now on he is to be chasing his language in his actions, and, in the nature of things, never catching up. I have said that the spectacle is not tragic. Tamburlaine's imagination vents itself in rhetoric which in turn re-kindles his imagination to still greater ambitions, and this process is shown as guaranteeing military success. But it is an amoral process. We get the point about the restless, limitless nature of human ambition and the impossibility of its being able to find any single correlative in action. But what does it all add up to in the end?

It is no use saying that it adds up to great poetry, even if not always great dramatic poetry, for the point at issue is just how great is this kind of poetry and why. Consider the speech in which Tamburlaine most fully equates kingship with limitless human aspiration :

> The thirst of reign and sweetness of a crown
> That caused the eldest son of heavenly Ops
> To thrust his doting father from his chair,
> And place himself in the imperial heaven,
> Mov'd me to manage arms against thy state.
> What better precedent than mighty Jove?
> Nature, that fram'd us of four elements
> Warring within our breasts for regiment,
> Doth teach us all to have aspiring minds :
> Our souls, whose faculties can comprehend
> The wondrous architecture of the world,
> And measure every wandering planet's course,
> Still climbing after knowledge infinite,
> And always moving as the restless spheres,
> Wills us to wear ourselves and never rest,
> Until we reach the ripest fruit of all,
> That perfect bliss and sole felicity,
> The sweet fruition of an earthly crown.

Critics have differed as to whether the conclusion of this passage is an anti-climax or a supreme climax. At the beginning of the speech, characteristically, Marlowe presses a new meaning on a Greek myth to make it serve as an illustration and an illumination of the inevitability of continuously aspiring ambition among men. The line "What better precedent than mighty Jove?" rings out as an arrogant challenge. He next goes on to say that the four elements of which man's physical nature is composed (according to medieval and Aristotelian physiology), since they are in continual conflict with each other, teach us all to have aspiring minds. We might say that the relation between conflict and aspiration is not made clear and there seems to be no reason why the former should suggest the latter, but there is a suppressed middle term, emulation, which might bridge the logical gap here. In any case the argument is not essentially rational, but rhetorical : Tamburlaine is seeking mythological, cosmic, and natural sanctions for human aspiration : human ambition forms part of the total wonder of nature. The Faustian lines

> Our souls, whose faculties can comprehend
> The wondrous architecture of the world,
> And measure every wandering planet's course,
> Still climbing after knowledge infinite,

are very impressive in their rising eloquence and the fine, steady abstraction of "Still climbing after knowledge infinite". We are made to feel the *insatiable* nature of human curiosity. The search is never-ending—

> Until we reach the ripest fruit of all,
> That perfect bliss and sole felicity,
> The sweet fruition of an earthly crown.

The play itself, of course, belies this. Tamburlaine collects crowns as a philatelist collects stamps and remains unsatisfied. The extraordinary force of the abstract words "perfect bliss and sole felicity", suggesting a theological conception of heavenly beatitude, and, reminding us of Milton's "When everything that is sincerely good and perfectly divine", hardly prepares us for what they are leading up to, "the sweet fruition of an earthly crown". Yet I do not think the passage ends in anti-climax. The *ripest fruit* of all, that *perfect bliss* and *sole felicity*, turns out to be the *sweet fruition* of an earthly crown.

The crown in this context is made, by its culminating position, into a symbol of ultimate human ambition. *This is what Tamburlaine (and Marlowe) mean, then, when they talk of a crown.* It is not the usual meaning of the word "crown" that limits the totality of meaning achieved by these lines ; on the contrary, it is the meaning set up by the preceding lines that determines in what sense we are to take the word "crown" when we come to it in its climactic position. Contemplated by the imagination, an earthly crown seems to be the guarantee of what a heavenly crown is conventionally assumed to promise—"perfect bliss and sole felicity". It is the imagination which invests words and objects with symbolic meaning. The word "crown" literally "means" a circle placed on the head of a king. But the word, like the word "king", can be used to contain an idea or an emotion. This is what Shakespeare does with the words in *Richard II*. But with Marlowe the idea and the emotion are larger than any practice of kingship would warrant. Acting out kingship in language or in coronation ceremony thus becomes a way of pointing to the nature of human aspiration. Indeed, language and gesture become the best kind of action because they can bear all that the imagination puts into them and are therefore not limited as even the greatest ordinary actions are bound to be. A coronation ceremony is always more moving than a king giving laws or in any other way exhibiting his power. And in the last resort it is in the ceremony of language that human aspiration finds fullest satisfaction. This is the point so splendidly made by—or rather embodied in—the passage quoted.

What, then, does it all add up to in the end? *Tamburlaine* is a play in which the virtuosity of the actor is more important than the moral nature of his actions. The hero tells us what he is going to do before he does it ; tells us what he is doing when he is doing it, and after he has done it tells us what he has done—and all in language whose grandiloquence makes almost every speech a ritual of aspiration. Successful action follows on the speech almost automatically, for speech of this kind can only spring from an irrepressible energy, a perpetual hunger for always going further and doing more, which *must* be satisfied. Those who fail are those with limited aims—contrary to the vulgar view that to limit one's aim is to make success more probable. Tamburlaine's antagonists are not only those with pettier minds ; they are also those—like Bajazeth, his most formidable opponent—whose aim is complacently to maintain their achieved power, which they take for granted as part of the permanent state of things. The language of Bajazeth is not unlike that of Tamburlaine : he must be an opponent to challenge Tamburlaine's imagination and also one whose overthrow marks a significant step in Tamburlaine's pursuit of his words by his actions.   One difference between the language of Bajazeth and that of Tamburlaine is that Tamburlaine's tends to be directed towards the future—what he wills to do and what he therefore will do, "For Will and Shall best fitteth Tamburlaine"—whereas the language of Bajazeth is more a complacent vaunting of what he is. When Bajazeth does talk of the future, it is in terms of intention—

> —We *mean to* take his morning's next arise
> For messenger he will not be reclaim'd,
> And *mean to* fetch thee in despite of him—

which sounds tentative beside Tamburlaine's

> I that am term'd the Scourge and Wrath of God,
> The only fear and terror of the world,
> Will first subdue the Turk, and then enlarge
> Those Christian captives which you keep as slaves.

In the verbal duel between Bajazeth and Tamburlaine this difference disappears, and both speak in terms of "will" and "shall".   The event shows which is the boaster.   It is however worth noting that Bajazeth projects his images of power in terms of number and quantity rather than in the cosmic and mythological imagery characteristic of Tamburlaine.

The scene immediately preceding the exchange of words between Tamburlaine and Bajazeth shows us Zenocrate, now deeply in love with Tamburlaine, being urged by Agydas to give up Tamburlaine in favour of her original Arabian king.   Agydas, significantly, has no appreciation of Tamburlaine's language.   When Zenocrate looks for "amorous discourse", he tells her, Tamburlaine

> Will rattle forth his facts of war and blood.

Marlowe is deliberately playing a dangerous game here, allowing us to hear this brilliantly contemptuous description of Tamburlaine's speech in the very middle of the play.   But he is confident that once we hear Tamburlaine's voice sounding again we shall dismiss this

belittling description. Even before this, he has Zenocrate reply, in
language that echoes Tamburlaine's own,

> As looks the sun through Nilus' flowing stream,
> Or when the Morning holds him in her arms,
> So looks my lordly love, fair Tamburlaine ;
> His talk much sweeter than the Muses' song
> They sung for honour 'gainst Pierides,
> Or when Minerva did with Neptune strive ;
> And higher would I rear my estimate
> Than Juno, sister to the highest god,
> If I were matched with mighty Tamburlaine.

Tamburlaine discovers Agydas trying to tempt Zenocrate away from
him, and to this man who belittles his language he addresses no words
but only sends a dagger as an invitation to him to kill himself. Agydas
gets the point :

> He needed not with words confirm my fear,
> For words are vain when working tools present
> The naked action of my threatened end.

There is a fine irony in Tamburlaine's refusal to use words to the man
who cannot appreciate them. One is reminded of a dialogue, earlier
in the play, between Mycetes and Meander.

> MYCETES.   Was there such brethren, sweet Meander, say,
>   That sprung of teeth of dragons venomous?
> MEANDER.   So poets say, my lord.
> MYCETES.   And 'tis a pretty toy to be a poet.

Miss Ellis-Fermor, in her note on this line in her edition, drew attention to what she considered its "biting irony", seeing it as a bitter
comment by Marlowe on the reputation and fate of poets. But surely
the irony does not lie here at all, but in the man who can neither speak
nor act both doubting mythology and despising poetry. Mythology
is the very stuff of much of Tamburlaine's speech, and his poetic
utterance is bound up with his aspiration and thus with his capacity
for action. Mycetes, incapable of poetic utterance and equally of
effective action, shows his lack of understanding of the relation between
language and action by his contemptuous remark about poets.

The slanging match between Zenocrate and the Turkish empress
Zabina is a rather crude acting out of this same correlation between

speech and action that is so important in the play : while their husbands fight it out on the field, they "manage words" in mutual taunting. Tamburlaine's humiliation and degradation of Bajazeth and Zabina and his complete victory over the Turkish forces is another acting out of his soaring ambition, yet it cannot be denied that there is an element of sadism in the detailed presentation of this cruel treatment. Bajazeth has counted on Mahomet to save him, and appeals desperately to the prophet for succour : but none comes. Man stands alone in Marlowe's universe and draws his strength from his own aspiring imagination. When Tamburlaine uses Bajazeth as a footstool and mounts on him to his throne, the gesture itself is striking—a gesture of overweening ambition and aspiration ; he is not content, however, to leave it at that, but breaks out into a speech whose rhetorical extravagance gives full meaning to his symbolic act :

> Now clear the triple region of the air,
> And let the majesty of heaven behold
> Their scourge and terror tread on emperors.
> Smile, stars that reign'd at my nativity,
> And dim the brightness of their neighbour lamps ;
> Disdain to borrow light of Cynthia,
> For I, the chiefest lamp of all the earth,
> First rising in the east with mild aspect,
> But fixed now in the meridian line,
> Will send up fire to your turning spheres,
> And cause the sun to borrow light of you.
> My sword struck fire from his coat of steel,
> Even in Bithynia, when I took this Turk ;
> As when a fiery exhalation,
> Wrapt in the bowels of a freezing cloud,
> Fighting for passage, makes the welkin crack,
> And casts a flash of lightning to the earth.
> But ere I march to wealthy Persia,
> Or leave Damascus and th' Egyptian fields,
> As was the fame of Clymene's brainsick son
> That almost brent the axletree of heaven,
> So shall our swords, our lances and our shot
> Fill all the air with fiery meteors ;
> Then, when the sky shall wax as red as blood,
> It shall be said I made it red myself,
> To make me think of naught but blood and war.

In any other kind of tragedy such a speech would represent the ultimate *hubris*. But, as I have insisted, Tamburlaine is not a true tragedy and is a wholly amoral play. This is inordinate aspiration in action : it is offered to us for our admiration, not necessarily for our approval.

There is an element not only of sadism but at times of sheer sensationalism in the later scenes with Bajazeth and Zabrina, which are carefully spaced so as to suggest a crescendo of humiliation to its ultimate point. The contrast between what these two were and what they have now become is not pointed, as it would be in a medieval tragedy, with the lesson of the uncertainty of fortune and the other usual accompaniments of accounts of the falls of princes, nor, after a certain stage, does it serve any more to symbolise Tamburlaine's achievement in overcoming the great Turkish emperor. An independent psychological interest comes in, and the scene in which, after Bajazeth has brained himself against his cage, Zabina goes mad and in a whirl of lunatic words follows his example, exist for its own sake ; it had many successors in Elizabethan drama.

Meanwhile, we have had the destruction of Damascus, with all its histronic accompaniments, and the defeat, and liberation for Zenocrate's sake, of Zenocrate's father, the Soldan of Egypt. As I have already argued, Tamburlaine's behaviour at Damascus is to be interpreted as showing him applying the appropriate rituals of destruction which are in turn the appropriate accompaniments of the rituals of his rise to ever increasing power. Zenocrate is unhappy, because these are her fellow Egyptians who have been slaughtered and she has not yet been reassured about her father. But we are not to see a genuine conflict here. Marlowe is not presenting Tamburlaine as torn between desire for military glory on the one hand and love of Zenocrate on the other ; there is no suggestion either of any sort of conflict between love and honour. Marlowe was no Corneille, and no Dryden. True, he shows us Zenocrate troubled about her father, and Tamburlaine troubled because Zenocrate is troubled. And Tamburlaine's distress produces one of the most admired speeches in the play. What he says in this speech is that his appreciation of female beauty is one thing which cannot be adequately represented in words. Hitherto, as we know, he has never had any difficulty in giving verbal embodiment to his ambitions, and he has not been able to savour them until he has given them verbal embodiment. Zenocrate, whom he had earlier described

in language suggesting her value and preciousness, is now seen to be
the possessor of a quality which troubles because the expression of it
in words lies beyond "the highest reaches of human wit". The
passage is a set piece—I cannot help feeling that it may have been
written earlier as a separate poem and then incorporated into the play
at this point—and the point it makes is not developed, nor is it related
to any other pattern of meaning in the play. Further, the latter part
of the speech is textually confused and in parts difficult to interpret.
It almost looks as though Marlowe did not know what to do with his
speech on beauty after he had introduced it. Here is the passage :

> What is beauty, saith my sufferings, then?
> If all the pens that ever poets held
> Had fed the feeling of their masters' thoughts,
> And every sweetness that inspir'd their hearts,
> Their minds and muses on admired themes ;
> If all the heavenly quintessence they still
> From their immortal flowers of poesy,
> Wherein as in a mirror we perceive
> The highest reaches of a human wit—
> If these had made one poem's period,
> And all combin'd in beauty's worthiness,
> Yet should there hover in their restless heads
> One thought, one grace, one wonder, at the least,
> Which into words no virtue can digest.
> But how unseemly is it for my sex,
> My discipline of arms and chivalry,
> My nature, and the terror of my name,
> To harbour thoughts effeminate and faint!
> Save only that in beauty's just applause,
> With whose instinct the soul of man is touched,
> And every warrior that is rapt with love
> Of fame, of valour, and of victory,
> Must needs have beauty beat on his conceits,
> I thus conceiving, and subduing both,
> That which hath stopt the tempest of the gods,
> Even from the fiery spangled veil of heaven,
> To feel the lovely warmth of shepherds' flames,
> And march in cottages of strowed weeds,
> Shall give the world to note, for all my birth,
> That virtue solely is the sum of glory,
> And fashions men with true nobility.

The first fourteen lines constitute a poem on the mystery and inexpressibility of beauty, very Elizabethan in feeling and imagery and conventional in movement and diction. Then Tamburlaine reproaches himself for harbouring effeminate thoughts, but goes on to defend himself by making the point that it is the working of beauty on the human imagination which leads men to their highest exploits. He ends by saying that he, who both responds to beauty and knows how to keep it in its proper place–that beauty which has led the gods to assume humble disguises—will announce to the world that it is the proper response to beauty which enables men to achieve true glory and nobility. It is difficult to feel that this speech really belongs to the play. How is this consistent with

> Nature, that fram'd us of four elements
> Warring within our breast for regiment,
> Doth teach us all to have aspiring minds

and the rest of that great vindication of the perpetually aspiring mind? Further, the conflict suggested here is not developed dramatically at all. Immediately after the speech he briefly baits Bejazeth, announces that for Zenocrate's sake he will spare her father, and goes off to win another victory. Then comes the spectacular scene of the suicide of both Bajazeth and Zabina, followed by a speech by Zenocrate in which we really see her with a divided mind. She is unhappy at the slaughter of the citizens of Damascus, and she is shaken to see the dead bodies of Bajazeth and Zabina. The sight leads her to fear for Tamburlaine : he has defied Fortune, and may in the end come to a sudden fall like "the Turk and his great empress". She asks both Jove and Mahomet to pardon Tamburlaine's "contempt of earthly fortune" and then— and this is the first and only touch of this in the whole play—shows some pity for Bajazeth and Zabina and regret that she "was not moved with ruth", for which she also asks pardon. Her main fear seems to be that Tamburlaine's contempt of fortune threatens them both. Immediately after this, the King of Arabia, mortally wounded, comes in to die at Zenocrate's feet, and Tamburlaine enters bringing in the captured and now liberated Soldan of Egypt, Zenocrate's father. Tamburlaine's worry about beauty and Zenocrate's about her husband's temerity receive no further mention. Indeed, Tamburlaine now breaks into one of his most thundering speeches, abounding in high images of power, in which he sees the multitude of those dead by his hand, including the culminating sight of the dead Bajazeth and Zabina and the dead king of Arabia, as "sights of power to grace my victory". For the first time we feel Tamburlaine's speech almost horrible, indeed inhuman, in its expression of limitless lust for power and his intoxication with the bare notion of triumphing and overcoming :

> The god of war resigns his room to me,
> Meaning to make me general of the world ;
> Jove, viewing me in arms, looks pale and wan,
> Fearing my power should pull him from his throne ;
> Where'er I come the fatal sisters sweat,
> And grisly death, by running to and fro
> To do their ceaseless homage to my sword ;
> And here in Afric, where it seldom rains,
> Since I arriv'd with my triumphant host,
> Have swelling clouds, drawn from wide gasping wounds,
> Been oft resolv'd in bloody purple showers,
> A meteor that might terrify the earth,
> And makes it quake at every drop it drinks ;
> Millions of souls sit on the banks of Styx,
> Waiting the back return of Charon's boat ;
> Hell and Elysium swarm with ghosts of men
> That I have sent from sundry foughten fields
> To spread my fame through hell and up to heaven ;
> And see, my lord, a sight of strange import
> Emperors and kings lie breathless at my feet ;
> The Turk and his great empress, as it seems,
> Left to themselves while we were at the fight,
> Have desperately despatched their slavish lives ;
> With them Arabia too hath left his life :
> All sights of power to grace my victory.
> And such are objects fit for Tamburlaine,
> Wherein, as in a mirror, may be seen
> His honour, that consists in shedding blood
> When men presume to manage arms with him.

It is immediately after this speech that the play ends with the crowning of Zenocrate and promise of her immediate marriage to Tamburlaine.

Tamburlaine is essentially a play about human aspiration, which is presented as something admirable, to be wondered at, and as something which can be fully rendered only in a special kind of rhetorical poetry in which, and only in which, the proper vehicle for the expression of this aspiration can be found. Action takes second place ; it is often either perfunctory, or the casual implementation of previous and succeeding speech about it, or stylised into a ritual which removes from it all moral implication. Human nature in its less strenuous aspects breaks in on occasion, but this forms no part of the grand design of the play but is the inevitable consequence of the dramatist's inability to sustain in a state of continuous excitement his vision of man as purely *homo ambitiosus* (in his translation of Ovid's *Elegies*, Marlowe renders *ambitiosus amor* of Elegy IV Book II as "my ambitious ranging mind"). It is indeed impossible to keep going a whole play without paying some attention to the more domestic elements in human nature. The dialogue between Bajazeth and Zabina in their extremity of torment and humiliation has a kind of affectionate sweetness which threatens the whole fabric of the play :

> Sweet Bajazeth, I will prolong thy life
> As long as any blood or spark of breath
> Can quench or cool the torments of my grief.

Zabina, who is here speaking, never falters in her tone of loving courtesy towards her degraded husband, so long as he is alive. This suggests a world of values in the light of which the value of aspiration as such demands to be judged with a moral judgment. But the whole point of *Tamburlaine* is that moral judgments are irrelevant. Aspiring man is for Marlowe man at his most impressive, and impressiveness of this sort has no relation at all to morality : it is *virtù*, not virtue in the present English sense of the word, that matters. But though aspiration does certainly represent an important and captivating aspect of man, and though the picture of the great conqueror as representing one mode of man "still climbing after knowledge infinite" is presented by Marlowe with extraordinary brilliance, the glare of naked and continuous desire for power, however that desire may be presented so as to symbolise a central aspect of the human condition, becomes in the end too unrelieved a light by which to look at human nature. There are moments when we feel that Marlowe himself realised this, but because at such moments Marlowe is deflected away from his grand design, it is difficult to integrate them into the play as a whole. To take up such moments and discuss them as though they represent a genuine psychological sophistication in the presentation of the characters seems to me to be quite unrealistic. To attempt to see subtleties in the development of Zenocrate's character or to find profound moral conflict implied in Tamburlaine's "What is beauty, saith my sufferings then" speech is to try to read the play for something other than it is, and this is not profitable. *Tamburlaine* is a dramatic poem about man as an aspiring animal, and so far as a play can be made out of this limited theme Marlowe has made one. The greatest drama does not, however, push a single viewpoint so relentlessly. However much we call into service our knowledge and appreciation of the way in which Renaissance humanism developed a new and exciting view of the significance of human aspiration, the fact remains that *homo ambitiosus* is in the end a bit of a bore. For all its splendour, *Tamburlaine* tires us before we have done with it.

"I put", wrote Thomas Hobbes in his *Leviathan*, "I put for a general inclination of all mankind, a perpetual and restless desire of power after power, that ceaseth only in death". Hobbes thought that this notion was his own sadly realistic discovery. But Marlowe had been there before him, noting the same fact not with sadness but triumphantly. In spite of the sustained note of triumph, however, even in Marlowe the sadness is there. What in the end is this fury of ambition, this boundless appetite for power, this high frenzy of rhetorical expression of lust for perpetually exceeding? It divides man from his fellows (in spite of Tamburlaine's capacity for loyalty and friendship), damps down the more valuable human responses, and rides roughshod over reason and morality. Marlowe cannot, in spite of all his endeavours, prevent a sense of this from breaking into his play, though it never becomes really part of it. *Tamburlaine* the play, like Tamburlaine the character, exhibits astonishing virtuosity : but in the end we feel that, in plays as in men, virtuosity is not enough.

4

Imagery and Meaning in
Antony and Cleopatra[1]

*A*ntony and Cleopatra is at once the most magnificent and the most
puzzling of Shakespeare's tragedies. Its magnificence resides in
the splendour and amplitude of its poetry, in the apparently
effortless brilliance with which language is employed in order to
search and illuminate the implications of the action ; it puzzles because
the action itself seems to be of no moral interest yet it compels a kind
of wondering attention which would normally be given only to a play
with a profoundly challenging moral pattern. Bradley sensed this
paradox when he asked, "Why is it that, although we close the book
in a triumph which is more than reconciliation, this is mingled, as we
look back on the story, with a sadness so peculiar, almost the sadness
of disenchantment?" And he added : "With all our admiration and
sympathy for the lovers we do not wish them to gain the world. It is
better for the world's sake, and not less for their own, that they should
fail and die." This is surely to simplify the problem to the point of dis-
tortion, for it is not that Antony and Cleopatra arouse our admiration
while doing wrong, so that we thrill to them yet cannot in conscience
wish them success. It is rather that in this play Shakespeare seems to
be building a moral universe out of non-moral materials. Yet I do
not think that we can answer Bradley merely by making a spirited
defence of the characters of the hero and heroine, as Dover Wilson
does, convincingly enough, if not altogether relevantly.

Shakespeare, taking the familiar story, and many details, from
North's *Plutarch*, turns it into a poetic drama in which the poetry
works continuously to give quite new dimensions to the action. In
no other tragedy of Shakespeare does the actual story, the summaris-

[1] Delivered at the Sorbonne, November 1961.

able plot, seem at such a distance from the way it emerges in the play. Of course a great work of literature, most of all a great poetic drama, is always very much more than its summarisable plot. But a prose account of the action of *Hamlet* or *Othello* or *Macbeth* would at least give us some faint idea of the kind of tragedy that we are here involved with ; certainly it would not lead us in the directly opposite direction and suggest a wholly different kind of play. This, however, is precisely what a prose account of the action of *Antony and Cleopatra* would do : if we read Plutarch's *Life of Antony* without thinking at all of Shakespeare's play (admittedly, this is now difficult for most of us to do) it suggests altogether different kinds of dramatic possibilities. In short, Shakespeare in this play puts poetic imagery to work in order to make the story tell far more than we could have conceived possible of this particular story and to involve it in aspects of the human situation from which the events themselves seem to be at the farthest possible remove. And *this*, I suggest, is what lies at the bottom of Bradley's disquiet—a disquiet which cannot be banished by any defence of the characters' behaviour or by pooh-poohing Bradley's Victorian morality. What strikes us, after we have given ourselves to the play and emerged from it again, is the incredibility of Shakespeare's achievement : it is the wonder of his having succeeded in making this action stretch to this meaning. It is impossible, and yet it happens. Coleridge considered the play "perhaps the most wonderful" of all Shakespeare's, and wonder is indeed one of our many reactions to it. He sticks to history minutely, argued Coleridge, yet in few even of his own plays does he impress "the notion of his giant strength so much, perhaps [there is] none in which he impresses it more strongly". Whether Shakespeare stuck to history as minutely as Coleridge thought is beside the point ; Coleridge here puts his finger on a central feature of the play—the wonder of Shakespeare's having made a play with this kind of life and richness and exploratory quality out of the particular tract of history and biography which he used.

Shakespeare's play is not, of course, as Dryden's was to be, about "All for Love, or the World Well Lost", though this is one strand woven into the total fabric. It is—to summarise it crudely—about the different roles that man can play on the various stages which human activity provides for him, and about the relation of these roles to the player's true identity. Shortly before his suicide, when Antony sees events as having cheated him out of his role both of lover and of conqueror, he expresses his sense of the dissolution of identity:

> Sometime we see a cloud that's dragonish,
> A vapour sometime, like a bear, or lion,
> A tower'd citadel, a pendent rock,
> A forked mountain, or blue promontory
> With trees upon 't, that nod unto the world,
> And mock our eyes with air.

He goes on to say that he

> made these wars for Egypt, and the queen,
> Whose heart I thought I had, for she had mine,

and having, as he believes, lost Cleopatra's heart, he no longer has a real identity as lover or as man of action. The melancholy music of the lines rises up to involve us in this sad sense of loss of self. When, however, he is informed by Mardian that Cleopatra has killed herself for love of him, his identity as lover is immediately re-established and he assumes this role again with a new confidence:

> I will o'ertake thee, Cleopatra, and
> Weep for my pardon. So it must be, for now
> All length is torture: since the torch is out,
> Lie down and stray no farther. Now all labour
> Mars what it does: yea, very force entangles
> Itself with strength: seal then, and all is done.
> Eros!—I come, my queen:—Eros!—Stay for me,
> Where souls do couch on flowers, we'll hand in hand,
> And with our sprightly port make the ghosts gaze:
> Dido, and her Aeneas, shall want troops,
> And all the haunt be ours.

At first it seems that the re-establishment of his identity as lover means the abandonment of his identity as soldier—"No more a soldier", he exclaims; but soon it becomes clear that in his resolution to follow Cleopatra to death he is at last adequately uniting both roles. Cleopatra has now assumed the role of conqueror, and he will imitate her:

> I, that with my sword
> Quarter'd the world, and o'er green Neptune's back
> With ships made cities, condemn myself, to lack
> The courage of a woman, less noble mind
> Than she which by her death our Caesar tells
> "I am conqueror of myself."

When he discovers that Cleopatra has not killed herself after all, he does not fall back into his earlier state of disillusion with her ; he remains the lover and the loved, ready to act out the last of love's gestures :

> I am dying, Egypt, dying ; only
> I here importune death awhile, until
> Of many thousand kisses, the poor last
> I lay upon thy lips.

Finally, at the moment of death, he reassumes the character of conqueror also :

> but please your thoughts
> In feeding them with those my former fortunes
> Wherein I liv'd : the greatest prince o' the world,
> The noblest ; and do now not basely die,
> Not cowardly put off my helmet to
> My countryman : a Roman, by a Roman
> Valiantly vanquish'd.

Cleopatra's great cry of grief at his death is the equivalent from her side of Antony's speech about the changing shapes of the clouds : no identities are now left in the world, no distinction between mighty and trivial ; she is overwhelmed in a patternless and so meaningless world in which all roles are interchangeable :

> O, wither'd is the garland of the war,
> The soldier's pole is fall'n : young boys and girls
> Are level now with men : the odds is gone,
> And there is nothing left remarkable
> Beneath the visiting moon.

Her love for Antony, we now realise, had been what gave meaning to reality for her ; it had been the top in a hierarchy of facts, and when Antony is gone there is no hierarchy, no order, and so no significance in reality. Her own position as queen equally becomes meaningless : she is

> No more but e'en a woman, and commanded
> By such poor passion as the maid that milks,
> And does the meanest chares.

At the end of the play Cleopatra re-establishes order by the culminating role-taking of her death. So Othello, once he has learned that it was Iago's malevolence and not the order-destroying and meaning-destroying fact of Desdemona's faithlessness that produced the

F

appearance of Desdemona's guilt, is enabled to assume again the role
of proud warrior : suicide is inevitable for him, as it is for Antony
and Cleopatra, yet it is now an act possessing meaning. (I might add,
in passing, that it seems to me that there has been much misguided
criticism of *Othello* and *Hamlet* in recent years by critics who wrongly
assume that, for Shakespeare, characters who act histrionically are
therefore acting immorally. A proper reading of *Antony and Cleopatra*
can help us to correct this error.)

Let me go back to the beginning of the play and see if I can trace
some of the ways in which Shakespeare uses poetic imagery to establish
his main patterns of meaning. The opening lines give us with startling
immediacy the stern Roman view of Antony's love for Cleopatra,
separating at once the Roman from the Egyptian word :

> Nay, but this dotage of our general's
> O'erflows the measure : those his goodly eyes,
> That o'er the files and musters of the war
> Have glow'd like plated Mars, now bend, now turn
> The office and devotion of their view
> Upon a tawny front : his captain's heart,
> Which in the scuffles of great fights hath burst
> The buckles on his breast, reneges all temper,
> And is become the bellows and the fan
> To cool a gipsy's lust.

Granville-Barker has well described the quality of the verse :

> This is as ample and virile in substance, as luminous and as consonant
> in its music as anything well could be. One tremendous sentence, the
> ends of the lines not answering to pauses either ; these, such as they
> are, fall midway . . . , so that fresh impulse may overleap the formal
> vision, and the force be the force of the whole. Note, too, the placing
> of the dominant "o'erflows the measure" and its complement "reneges
> all temper" with the doubled parenthesis between them, and how the
> "now bend, now turn" saves this from slackness ; how "files and
> musters" and "office and devotion" strengthen the beat of the verse,
> with "plated Mars" coming like the sudden blare of a trumpet, and
> "burst the buckles on his breast" to sound the exploding indignation
> which culminates in the deadly
>
> And is become the bellows and the fan
> To cool a gipsy's lust.

Granville-Barker has noted how the force of the imagery here is carried over to the reader or hearer. But what of the imagery itself? The word "dotage" strikes hard in the very first line—a damning and degrading word. But note that it is "this dotage of our general's". Antony is still, to the Roman onlooker, "our general": there is a shared pride in that word "our" and a deliberate placing in the hierarchy of command in the word "general". The general is a general, but his observed behaviour is to be described by this viewer as dotage. This *viewer*, because when Philo says "*this* dotage" he is pointing at what he sees, drawing his companion's attention to the visible paradox, a general, yet in his dotage. Antony is seen by Philo as playing two contrary roles at the same time—and this is not in accordance with the proper proportions of things, it "o'erflows the measure". It would be proportionate for a general to love, but not for him to *dote*. For a general to dote "reneges all temper", that is, it renounces all decent self-restraint, it is disproportionate, an improper placing of a particular kind of behaviour in the hierarchy of human activities and emotions.

A general has his proper "office and devotion", his appropriate service and loyalty. For a general's eyes—"goodly eyes", it is emphasised, that have in the past appropriately and suitably "glowed like plated Mars"—now to turn

> The office and devotion of their view
> Upon a tawny front

is again outrageous indecorum, wild disproportion. This disproportion is emphasised again and brought to a climax with

> his captain's heart,
> Which in the scuffles of great fights hath burst,
> The buckles on his breast, reneges all temper,
> And is become the bellows and the fan
> To cool a gipsy's lust.

What has military glory to do with such domestic objects as a bellows and a fan? The juxtaposition is deliberately outrageous. Similarly, the captain's heart put at the service of a gipsy's lust reiterates the disproportion, the total scrambling of that hierarchy which gives people and objects their proper virtue and their proper meaning. Yet "tawny front" can suggest not only "dusky face" but also a leonine façade, and "gipsy" is etymologically and phonetically linked with the noble adjective "Egyptian". While Philo's language suggests his shocked awareness of a supreme disproportion, it also suggests that this is one man's interpretation. "Egyptian" is wilfully degraded into "gipsy". As the spectacle of the two lovers moves across to the middle of the stage to Philo's cry of "Look, where they come"—the lovers are now before our eyes as well as his—Philo's sense of the disproportion involved becomes agonising :

> Take but good note, and you shall see in him
> The triple pillar of the world transform'd
> Into a strumpet's fool.

And he invites his companion, in biblical-sounding language, to "behold and see".

But it is we, the audience or the reader, who now both see and hear. And what is it that we hear?

> CLEOPATRA.   If it be love indeed, tell me how much.
> ANTONY.   There's beggary in love that can be reckon'd.
> CLEOPATRA.   I'll set a bourn how far to be belov'd.
> ANTONY.   Then must thou needs find out new heaven, new earth.

We move at once from the Roman soldier's view of Antony's behaviour to the view of the lovers themselves. Here, too, is disproportion, but disproportion of a very different kind from that seen by Philo. Antony declares that there is no limit to his love, that to measure it would involve going beyond the confines of both heaven and earth. This indeed "reneges all temper"—but in glory, not in a shocking confusion of categories. The public entry of Antony and Cleopatra is a posed affair; it is preceded by a flourish of trumpets and accompanied by all the panoply of a royal progress; the lovers are acting out their love. To part of the audience—Philo and Demetrius, the shocked Roman soldiers—the role represents a monstrous confounding of categories; to the actors themselves, it is a glorious extravagance and subsumes everything else; to us who read or watch the play—well, what is it to us? Whose side are we on? We are jolted from Philo's offensively debasing comments to the sight and sound of the two lovers protesting their love. "All the world loves a lover", the proverb goes, and one naturally takes the lovers' side. But with Philo's words ringing in our ears we remain watchful, eager, interested : what is the true identity of this pair?

No pause for speculation is allowed. At once an attendant enters, saying

> News, my good lord, from Rome

—from that Rome whose representative has just so devastatingly described Antony's behaviour. The brisk official announcement crashes into the world of amorous extravagance that the lovers' dialogue has been building up. Antony's barked, annoyed response—"Grates me, the sum"—shows him forced suddenly out of one role into another which he is most reluctant to play. At this Cleopatra suddenly changes too, quite unexpectedly yet wholly convincingly, into the playful, teasing mocker of her lover :

> Nay, hear them, Antony :
> Fulvia perchance is angry ; or who knows
> If the scarce-bearded Caesar have not sent
> His powerful mandate to you, "do this, or this ;
> Take in that kingdom, and enfranchise that ;
> Perform't, or else we damn thee."

This shocks Antony out of his second role—the lover whose love-making is broken into by the claims of business—into yet a third, the surprised and puzzled lover :

> How, my love?

With what wonderful economy does Shakespeare capture this third movement of mind and feeling in Antony. He is surprised out of his annoyance with the interrupter, wondering what Cleopatra is up to. She soon shows him, as she goes on :

> Perchance? nay, and most like :
> You must not stay here longer, your dismission
> Is come from Caesar, therefore hear it, Antony.
> Where's Fulvia's process? Caesar's I would say. Both?
> Call in the messengers. As I am Egypt's queen,
> Thou blushest, Antony, and that blood of thine
> Is Caesar's homager : else so thy cheek pays shame
> When shrill-tongued Fulvia scolds. The messengers!

She ends, note, by brusquely telling him to attend to the messengers : but she has made sure that, for the time being at least, he won't. Her mocking references to Fulvia, Antony's deserted wife—and we remember that Plutarch has described Fulvia as "a woman not so basely minded to spend her time in spinning and housewivery, and was not contented to master her husband at home but would also rule him in his office abroad"—sting Antony into rejection of all that Rome means. In his next speech he confirms Philo's view of the monstrous disproportion of his behaviour in a remarkable outburst which gains our sympathy not by any explicit or implicit moral justification but by its taking in all of human existence by the way and then including and surpassing it :

> Let Rome in Tiber melt, and the wide arch
> Of the rang'd empire fall ! Here is my space,
> Kingdoms are clay : our dungy earth alike
> Feeds beast as man ; the nobleness of life
> Is to do thus : when such a mutual pair,
> And such a twain can do't, in which I bind,
> On pain of punishment, the world to weet
> We stand up peerless.

When Coleridge, in the passage I have already quoted, referred to Shakespeare's "impressing the notion of giant strength" in this play, he added : "This is owing to the manner in which it is sustained throughout—that he *lives* in and through the play—to the numerous momentary flashes of nature counteracting the historic abstraction, ..." Here is the living in and through the play, here are the flashes of nature. "Let . . . the wide arch of the rang'd empire fall." This is hyperbole with real content. "Rang'd" suggests "ordered" as well as "widely ranging". The ordered variety of political life, which is how Rome lies in the imagination, must give way to the subsuming of all order and all variety in the oneness of this present experience, which is how the passion of love fills the imagination. It is the obverse of truth that John Donne expressed :

> For love, all love of other sights controules,
> And makes one little roome, an every where.

All nobility of action is subsumed in the embrace of "such a noble pair". If the two poles between which Antony moves are Rome and Egypt, for the moment the Roman pole is annihilated. But Antony has a long way to go before he can find a role which combines his character of man of action and lover, which *justifies* him (not perhaps in a moral sense but in the sense that it accommodates his full *psyche*) :

the chain of events which finally drives him to suicide is made, in virtue of the poetic imagery in the play, to be the only way in which his various roles can come together in the same action. At this stage, we see him changing parts, but every change is accompanied by some awareness of what is being given up by not participating in other kinds of human action. How compelling and inclusive is the phrase "our dungy earth alike / Feeds beast as man", taking as it does into its purview in one sweep of perception the very basis of human and animal life and their common dependence on this "dungy earth". And how that phrase "dungy earth" stresses the coarse and common, yet rich and life-giving, elements that link the highest with the lowest in any hierarchy. In a sense Antony is not here abandoning everything in the world by his and Cleopatra's mutual love : he is taking it all with him. But only in a sense : as the play moves on Shakespeare develops more and more ways of taking all life with him in presenting the adventures of this couple. Between this speech and the recurrence of the image in a different context in Cleopatra's speech in Act V, scene II, whole worlds of meaning have been established :

> My desolation does begin to make
> A better life : 'tis paltry to be Caesar :
> Not being Fortune, he's but Fortune's knave,
> A minister of her will : and it is great
> To do that thing that ends all other deeds,
> Which shackles accidents, and bolts up change ;
> Which sleeps, and never palates more the dung,
> The beggar's nurse, and Caesar's.

Here the search for a timeless identity, "which shackles accidents, and bolts up change", is movingly linked to a profound sense of the common necessities of all human existence. And when the dying Cleopatra, with the aspic at her breast, exclaims

> Peace, peace!
> Dost thou not see my baby at my breast,
> That sucks the nurse asleep?

the imagery takes on yet another new dimension, so that not only does Cleopatra establish herself at the end as combining the roles of mistress and wife, of courtesan and queen, of Egyptian and Roman, of live-giver and life-taker, but this final unification of roles is linked —in ways that go far beyond the actual story—to a compassionate awareness of the sad yet satisfying realities of human needs and human experience.

But to return to the dialogue in Act I, scene i. Antony's moment of abandon to his vision of his and Cleopatra's mutual love cannot be sustained, for it cannot at this stage correspond to all the demands of his and Cleopatra's nature. He again repudiates his Roman business and then, by associating love with pleasure and pleasure with mere sport, modulates rapidly from the lover to the mere hedonist:

> There's not a minute of our lives should stretch
> Without some pleasure now. What sport tonight?

Cleopatra with continuing provocativeness acts the part of his Roman conscience—"Hear the ambassadors" is her only reply to the speech just quoted—but Antony, who has moved from passion to hedonism to joviality, insists on taking this as simply part of her attractive variety:

> Fie, wrangling queen!
> Whom everything becomes, to chide, to laugh,
> To weep: how every passion fully strives
> To make itself, in thee, fair and admired!

This topic of Cleopatra's infinite variety is to sound again and again, in many different ways, throughout the play before the hero and the heroine come to rest in the final and fatal gesture that can make variety into true identity. At this stage in the play Shakespeare deftly moves the royal lovers off the stage to let us hear again the two tough Roman soldiers whose comments had opened the action.

> I am full sorry
> That he approves the common liar, who
> Thus speaks of him at Rome,

says Demetrius, giving another shake to the kaleidoscope so that we now see Antony neither as the debauched general nor as the passionate lover but simply as a nasty item in a gossip column.

We move straight from this splendid opening, with its shifting points of view and provocative contrasts between the former and the present Antony and between the Roman and the Egyptian view, to be given what Granville-Barker calls "a taste of the chattering, shiftless, sensual, credulous Court, with its trulls and wizards and effeminates". The dialogue is in prose before Cleopatra's entrance, and it is indeed low chatter, though even here the quiet, almost but not quite embittered, realism of Enobarbus' speech stands out : "Mine, and most of our fortunes to-night, shall be—drunk to bed." This, then, it would seem, is the atmosphere that has bred Cleopatra. The queen enters, seeking Antony, aware that "A Roman thought hath struck him", and worried. She prepares her tactics, bidding Enobarbus fetch Antony and then sweeping out as Antony enters. Antony, when he appears, is purely Roman : the blank verse he speaks is brisk and business-like, moving in short sentences. The news from Rome shames him. He is shaken into wishing to hear Cleopatra named "as she is call'd in Rome" and to see himself through Fulvia's eyes. He has changed roles very thoroughly, and the atmosphere of the Egyptian Court, to which we have just been exposed, helps to make us sympathise. When Cleopatra reappears she has already been diminished, not only by the Court atmosphere and by Antony's Roman speech, but—and most of all—by Enobarbus' sardonic commentary on her behaviour and motives. Her tricks are all in vain, and after trying out a variety of moods and responses she is firmly shut up by Antony's Roman "Quarrel no more, but be prepared to know / The purposes I bear." She then tries the pathetic—

> Sir, you and I must part, but that's not it :
> Sir, you and I have lov'd, but there's not it ;—

and in the end, unable to deflect him from his "Roman thought", she acts the goddess of Victory and leaves him with the memory of an impressive parting :

> Upon your sword
> Sit laurel victory, and smooth success
> Be strew'd before your feet !

But Antony has already come to see himself as Philo and Demetrius had seen him at the play's opening ; we have heard him repeat Philo's very word, "dotage"—

> These strong Egyptian fetters I must break,
> Or lose myself in dotage.

At this point it looks as though the play is to be a tug-of-war comedy, with Antony being pulled now by Egyptian sensuality, now by Roman duty. And indeed, there is an element of this in the play, and some critics have seen this element as its main theme. But this is surely to take too narrow a view, a view, moreover, which makes nonsense of some of the play's finest features as well as of the responses of most careful readers. Of course one might take a mechanical view of the pattern of action and argue that because in the end Antony plays a Roman part (committing suicide) in Egypt for love of his Egyptian Queen he reconciles Rome and Egypt in his death, while Cleopatra, who similarly dies a Roman death in vindication of her Egyptian grandeur, similarly unites the two worlds. But this misses out so much that it cannot begin to be a proper account of what really goes on in the play. True, the conflict between Rome and Egypt *is* important in the play ; it is also true that, as has often been noted, this is the most spacious of the plays, and the whole known Roman world is involved. But any attempt to see the play as merely a balancing of opposites, geographical and psychological, impoverishes it intolerably and also results in the sharpening of the dilemma I described at the beginning. *Antony and Cleopatra* is a play about ways of confronting experience, about variety and identity.

In Act I, scene IV we suddenly see Antony in yet another light, when Octavius Caesar refers to him as "our great competitor", and this is followed by further images of disproportion applied to Antony—"tumble on the bed of Ptolemy", "give a kingdom for a mirth", and so on ; yet with these words still in our ears we are brought back to Alexandria to hear Cleopatra, seeing Antony's meaning for her more clearly at a distance, describe him as

> The demi-Atlas of this earth, the arm
> And burgonet of men

—a first foretaste of the grand mythological description she gives of him after his death to Dolabella :

> His legs bestrid the ocean, his rear'd arm
> Crested the world : his voice was propertied
> As all the tuned spheres, and that to friends :
> But when he meant to quail, and shake the orb,
> He was as rattling thunder. For his bounty,
> There was no winter in 't : an autumn 'twas
> That grew the more by reaping : his delights
> Were dolphin-like, they show'd his back above
> The element they lived in : in his livery
> Walk'd crowns and crownets : realms and islands were
> As plates dropp'd from his pocket.

These tremendous images of power, benevolence, and sensuality—or of greatness, love, and joy—sum up the different aspects of Antony's identity, which are seen together, as co-existing, at last after his death. In life they interfered with each other, and can only be described separately. Nevertheless, the introduction of the figure of "the demi-Atlas of this earth" so soon after Octavius Caesar's complaints about what Antony has declined to, is deliberate and effective. We should note, too, that even Caesar shows himself fully aware of the heroic Antony, though he sees him as the Antony who was and who may be again, not as the present Antony:

> Antony,
> Leave thy lascivious wassails. When thou once
> Was beaten from Modena, where thou slew'st
> Hirtius and Pansa, consuls, at thy heel
> Did famine follow, whom thou fought'st against,
> Though daintily brought up, with patience more
> Than savages could suffer. Thou didst drink
> The stale of horses, and the gilded puddle
> Which beasts would cough at: thy palate then did deign
> The roughest berry, on the rudest hedge;
> Yea, like the stag, when snow the pasture sheets,
> The barks of trees thou browsed. On the Alps
> It is reported thou didst eat strange flesh,
> Which some did die to look on: and all this—
> It wounds thine honour that I speak it now—
> Was borne so like a soldier, that thy cheek
> So much as lank'd not.

This is not only imagery suggestive of almost super-human heroism: it is also violently anti-sensual imagery. The contrast between "lascivious wassails" and "thy palate then did deign / The roughest berry" is absolute. Victory in Egypt is associated with riotous celebration; in Rome with endurance. Cleopatra at the end of the play combines both these notions in her death, which is both a suffering and a ceremony.

When Caesar and Antony confront each other in Rome, Antony admits the most important charge—that in Egypt he had not sufficiently known himself:

> And then when poisoned hours had bound me up
> From mine own knowledge.

Caesar, cold and passionless, never has any doubt of his own identity ; that is one of the advantages of having such a limited character. Lepidus' character consists in wanting to like and be liked by everybody ; he has no real identity at all.   Not that Shakespeare presents all this schematically.   The presentation teems with life at every point, and some of the situations in which Lepidus is involved are richly comic.

Meanwhile, Antony acts out his re-acquired *persona* of the good Roman leader and dutiful family man.   He marries Caesar's sister Octavia, and is all courtesy and affection.   But Enobarbus has been with the back-room boys satisfying their eager curiosity about Egypt. It is somewhat reminiscent of late Victorian—or even twentieth century—English businessmen interrogating one of their number who has returned from a visit to Paris.   "Is it really true what they say about it?   Can you really see this and do that?"   "Eight wild boars roasted whole at a breakfast, and but twelve persons there.   Is this true?" asks Maecenas : the detail is lifted boldly from Plutarch but Shakespeare puts it to his own use.   Enobarbus is being pumped about Egypt, and in replying, this sardonic realist with no illusions tells the simple truth about Cleopatra's irresistible seductiveness.   It is into his mouth that Shakespeare puts the magnificent and well-known description of Antony's first meeting with Cleopatra (again from Plutarch, but how transmuted!), thus guaranteeing its truth ; it is Enobarbus too who evokes her quintessential sex appeal with the brief but brilliant account of her captivating breathlessness after hopping "forty paces through the public street", and above all it is Enobarbus who replies to Maecenas' "Now Antony must leave her utterly" with

> Never ; he will not :
> Age cannot wither her, nor custom stale
> Her infinite variety : other women cloy
> The appetites they feed, but she makes hungry,
> Where most she satisfies.   For vilest things
> Become themselves in her, that the holy priests
> Bless her, when she is riggish.

This is not role-taking : it is the considered opinion of a hard-boiled campaigner, and in the light of it we know that Antony has a long way to go before his different *personae* can unite.

If *we* are never allowed to forget Cleopatra, how can Antony?   It takes only a casual encounter with an Egyptian soothsayer—whether sent by Cleopatra to weaken Antony's Roman will or not Shakespeare doesn't say—to turn him to Egypt again :

> I will to Egypt ;
> And though I make this marriage for my peace,
> I' the east my pleasure lies.

Mere sensuality is drawing him, it appears. Never up to this point has the love theme, as Antony reflects it, seemed so tawdry. It almost seems as though there is an obvious moral pattern emerging, with Rome on the good side and Egypt on the bad. This is further suggested by the following scene in Alexandria showing Cleopatra's reaction to the news of Antony's marriage to Octavia. Yet, after all her tantrums, with her

> Pity me, Charmian,
> But do not speak to me,

a new note of quiet genuiness emerges in Cleopatra's love for Antony. And if we come to feel that the political world of Roman efficiency represents the moral good in this conflict between Rome and Egypt, we are soon brought to the scene in Pompey's galley in which power and politics are reduced to their lowest level. Antony fools the drunken Lepidus by talking meaningless nonsense in reply to Lepidus' questions about Egypt ; Menas tries to persuade Pompey to slaughter his guests and so secure the sole rule of the world, and Pompey replies that Menas should have done it first and told him about it afterwards ; the reluctant Caesar is persuaded to join in the heavy drinking. Lepidus, "the third part of the world", has already been carried off drunk. And finally Enobarbus persuades Caesar to join in a dance with Antony and Pompey while a boy sings a drinking song. The utter emptiness of this revelry is desolating, and it casts a bleak light on the whole Roman world. When the song and dance are over Caesar says he has had enough :

> What would you more? Pompey, good-night.
> Good brother,
> Let me request you off : our graver business
> Frowns at this levity.

Menas and Enobarbus retire to the former's cabin for more music and drinking.

In the light of this dreary and almost enforced celebration we think of Enobarbus' description of Cleopatra's first welcome to Antony or the later presentation [Act IV, scene VIII] of Antony's response to temporary victory and realise that there is another aspect to Egyptian revelry than the dissolute chatter of Act I, scene II. Egyptian celebration has a humanity and a fullness wholly lacking on Pompey's galley.

> Enter the city, clip your wives, your friends,
> Tell them your feats, whilst they with joyful tears
> Wash the congealment from your wounds, and kiss
> The honour'd gashes whole,

exclaims Antony in genial triumph to his men and, to Cleopatra when she enters :

> My nightingale,
> We have beat them to their beds. What, girl, though grey
> Do something mingle with our younger brown, yet ha' we
> A brain that nourishes our nerves, and can
> Get goal for goal of youth. Behold this man,
> Commend unto his lips thy favouring hand :
> Kiss it, my warrior : he hath fought to-day
> As if a god in hate of mankind had
> Destroy'd in such a shape.

And Antony goes on to proclaim a victory celebration :

> Give me thy hand,
> Through Alexandria make a jolly march,
> Bear our hack'd targets like the men that owe them.
> Had our great palace the capacity
> To camp this host, we all would sup together,
> And drink carouses to the next day's fate,
> Which promises royal peril. Trumpeters,
> With brazen din blast you the city's ear,
> Make mingle with our rattling tabourines,
> That heaven and earth may strike their sounds together,
> Applauding our approach.

Kissing, touching, and shaking of hands are frequent where Antony is the centre of a celebratory scene : it is the human touch, the contact, the insistence on sharing feeling. So against "I' the east my pleasure lies" we must set on the one hand Roman pleasure as symbolised by the scene in Pompey's galley and on the other the warm human responsiveness to environment which Antony evinces in so many of his Egyptian moods. Antony's behaviour in the scene just referred to, when he joyfully celebrates a belated and temporary success which can already be seen as the prelude to almost certain defeat, can be interpreted (and has been interpreted) as the old roué breaking up, losing his grip and his sense of proportion. But surely this is to apply an irrelevant kind of psychologising to the development of the action. Shakespeare's concern here, it seems to me, is to keep providing Antony with ever changing emotional environments, to bring out all the weaknesses and strengths of his character, as a prelude to his finding his integrating identity in death. There is of course a sense of decline ; Antony's power and fortune are shown as waning together, and the ups and downs in his moods become as a result increasingly violent. But the latter part of the play is not simply a psychological study of the decline of the sensual man in intellectual and emotional stability as his fortunes decline (as Granville-Barker, brilliant thought his study of the play is, seems to imply). If it were that, it would be merely pathetic, and it would be hard to account for the note of triumph that rises more than once as the play moves to its conclusion. The play is in fact both triumph and tragedy ; Antony, and more especially Cleopatra, achieve in death what they have been unable to achieve in life : the triumph lies in the achievement, the tragedy in that the price of the achievement is death. In the last analysis the play rises above morality to strike a blow in vindication of the human species. Queen or courtesan or lover or sensualist, or all of these, Cleopatra in her death does not let humankind down.

When Antony returns to Egypt, his defection is announced by Caesar as involving total surrender to oriental perversity and showmanship. The scene opens in the middle of his catalogue :

Contemning Rome he has done all this, and more
In Alexandria : here's the manner of 't :
I' the market-place, on a tribunal silver'd,
Cleopatra and himself in chairs of gold
Were publicly enthron'd : at the feet sat
Caesarion, whom they call my father's son,
And all the unlawful issue that their lust
Since then hath made between them. Unto her
He gave the stablishment of Egypt, made her
Of Lower Syria, Cyprus, Lydia,
Absolute queen.

Quite apart from the contempt of Caesar which this implies, it offends
the Romans because it is not Caesar's cool use of power but the
histrionic public exhibition of power, acting out a ceremony of power
"in the public eye" (in Maecenas' incredulous phrase). This is an
important aspect of Antony's character : speech and gesture are for
him part of action ; we make love partly by talking about it, we enjoy
power by announcing it with proper pageantry. Caesar goes on to
report in horror :

> I' the common show-place, where they exercise,
> His sons he there proclaim'd the kings of kings ;
> Great Media, Parthia, and Armenia,
> He gave to Alexander ; to Ptolemy he assign'd
> Syria, Cilicia, and Phoenicia : she
> In the habiliments of the goddess Isis
> That day appear'd, and oft before gave audience,
> As 'tis reported, so.

This is acting, role-taking. The grandeur of the ceremonies seems to
come through even Caesar's repugnant description. He waits, however, for Octavia's arrival to reduce all this at one blow to what
seems to him its proper meaning :

> He hath given his empire
> Up to a whore, who now are levying
> The kings o' the earth for war. He hath assembled
> Bocchus, the king of Libya, Archelaus
> Of Cappadocia, Philadelphos, king
> Of Paphlagonia ; the Thracian king Adallas ;
> King Manchus of Arabia, King of Pont,
> Herod of Jewry ; Mithridates, king
> Of Comagene, Polemon and Amyntas,
> The kings of Mede and Lycaonia,
> With a more larger list of sceptres.

The litany of eastern names suggests both exotic power and sinister
threat to the familiar Roman world ; but the chief force of the speech
comes in the shocked association of the words "empire" and "whore".
The "kings o' the earth"—how abstractly absolute the phrase is ; the
largeness and grandeur of the company seem unlimited. For Caesar,
a thing is either one thing or another, and everything should belong
to its proper place. A whore to whom an empire has been given up is

perhaps made by that fact into something else : certainly, there is a transcending of normal categories. And this is the point. The out-landish assembly of the kings of the earth is monstrous enough, but that all this should be done in the name of a whore is an outrageous confounding of categories. One feels that this, rather than Antony's disloyalty, is Caesar's real complaint. It is not that it is totally ridiculous to call Cleopatra a whore. Antony sees her as such on occasion : he uses language much less moderate than Caesar's when he imagines that she has betrayed him. "Triple-turned whore", he calls her. But Antony, even in his moments of highest rage with Cleopatra, is aware that the identity he fastens on her in his abuse of her is but one of her identities—"What's her name, / Since she was Cleopatra?" He can apply to her a term much worse than "whore", employing that contemptuous food imagery which reduces a woman to a mere object to satisfy the appetite :

> I found you as a morsel, cold upon
> Dead Caesar's trencher : nay, you were a fragment
> Of Gnaeus Pompey's, besides what hotter hours,
> Unregister'd in vulgar fame, you have
> Luxuriously pick'd out.

Antony's emotional vagaries in the long movement of his decline exhibit him as beyond the control of any stabilising self ; it is almost as though Shakespeare is making the point that in order to gain one's identity one must lose it. Antony is seen by his friend Scarus, whose military advice he rejects as he rejects everybody's except Cleopatra's, as "the noble ruin of her (i.e., Cleopatra's) magic", and Shakespeare makes it clear that this is one aspect of the truth. Antony's military judgment is overborne by Cleopatra's reckless desires and intuitions. Even Enobarbus breaks out of his sardonic acquiescence in whatever goes on, to expostulate with Cleopatra herself in a tone of rising anxiety : notice how effectively Shakespeare uses his urgent repetitions ;

CLEOPATRA. I will be even with thee, doubt it not.
ENOBARBUS. But why, why, why?
CLEOPATRA. Thou hast forspoke my being in these wars,
            And say'st it is not fit.
ENOBARBUS. Well, is it, is it?

Soldier and lover are here contradictory roles, which must be acted

G

separately. To attempt to act them out simultaneously is to risk ruin-
ing both. Shakespeare spares us nothing—the bickering, the in-
fatuate action, the changes of mood, the melodramatic gesturing. Yet
the poetic imagery works in another direction, not so much in its
actual verbal suggestions as in its rising energy and human compre-
hensiveness. And at least Antony acts all his own parts. His chief
reason for scorning Octavius Caesar is that he plays simply the role
of cunning policy spinner and refuses to prove himself in any other
capacity :

> his coin, ships, legions,
> May be a coward's, whose ministers would prevail
> Under the service of a child, as soon
> As i' the command of Caesar : I dare him therefore
> To lay his gay comparisons apart
> And answer me declin'd, sword against sword,
> Ourselves alone.

Of course, Caesar will not take so preposterous a risk—

> Caesar to Antony : let the old ruffian know,
> I have many other ways to die.

Antony has descended to "old ruffian" now : but it would never
occur to Caesar that there is—perhaps must be—an element of the
ruffian in every good soldier. He keeps his categories too separate for
that kind of thought to be able to emerge. As for Caesar's "gay
comparisons", it is only Antony's language that makes them so : the
very notion is Antonine, not Caesarian.

The richness of Antony's humanity increases with the instability
of his attitudes. His rage with the presumptuous Thidias, who dares
to kiss Cleopatra's hand, is of course partly the result of Thidias' being
Caesar's messenger and of Cleopatra's looking kindly on him—he
himself shortly afterwards gives Cleopatra Scarus' hand to kiss. But
more than that, it is a release of something humanly real within him,
and his expression of it has a ring of appeal about it, appeal to our
understanding of his emotional predicament, of the full human-ness of
his situation :

> If that thy father live, let him repent
> Thou wast not made his daughter, and be thou sorry
> To follow Caesar in his triumph, since
> Thou hast been whipp'd for following him : henceforth

The white hand of a lady fever thee,
Shake thou to look on 't. Get thee back to Caesar,
Tell him thy entertainment : look thou say
He makes me angry with him. For he seems
Proud and disdainful, harping on what I am
Not what he knew I was. He makes me angry,
And at this time most easy 'tis to do 't :
When my good stars, that were my former guides,
Have empty left their orbs, and shot their fires
Into the abysm of hell.

It is interesting to compare this with the version in North's
Plutarch from which Shakespeare took the incident. "He was longer
in talke with her then any man else was, and the Queene her selfe also
did him great honor : insomuch as he made Antonius gealous of him.
Whereupon Antonius caused him to be taken and well favouredly
whipped, and so sent him unto Caesar : and bad him tell him that he
made him angrie with him, bicause he shewed him selfe prowde and
disdainfull towards him, and now specially when he was easie to be
angered, by reason of his present miserie."

The phrase "harping on what I am / Not what he knew I was" has
no equivalent in Plutarch. Antony's consciousness of his different
selves represents an important part of Shakespeare's intention. At the
same time Antony's almost genial acknowledgement of his own
weakness has not only an engaging confessional aspect but also draws
on its rhythm and movement to achieve a suggestion of human
fallibility which increases rather than diminishes Antony's quality as
a man :

He makes me angry,
And at this time most easy 'tis to do 't : . . .

When Cleopatra approaches him, hoping that his angry mood has
passed, he is still talking to himself :

Alack, our terrene moon
Is now eclips'd, and it portends alone
The fall of Antony !

It is Cleopatra who is the moon—the changeable planet. (We recall
Juliet's reproof to Romeo :

O, swear not by the moon, th' inconstant moon,
That monthly changes in her circled orb . . .)

But while he is lamenting Cleopatra's changeableness, she is awaiting the change in him that will bring him back to a full recognition of her love for him : "I must stay his time." He accuses her of flattering Caesar, and she replies simply : "Not know me yet?" To which in turn he replies with another simple question : "Cold-hearted toward me?" Her answer to this, beginning with the quietly moving "Ah, dear, if I be so, . . ." brings him round at once. "I am satisfied", is all he says to conclude the dispute, then proceeds at once to talk about his military plans. Having declared these, he suddenly realises just who Cleopatra is and where he stands in relation to her :

> Where hast thou been, my heart? Dost thou hear, lady?
> If from the field I shall return once more
> To kiss these lips, I will appear in blood,
> I, and my sword, will earn our chronicle :
> There's hope in 't yet.

He is both warrior and lover now, and well may Cleopatra exclaim "That's my brave lord!" This in turn encourages Antony to move to his third role, that of reveller :

> I will be treble-sinew'd, hearted, breath'd,
> And fight maliciously : for when mine hours
> Were nice and lucky, men did ransom lives
> Of me for jests : but now, I'll set my teeth,
> And send to darkness all that stop me. Come,
> Let's have one other gaudy night : call to me
> All my sad captains, fill our bowls once more ;
> Let's mock the midnight bell.

More role-taking now takes place on a very simple and moving plane. Cleopatra adjusts herself to Antony's recovered confidence :

> It is my birth-day,
> I had thought t' have held it poor. But since my lord
> Is Antony again, I will be Cleopatra.

Cleopatra's reference to her birthday is almost pathos, but it rises at once to grandeur with "But since my lord / Is Antony again, I will be Cleopatra." The question posed by the play is, what do these two characters finally add up to? When Antony is Antony again and Cleopatra Cleopatra who *are* they? One cannot give any answer less than the total meaning of the play.

Enobarbus, the "realist", gives his comment on this dialogue. He knows his Antony; his shrewd and knowing mind give its ironic diagnosis:

Now he'll outstare the lightning; to be furious
Is to be frighted out of fear, and in that mood
The dove will peck the estridge; and I see still,
A diminution in our captain's brain
Restores his heart; when valour preys on reason,
It eats the sword it fights with: I will seek
Some way to leave him.

But it is the realist who does not see the reality, and Enobarbus' death in an agony of remorse for having deserted Antony in the name of *Realpolitik* is Shakespeare's final comment on this interpretation.

The strangely haunting scene in which the soldiers hear the music which signifies the departure of "the god Hercules, whom Antony lov'd" projects the loss of faith in Antony's success even by those who love him: this is one soldier's view of their leader. Antony has already started to play an elegiac role before his men, and this is a consequence of it.

The death of Antony leaves a whole act for Cleopatra's duel with Caesar before she finally outwits him and dies in her own way and in her own time. It is an act in which she plays continuously shifting roles, and while these are obviously related to the exigencies of her conflict with Caesar and the fluctuations in her position, they also show her exhibiting varied facets of her character before deciding on the final pose she will adopt before the world and before history. She is not fooled by Caesar or by anybody, despite superficial evidence to the contrary. In the scene with Caesar and Seleucus where she is clearly playing a part designed to fool Caesar into thinking that she wants to live and make the best bargain possible for herself, she exclaims contemptuously to her ladies in waiting: "He words me, girls, he words me". Caesar is not an accomplished actor—he is not used to role-taking—and he gives himself away. "Feed and sleep", he tells Cleopatra, thinking that the exhortation will disarm and soothe her. But the words suggest the treatment one gives to a caged beast and give away, what Dolabella is easily charmed by Cleopatra into confirming, that Caesar intends to lead Cleopatra and her children as captives in his triumphal procession. This role, for all her infinite

variety, is one Cleopatra will never play. If she does not arrange her
last act properly, the Romans will put her in *their* play :

> Nay, 'tis most certain, Iras : saucy lictors
> Will catch at us like strumpets, and scald rhymers
> Ballad us out o' tune. The quick comedians
> Extemporally will stage us, and present
> Our Alexandrian revels : Antony
> Shall be brought drunken forth, and I shall see
> Some squeaking Cleopatra boy my greatness
> I' the posture of a whore.

The pageant of her death which she arranges is a sufficient antidote
to this. Preceded as it is by the characteristically enlarging dialogue
with the clown who brings the figs—enlarging, that is, the human
implications of the action—she goes through death to Antony whom
at last she can call by the one name she was never able to call him in
life—"Husband, I come". The splendour and dignity of the final
ritual brings together in a great vindication the varied meanings of her
histrionic career and temperament :

> Give me my robe, put on my crown, I have
> Immortal longings in me.

It is both a subsuming and a sublimating ritual. Love and loyalty and
courage and queenliness are here together at last. And so is sexyness
and sensuality, for this is a vindication through *wholeness*, not through
a choice of the "proper" and the respectable elements only. Iras dies
first and Cleopatra exclaims :

> This proves me base :
> If she first meet the curled Antony,
> He'll make demand of her, and spend that kiss
> Which is my heaven to have.

This almost flippant sensuality has its place in the summing up, which
transcends morality. Charmian, who dies last, lingers to set her dead
mistress's crown straight :

> > Your crown's awry,
> I'll mend it, and then play.

"Play" means play her part in the supreme pageant of ceremonial death and at the same time refers back, with controlled pathos, to Cleopatra's earlier

> And when thou hast done this chare, I'll give thee leave
> To play till doomsday : . . .

When Caesar arrives, the striking and moving spectacle of the dead queen in all her regal splendour flanked by her two dead handmaidens forces even this cold schemer to see her in the great inclusive role she has arranged for herself. Love, which in the Roman view of the matter has hitherto been opposed to duty, the enemy of action and dignity and honour, is now at last, and by the very epitome of Roman authority and efficiency, pronounced to be part of history and of honour :

> Take up her bed,
> And bear her women from the monument ;
> She shall be buried by her Antony.
> No grave upon the earth shall clip in it
> A pair so famous : high events as these
> Strike those that make them : and their story is
> No less in pity than his glory which
> Brought them to be lamented. Our army shall
> In solemn show attend this funeral,
> And then to Rome. Come, Dolabella, see
> High order, in this great solemnity.

"Famous", "high", "glory", "solemn", "order", "solemnity"—these are the terms which Caesar now applies to a love story which earlier he had dismissed as "lascivious wassails". Is the play about human frailty or human glory? We are left with the feeling that one depends on the other, an insight too subtly generous for any known morality.

5

Some Aspects of Milton's Pastoral Imagery[1]

The relation between tradition and the individual talent—to use the terms made familiar by T. S. Eliot—is of a rather special order in the poetry of John Milton. He is the most learned of English poets, soaked in classical as well as biblical literature, and the problem of accommodating his load of learning to his poetic originality was not easy. Indeed, part of the modern attack on Milton derives from a belief in the excessive part played in his work by tradition, or at least by a use of classical precedent and a sense of language more Latin than English. Eventually, in *Paradise Lost, Paradise Regained,* and *Samson Agonistes,* he found his own kind of originality : but his later poetry, particularly that written after the Restoration, shows a certain loss of geniality and of aesthetic play resulting from his disillusion with the course of English history. If in his earlier poetry we find the relation between tradition and the individual talent more uncertain, we find there also a greater freedom of manœuvre and at the same time an awareness of, almost an obsession with, the poem as an art object, as artifact, that leads him to subsume both his knowledge and his moral feelings in his art, to operate uninhibitedly as poet rather than as the poet-prophet he later became. Much important work has been done recently on *Paradise Lost* and on the later poetry in general ; but Milton's problem in establishing himself as a native English poet on almost too solid classical foundations is essentially a problem he faced in his earlier poetry, and this is therefore what I propose to look at.

The question of precedent and practice and their mutual relationship

[1] Delivered at the International Association of University Professors of English, Venice, August 1965.

can be usefully approached from the point of view of Milton's pastoral imagery, for by Milton's day nothing could be more traditional than the pastoral yet at the same time there can be no doubt that Milton responded with delight and with a variety of other emotions to the sights and sounds of the living countryside in Cambridgeshire during his student days and on and around his father's estate at Horton in the years immediately following. It may well be that the delay in blossoming forth as a poet, of which Milton as we know was extremely conscious and about which he was at times positively defensive, resulted, in some degree at least, from the difficulty he found in fusing what Chaucer called "auctoritee" and "experience", books and life. At any rate we find in his early poems a moving between the two, sometimes an uncertain and even wild moving, that shows him looking for a means of equilibrium.

There is something else about the pastoral that is worth emphasising at the outset. Though the poems of Theocritus and the Eclogues of Virgil do not represent the supreme heights of classical literature, they are nevertheless shot through with a sense of poetry as an *art*, to be valued and rewarded as such. The goatherd in the first eclogue of Theocritus pleads with Thyrsis to sing him his song, and offers him as an inducement a wonderfully carved wooden cup which is itself, like the song, a work of art. The description of the carving on the cup is itself most cunningly wrought, and the ballad of "The Affliction of Daphnis" which Thyrsis is thus prevailed upon to sing is also, though in a very different way, a beautifully formal work. Virgil takes over this tradition in his third eclogue, wagering as a prize in a singing contest a pair of beechwood cups carved by the divine Alcimedon, on each of which "a pliant vine overlaid with skilful chisel clothes the clusters spread by the pale ivy" :

> pocula ponam
> fagina, caelatum divini opus Alcimedontis :
> lenta quibus torno facili super addita vitis
> diffusos hedera vestit pallente corymbos.

(We meet that intertwining vine and ivy, incidentally, in *Lycidas*, "the gadding Vine o'regrown", as we are to meet so much of Virgil's plant imagery in the early Milton.)

The point I am making here is that in the Greek and Latin tradition of bucolic poetry there is a view of the importance and the value of

art and of the work of art as something skilfully made and valued
purely for the skill exhibited and that Milton was clearly influenced by
this. Milton, of course, knew Theocritus, and he knew deeply and
intimately Virgil's Eclogues. It is worth pointing out that the Virgilian
source for the opening lines of *Lycidas*—

> et vos, o lauri, carpam et te, proxima myrte
> Yet once more, O ye Laurels, and once more
> Ye Myrtles brown—

comes from Virgil's second eclogue, which is a homosexual love poem,
and that the Latin epigraph to *Comus*, a poem in praise of chastity,
comes from the same eclogue. Now this is very odd. We know
about the young Milton's passionate belief in chastity; we know of
his scrupulously pure way of life while at Cambridge, his refusal to
join in the horseplay of his fellow-undergraduates, his nickname of
"the Lady of Christ's". Yet the classical poem which he raids most
obviously in the two most important poems of his young manhood is
one of which the Victorian classical scholar John Conington wrote:
"We should be glad to believe it to be purely imaginary, though even
then it is sufficiently degrading to Virgil." I am not arguing that we
ought to agree with Conington; I am suggesting that the paradox
implied by Milton's almost exhibitionist use of such a poem can only
be resolved if we realise that at this stage in Milton's poetic career
classical poetry stood for an ideal of art, of formal excellence, and that
his main concern in drawing on classical poetry was to find help in
making good poems, not to produce a work "doctrinal to a nation".

It will be argued at once that a view of a poem as an artifact which
is not related to the deepest perceptions and emotions of the poet is
essentially a barren view which will result in mere exercises and not
in great poetry. I do not propose to dispute the aesthetics of the case
here. Indeed, I will concede that the bulk of Milton's early poems
are exercises—*études*, *Übungen*—in which he is flexing his poetic
muscles, and that those of them which become great poems do so
almost accidentally, as those of us who have practised a musical
instrument may suddenly realise that what we began to play as a
"study" is a "piece". This does not mean that the anguished sense of
being cut off with poetic ambition unfulfilled that we get in *Lycidas* or
the praise of chastity in *Comus* is not sincere: each comes, I am sure,
from the depths of Milton's being. But in neither case did he set out

to write a poem or a masque on that theme. The theme emerged :
the relation between tradition and the individual *feeling* worked itself
out in its own way as the work was being written. *Comus* was an
entertainment commissioned as a compliment to the Earl of Bridge-
water on his inauguration as Lord President of Wales ; *Lycidas* was
a duty piece done for a volume of memorial poems to Edward King.
In producing such works Milton would inevitably endeavour to show
his paces by demonstrating his skill in handling an accepted convention. Each was presented as an artifact designed for a specific occasion ;
if in the course of its creation each also became something more than a
ceremonial exercise—well, that is liable to happen when great poets
undertake routine commissions.

If there had been no Civil War in England and Milton had remained
in a social milieu in which he would have been expected to operate as a
poet, counterpointing the demands of his audience against the prompt-
ings of his own genius, he would surely have continued to develop
new ways of making "exercises" into "pieces". As it is, history first
virtually silenced him as a poet then released him into a privacy in
which he was no longer a poet operating in the give-and-take of a
traditional social milieu but a solitary prophet with his vision turned
inward even though his voice was sent out to any who would hear.
The later Milton is thus a special case : at this stage in his life he could
do what he liked with tradition, classical or Christian, and did not
have to accommodate himself to a particular socio-literary scene. It is
in the poems of the earlier Milton that we see learning and originality
exploring ways of coming to terms with each other.

It is in his Latin Elegies that we see most clearly the young Milton
drawing on his knowledge of classical literature in order to construct
exhibitionist exercises in which he shows off both his knowledge and
his skill. There is something engaging and slightly comic in the
fourth Elegy, a Latin verse letter addressed to his old tutor Thomas
Young, with its fluent hexameters and pentameters and its riot of
classical imagery :

> Primus ego Aonios illo praeunte recessus
> Lustrabam, et bifidi sacra vireta jugi,
> Pieriosque hausi latices, Clioque favente,
> Castalio sparsi laeta ter ora mero.

"Under his guidance I first visited the Aonian vales and the sacred

sward of the twin-peaked mountains, drank of the Pierian spring and
by Clio's grace thrice wet my joyful lips with Castalian wine." This
is how he reminds Thomas Young (who, one must remember, was a
Presbyterian divine) of the classical literature he had read under his
tutelage. The imagery in this poem is taken from a variety of sources :
the conclusion combines Ovid and the Bible :

> Namque eris ipse Dei radiante sub aegide tutus,
> Ille tibi custos, et pugil ille tibi ;
> Ille Sionaeae qui tot sub moenibus arcis
> Assyrios fudit nocte silente viros ; . . .

"For you yourself will be safe under the bright aegis of God ; He will
be your guardian and your defender. He who under the walls of the
citadel of Zion routed the Assyrian warriors in the silent night . . ."

A more interesting example is the fifth elegy, the famous *In
Adventum Veris*. Though Ovidian in style almost to the point of
parody, this rapturous welcome to spring nevertheless pulses with
genuine feeling. At the same time, it does not contain a single image
derived from observation of the English countryside. Everything is
turned into classical mythology and classical literary landscape. The
poem is exuberantly exhibitionist; the young Milton is showing how he
can handle a traditional Latin apparatus. Yet the eager rush with which
he collects and manipulates his classical imagery suggests genuine
excitement. Whether the excitement is about spring and the new
movement of life it brings to the countryside or, as seems more likely,
about his own poetic virtuosity and its promise of creativity, is
debatable. Perhaps the thought of earth renewing itself in spring
suggested to him inevitably the putting forth of poetic power, or
perhaps the movement was in the other direction and a sense of poetic
power found its proper "objective correlative" in thoughts of spring.
Certainly the connexion between spring and his own poetic activity
is made quite explicitly :

> Fallor? an et nobis redeunt in carmina vires,
> Ingeniumque mihi munere veris adest?

"Am I deceived? Or are my powers of song also returning, and is my
inspiration here by the grace of spring?" And so he writes an Ovidian
spring-song as a salute to his own budding talent—an *étude*, a show-
piece, and a manifesto.

The other Latin elegies, for all their occasional moments of personal confession, are clever exercises, with just a hint now and then that the exercises may be a sublimation of a personal emotion. It has often been noted that the young Milton expressed in Latin feelings about sex and love that he never expressed in his English poetry. The "active Love with irridescent wings"—*pictis Amor impiger alis*—that stands by his bedside in Elegy VII is heavily literary; it, too, is associated with spring, specifically with May Day. Does this mean, as has been more than once suggested, that Milton dared to express himself more freely in Latin than in English? I do not think that the situation is as simple as that. A poem in Latin was for him an evident artifact, the kind of artifact that a 'prentice poet would want to experiment with. A poet who could quote from a Latin homosexual love poem as epigraph to a masque in praise of chastity clearly thought of Latin poetry, as employed by a modern English poet, as a special case. Knowledge of it was proof of art, not confession of identity of point of view. Later Milton was to find profounder ways of counterpointing Christian and pagan imagery and utilising the imagination of the classical world as a means of strengthening and balancing his own Christian viewpoint. This is a large question, and involves a long tradition of Christian use of pagan classical authors about which much has been written.

We have not, however, settled the use of classical themes and images in Milton's Latin poetry when we say that these poems were exhibitionist artifacts which inevitably on occasion showed some genuine personal feeling, if not directly then by the very fact that they appear to have been written with such excitement. For the *Epitaphium Damonis*, a highly stylised pastoral elegy written on Greek and Latin models to bewail the death of his dear friend Charles Diodati, is perhaps the most personal poem Milton ever wrote. It is about Diodati in a way that *Lycidas* is not about Edward King. He refers in the opening lines, rather flamboyantly, to Moschus' *Lament for Bion*, but by far the stronger influence is Virgil, in whose third and eighth eclogues he found the name Damon. Of the riot of classical names we find in the poem—Pales, Faunus, Pan, Tityrus, Alphesiboeus, Aegon, Amyntas, Mopsus, Hyas, Dryope, Aegle, Menalcas, Lycidas, and others—many are found in both Theocritus and Virgil, some are only in Virgil or other Roman writers, and there is no Theocritian name in Milton's poem that is not also found, generally more frequently, also in Virgil's eclogues. The inspiration is clearly more Latin than Greek, which is reasonable enough in a poem written in Latin. That Milton, genuinely moved by the death of a dear friend, should have written a Virgilian pastoral elegy replete with classical names taken from Virgil's fifth and, to a lesser degree, his tenth eclogue, suggests that classical literature was more to him than a field for exhibitionist imitation. It seems to me, reading and pondering this poem some years after collecting my main thoughts about Milton in a book on the poet, that while of course a case can always be made for Milton's having tried to sublimate his grief in a formal exercise, the case of the *Epitaphium Damonis* is more complicated than that. The personal note rises in a new way with the question *Pectora cui credam?* "To whom shall I now confide my heart?" He had wanted to tell his friend about his plans for writing a national epic on ancient British themes. The loss of his confidant, the loss of the friend to whom he confided his secret poetic ambitions, forces him to put these ambitions into a poem and tell the world. When he begins to do so, the imagery begins to move away from the classical world and to name features of the English landscape, especially English rivers, the Ouse, the Severn, the Trent *et Thamesis meus ante omnes*, "and my own Thames above all". And yet to say that Milton moves from exercise to confession in this poem is a misleading over-simplification. His imagination was clearly deeply touched by the classical elegiac notion of the poet as shepherd, because he saw shepherds as *companions*, as *artists* (singers of artful songs), and as *guardians* (of flocks). These three facets of the shepherd's role had already fused in his imagination to produce in *Lycidas* a concept of the poet-priest which remained central in Milton's imagination. In the *Epitaphium Damonis* the guardian-priest element is less stressed (though the refrain indicates that the poet has to neglect his sheep because of his grief for his dead friend); companionship, emulation, what we would today call literary friendship, is the aspect of the shepherd symbolism that he concentrates on. And wouldn't the turning of an accomplished Latin poem on this theme be precisely what Charles Diodati would have admired?

But I must not spend too long on the Latin poems, even though they point up the paradox of "study" and "piece" in a rather special way. The development of Milton's use of pastoral imagery in his English poems is more interesting. There is nothing that need detain us in the poem *On the Death of a Fair Infant dying of a Cough*, for the opening comparison of the dead infant to a flower, a "soft silken Primrose", is part of a rather baroque image cluster that derives no real force from the nature image : Phineas Fletcher rather than the Greek and Latin classics is the inspiration here, though there are also some suggestions of Ovid. More interesting is the *Vacation Exercise* in which he pledges his allegiance to his native English language and ends with a list of English rivers which is something more than a Draytonian exercise in patriotic topography, with appropriate local myths brought in ; it suggests, however faintly, a deliberate desire to pit the English land-scape against the classical. The fruits of these we find in *L'Allegro* and *Il Penseroso* where classical myth and English rustic scenery march in a new way.

The *Nativity Ode* belongs to a different strand in the development of Milton's imagery—the strand represented at an earlier stage by the poem *On the Death of a Fair Infant*. When Milton writes

Nature in aw to him
Had doff't her gawdy trim

he is very far away from the world of nature as depicted by Theocritus or Virgil, in spite of the almost pagan personification of Nature. Similarly, the picture of earth hiding her guilty front with innocent snow is a baroque pathetic fallacy which is at the same time primitive and sophisticated. Most of all we find in the lines

The Shepherd on the Lawn,
Or ere the point of dawn,
Sate simply chatting in a rustick row

a kind of wilful pictorial naïveté that is worlds apart from anything in the portraits of shepherds by Theocritus or Virgil, in spite of the introduction of "the mighty Pan" immediately afterwards. There does, however, seem to be an almost throwaway reference to classical pastoral in the lines

Perhaps their loves, or els their sheep,
Was all that did their silly thoughts so busie keep.

There is a deliberate demoting of the shepherds here, to emphasise the contrast between these simple characters and the mighty revelation that is to be made to them. (For Milton, incidentally, the birth of Christ was a mighty revelation, not a cradle scene : he thought of the

Christ-child as a hero like Hercules in his cradle.) The shepherds here are thus neither poet-guardians nor figures in a classical landscape : they are emblems of simplicity, and that is all they need to be in this context.

The *Epitaph on the Marchioness of Winchester*, with its lapidary Jonsonian quality, gave no scope for any further experiment in counterpointing the conventional and the natural in pastoral imagery. Everything here is subdued to the quiet formality of diction and rhythm :

> So have I seen some tender slip
> Sav'd with care from Winters nip,
> The pride of her carnation train,
> Pluck't by some unheedy swain,
> Who onely thought to crop the flowr
> New shot up from vernall showr ;
> But the fair blossom hangs the head
> Side-ways as on a dying bed,
> And those Pearls of dew she wears,
> Prove to be presaging tears
> Which the sad morn had let fall
> On her hast'ning funerall.

The plucked flower here is a highly stylised object derived from a long tradition of emblematic (rather than symbolic) use of such things. The phrase "vernall showr" is in a forward-looking rather than a backward-looking tradition, looking to a vocabulary of natural imagery that was to culminate in the early Pope. It is interesting to see how Milton accommodates biblical characters to this formalised imagery. The biblical Rachel becomes "that fair Syrian Shepherdess", a complete octosyllabic line in itself, in which the individuality of the character is smoothed away to make her an emblematic pastoral figure, yet at the same time, by the use of the demonstrative "that", Milton suggests that of course we all know whom he is talking about, since he is drawing on a known story. One might compare this rather elementary (but highly effective) essay in formalising and in a sense classicising a biblical reference with the more complex ways in which Milton in *Paradise Lost* was to use classical literature in giving depth to his biblical characters.

The little song *On May Morning* is different from anything we have so far looked at. While the morning star and the personified May throwing flowers from her lap might well belong to a classical tradition, the feel of these lines is very English, and more in the tradition of medieval spring songs than anything classical :

> Now the bright morning Star, Dayes harbinger,
> Comes dancing from the East, and leads with her
> The Flowry *May*, who from her green lap throws
> The yellow Cowslip, and the pale Primrose.
>> Hail bounteous *May* that dost inspire
>> Mirth and youth, and warm desire,
>> Woods and Groves, are of thy dressing,
>> Hill and Dale, doth boast thy blessing.
> Thus we salute thee with our early Song,
> And welcom thee, and wish thee long.

Milton had used the primrose in his poem *On the Death of a Fair Infant*, but there it was pure emblem. Here it is set beside "the yellow cowslip" and is clearly a flower of the English countryside. Neither cowslip nor primrose is found in classical pastoral poetry : both are species of the *primula*, which is a medieval Latin and not a classical word. I have amused myself by going through the Greek pastoral poets and Virgil's Eclogues and listing the names of all the flowers, plants, and trees found there, and then putting this list beside a list of flowers, plants, and trees found in Milton's early poetry. As might have been expected, a large number are common to Greece, Rome, and England, and when found in Milton might derive from personal observation or from his classical reading. Some occur only in classical literature—the μυρίκη or tamarisk (Virgil's *humilis myrica*), the αἰγίπυρος or red goat-flower, the κνύζα or fleabane, for example (all in Theocritus), the *colocasium* or Egyptian lily of Virgil, among many others. Surprisingly, a considerable number of flowers mentioned by Theocritus, Moschus, and Virgil are common in England but are not mentioned by Milton. Cyclamen (κυκλάμινος), anemone (ἀνεμώνη), and humble parsley (σέλινον) are common in Theocritus but not in Milton, and Virgil has *vaccinium*, the blueberry or whortleberry, *baccar*, the fox-glove, *papaver*, the poppy (the μάκων of Theocritus), that I have not found in the early Milton. Of trees, Theocritus has the elm, the oak, the pine, the poplar (both the black poplar, αἴγειρος, and the white poplar λεύκη), the fir, and the plane ; Virgil has the beech, the elm, the poplar, the ash, the fir, the oak, the willow, the alder, the cypress. Ivy is common in both Theocritus and Virgil (the Greek κισσός, Attic κιττός, Latin *hedera*), and Virgil is fond of the dense

H

hazel (*inter densas corylos*), the thorn (*spinetum, spina*), and of course the laurel and the myrtle.

Now even when we cannot find in Milton a particular tree or shrub mentioned by Virgil we often find a vegetation image which suggests the way Virgil describes a particular tree or shrub. Sometimes we feel that observation of the English rural scene is mingled with echoes of classical reading, and that just as landscape painters have taught us how to look at a landscape, so classical descriptions of flowers and trees taught Milton—in part at least—how to look at the vegetation of his native countryside. I sometimes wonder, too, whether some of the botanical errors attributed to Milton are not the result of this blending of classical and English. For example, in *L'Allegro*, we have the lines

> Through the Sweet-Briar, or the Vine,
> Or the twisted Eglantine.

Now, as commentators have rightly pointed out, sweet-briar and eglantine are the same thing. By eglantine did Milton perhaps mean honeysuckle? The *Oxford English Dictionary* gives the first meaning of "eglantine" as "the sweet-briar" and a possible second meaning, with a specific reference to this passage of Milton's, as "honeysuckle". Milton was clearly thinking of some kind of climbing flower. Had he in mind, perhaps, Theocritus' ἐλίχρυσος, the helichryse, a creeping plant with yellow flowers akin to the everlastings or immortelles of the seventeenth-century English gardener? Or consider a phrase from the third eclogue of Virgil: *tu post carecta latebas*, "you were lying hidden behind the sedges". The Larin *carectum* means "a bed of sedge". The "bonnet sedge" worn by Camus in *Lycidas* is generally, and appropriately, said to suggest the sedge by the River Cam, but is it not likely that behind the Cam Milton saw also the Virgilian landscape? Or consider these lines from *Lycidas* :

> Thee Shepherd, thee the Woods, and desert Caves,
> With wilde Thyme and the gadding Vine o'regrown,
> And all their echoes mourn.
> The Willows, and the Hazle Copses green,
> Shall now no more be seen, . . .

Every schoolboy knows the Virgilian parallel to the first of these lines :

> ipsae te, Tityre, pinus,
> Ipsi te fontes, ipsa haec arbusta vocabant.

"Thee, Tityrus, the very pines, the very fountains, the very trees sighed for." But what about the actual vegetation cited? The woods of course are the *arbusta* as well as the *silvae* that abound in Virgil. The caves are not found in this particular eclogue. But it was in an *antrum*, a cave, that in the fifth eclogue Menalcas and Mopsus sing their famous lament for Daphnis—a pastoral elegy which was clearly one of the models for Milton's poem. As for "wilde Thyme", this is *serpyllum*, one of the herbs pounded up by Thestylis to make a soup for the reapers in the second eclogue. (Incidentally, Thestylis' herbal brew surely lies behind these lines from *L'Allegro* :

> Where *Corydon* and *Thyrsis* met,
> Are at their savory dinner set
> Of Hearbs, and other Country Messes,
> Which the neat-handed *Phillis* dresses.

This is very reminiscent of Virgil's

> allia serpyllumque herbas contundit olentes.

Allium, garlic, is not found in Milton. He prefers to leave the ingredients of this particular "savory dinner" nameless.) I have already commented on the phrase "the gadding Vine o'regrown" and related it to Virgil's

> lenta quibus torno facili super addita vitis
> diffusos hedera vestit pallente corymbos.

The willows suggest the *lenta salix*, "pliant willow", of Virgil's fifth eclogue, and though Milton does not give directly the significance of the adjective "lentus" (which means "slow" and "lazy" as well as "pliant") the fact that he goes on to suggest that the trees are now still and are no longer

> Fanning their joyous Leaves to thy soft layes

might mean that Virgil's adjective for the willow was lying somewhere in the back of his mind. The "Hazle Copses" are, of course, Virgil's *densae coryli*.

The passage from *Lycidas* that I have just quoted is a good example of the formal use of vegetation for a literary purpose : the context is such that we do not expect a realistic treatment of familiar trees and flowers. The inversion, the pathetic fallacy, the place of this passage in the poem as a whole, all suggest the rhetorical function of this use of natural imagery. But in *L'Allegro* and *Il Penseroso* Milton is very much in England, observing the landscape with which he was familiar, in spite of the deliberately excessive classical imagery of the opening. The dismissal of Melancholy with reference to Cerberus, Stygian Cave, and Cimmerian desert, is an exuberant, almost comic preamble to the poem proper, which really begins with the smooth octosyllables which follow the violent prelude :

> But come thou Goddes fair and free,
> In Heav'n ycleap'd *Euphrosyne.*

So far, and indeed for the next dozen lines, we are still in the world of classical myth. The mutation to an English atmosphere comes with the line

> So bucksom, blith, and debonair,

in which the mythological genealogy of Euphrosyne or Mirth gives way suddenly to an account of an English country lass. The lines that follow, with their reference to

> Quips and Cranks, and wanton Wiles,
> Nods, and Becks, and Wreathed Smiles,

evoke a very English sort of mirth ; yet Milton goes on to describe these very nods and smiles as

> Such that hang on *Hebe's* cheek.

We are back in the world of classical mythology again, but this time the atmosphere remains English; we know that Hebe is the goddess of youth and cup-bearer to the gods, but in this context she is an English rustic wench. From this point on the landscape becomes more emphatically English. The flight of the lark, the rise of the "dappled dawn", the window surrounded by climbing plants, the crow of the cock, the sound of the hunters—all this clearly comes from Milton's own experience of English country life. Even though the later stages of sunrise are described in deliberately stately manner—

> Wher the great Sun begins his state,
> Rob'd in flames, and Amber light,
> The clouds in thousand Liveries dight—

it is an English stateliness, with images drawn from English court and Great House ceremonial. And now even when he stylises his rustic picture to fix it as the perfect pastoral, the stylisation derives from English images :

> While the Plowman neer at hand,
> Whistles ore the Furrow'd Land,
> And the Milkmaid singeth blithe,
> And the Mower whets his sithe,
> And every Shepherd tells his tale
> Under the Hawthorn in the dale.

There are echoes of English folklore here, just as there are evocations of the English "lantskip" in "Russet Lawns, and Fallows Gray" and in

> Meadows trim with Daisies pide,
> Shallow Brooks, with Rivers wide,

and there are suggestions of medieval romance in

> Towers, and Battlements it sees
> Blossom'd high in tufted Trees,
> Wher perhaps som beauty lies,
> The Cynosure of neighbouring eyes.

The beauty suggests the Sleeping Beauty of medieval legend, and has nothing to do with the classical world. But then, just as we feel sure we are firmly anchored in England, we find

> Hard by, a Cottage chimney smokes,
> From between two aged Okes,
> Where *Corydon* and *Thyrsis* met,
> Are at their savory dinner set,

and then we get the lines about the neat-handed Phillis and her country messes to which I have already referred. The cottage between the two oak trees is a highly stylised image of rustic content, stylised to a point where it in fact transcends local landscape and becomes an embodiment of a universal concept of peaceful rusticity. Yet the poem has only partly modulated back to a classical world. Though Phillis leaves her bower

> With *Thestylis* to bind the Sheaves

neither she nor her classically-named companion really inhabits the world of Theocritus or Virgil. This is made quite clear by what follows :

Or if the earlier season lead
To the tann'd Haycock in the Mead,
Som times with secure delight
The up-land Hamlets will invite,
When the merry Bells ring round,
And the jolly rebecks sound
To many a youth, and many a maid,
Dancing in the Chequer'd Shade ;
And young and old come forth to play
On a Sunshine Holiday.

The bells are English bells, the rebecks are English musical instruments, the "Chequer'd shade" is a beautiful example of the deliberate patterning of an observed phenomenon (sunshine through the leaves of trees), and the Sunshine Holiday sums up a whole world of English traditional rustic festivity.   The following lines further intensify this English feeling; the "Spicy Nut-brown Ale", the stories of Queen Mab and the "drudging Goblin", the atmosphere of evening story-telling among a rustic community steeped in local lore, all contribute to the English effect. This marks the high point of the poem's native imagery ; Milton now begins to work back skilfully towards the classical world from a description of feats of arms in medieval romantic fashion, through wedding pageants, to drama, music, and poetry.   As the arts take control the classical images grow, until at last we are with Orpheus and Eurydice. *Il Penseroso*, dealing as it does with the life of the meditative man in studious retirement, shows less of this modulation from classical to native and back again ; here the native tradition is represented only by the world of medieval romance and medieval English architecture ; on the whole this poem is more consistently nourished from classical sources, both in imagery and in general use of language, than *L'Allegro*. Yet even in *Il Penseroso* there is one passage, coming oddly enough immediately after a reference to the myth of Cephalus and Aurora, which is based on personal observation :

Or usher'd with a shower still,
When the gust hath blown his fill,
Ending on the russling Leaves,
With minute drops from off the Eaves.

In *Arcades* Milton faced a special problem. He had been invited to use the convention of the masque (a form which by tradition had to make abundant use of classical mythology) and set it in the grounds of an English country house on the occasion of a family party. The whole point of the exercise was to transplant classical names and references to the present situation, and to do this with a formal grace. The scene is deliberately transformed into Arcadia, and the means of the transformation is the classical imagery. The one line which suggests the formalising of an observed English phenomenon rather than the deliberate transformation of an English scene into a classical one is

O're the smooth enameld green.

This is surely the well-kept lawn of an English country estate. Well watered and close cropped grass on a level surface—a phenomenon commoner in England then in almost any other country—does represent a sort of turning of nature into art, of grass into enamel. I remember when I lectured on Milton in America how the students protested against my specifying this image as based on observation : in America, where summer browns the grass and to cut it too close is to find it burning up completely, the combination of absolute smoothness with absolute greenness in a lawn is very rare. But anyone who has seen a well kept English lawn knows exactly what Milton meant by "the smooth enameld green".

Comus is a much more complex masque than *Arcades*, and here Milton is not simply classicising an English scene. The counterpointing of classical and native here is more elaborately and more interestingly achieved than anywhere else in Milton. Sometimes there is a geographical imagination at work, as there is so often in *Paradise Lost* and *Paradise Regained*. The description of Wales as

all this tract that fronts the falling Sun

shows him looking at the landscape from far above, through the eyes of the attendant spirit who looks down on "the starry threshold of *Joves* Court". This gives another dimension to his imagery, to be exploited in his later work in many ways. There is the landscape observed, there is the landscape seen in the light of classical pastoral scenery, and there is the landscape imagined as a relief map, as though seen from an aeroplane. At each of these three levels different degrees of stylisation are possible. Sometimes the sense of capturing an actual experience or observation emerges from a passage couched in abstract formal terms, as in these lines :

> but their way
> Lies through the perplex't paths of this drear Wood,
> The nodding horror of whose shady brows
> Threats the forlorn and wandring Passinger.

"Nodding horror" is an abstract phrase suggesting a concrete image —a nodding bough of a tree seen in the dark of a close wood as a mysterious threat. Milton's genius for employing abstract phrases full of concrete suggestion was not fully developed at this stage, but we see something of it nevertheless in *Comus*.

The language of Comus himself is much more redolent of the actual English countryside and of satisfaction with the sights and sounds of rustic England than that of any other character. In his first speech, beginning

> The Star that bids the Shepherd fold,

there is some cosmic imagery and some classical imagery, and a considerable amount of imagery suggestive of English rustic festivity and folklore. Later on he conveys Milton's own sense of satisfaction at rustic work well done in a language both highly formal and highly evocative :

> what time the labour'd Oxe
> In his loose traces from the furrow came,
> And the swink'd hedger at his supper sate.

Soon after this we get the famous passage in which we have echoes both of Shakespeare's Puck and of the Spenserian pastoralists but which conveys a sense of personal intimacy with rural England that for the moment makes Comus a thoroughly attractive figure :

> I know each lane, and every alley green
> Dingle, or bushy dell of this wilde Wood,
> And every bosky bourn from side to side . . .

We get, too, in the speech of the second brother, a sense of the pleasure taken in *familiar* rustic sounds :

> might we but hear
> The folded flocks pen'd in their watled cotes,
> Or sound of pastoral reed with oaten stops,
> Or whistle from the Lodge, or village cock
> Count the night watches to his feathery Dames, . . .

The "pastoral reed with oaten stops" comes from Theocritus and Virgil; but the passage as a whole suggests a loving familiarity with a native English countryside. The elder brother's language tends to be much more consistently drawn from classical precedent:

> *Thyrsis?* Whose artful strains have oft delaid
> The huddling brook to hear his madrigal,
> And sweeten's every muskrose of the dale,
> How cam'st thou here good Swain? hath any ram
> Slipt from the fold, or young Kid lost his dam.
> Or straggling weather the pen't flock forsook?

The misfortunes of ram and kid here are literary misfortunes, although the muskrose is English.

One could go through *Comus* charting the rise and fall of classical and native images, noting where they reinforce each other and where one kind gives way to the other. Anyone doing so will be surprised at the number of times that, when the idiom seems set in one direction, it either gradually or suddenly or even simultaneously moves towards the other. Comus' line

> Brisk as the *April* buds in Primrose-season

seems part of a purely English context, yet a few lines further on we find

> Not that *Nepenthes* which the wife of *Thone,*
> In *Egypt* gave to *Jove*-born *Helena* . . .

Milton keeps surprising us. Sabrina's song is derived from local English mythology: her story is told in Book II of the *Faery Queen.* The garlands the shepherds throw into her stream on their holidays

> Of pancies, pinks, and gaudy Daffadils

are of English flowers. Yet Sabrina herself is a highly literary character. The appeal to her is couched in terms of classical deities; Sabrina's reply shows her a classical nymph set in an English river-scene. The songs after the final anti-masque refer to Mercury and "the mincing Dryades", and the Spirit's final speech mingles reminiscences of both Puck and Ariel with references to Hesperus, Hyacinth, Cupid, Psyche, and Jove.

I do not propose to say much about *Lycidas*, for that pastoral elegy has been written about more than any other of Milton's earlier poems, and recently C. A. Patrides edited a book consisting entirely of essays on the poem. The relation of that poem to the pastoral tradition— Greek, Latin, Italian, English, classical, and Renaissance—has been explored over and over again. I have nothing new to say about Milton's sources. But I do suggest that it is worth looking more carefully than is usually done at the way he uses and combines his sources. The much discussed flower passage, beginning

> Bring the rathe Primrose that forsaken dies

includes English flowers not to be found in Theocritus or Virgil, a flower such as the violet found equally in the classics and in the English countryside, and the mythical classical flower amaranthus. We can all point to the classical precedents for this list of flowers; more interesting for my present purpose is the choice of flowers and the way each is given an adjective or a descriptive phrase as flowers so often are in the classical pastoral even though the actual description may be original. The poem ends with a distinct echo of the conclusion of Virgil's first eclogue.

> And now the Sun had stretch'd out all the hills

is clearly Virgil's

> maioresque cadunt altis de montibus umbrae.

Yet Milton leaves us with a feeling of an English landscape. The "uncouth Swain" singing "to th' Okes and rills" is not somehow either a Theocritian or a Virgilian shepherd (the very English word "uncouth" helps, as it were, to de-classicise him) and the line

> When the still morn went out with Sandals gray

does not quite evoke for us Aurora, but rather a grey English dawn. Even though it is a "*Dorick* lay" that the swain has sung, the English overtones sound out as the poem comes to its close. Those overtones are orchestrated and not negated by their classical background. The most effective achievement of that kind of orchestration, representing a counterpointing of tradition and personal feeling, remained on the technical side Milton's main poetic ambition.

6

Carlyle and the Victorian Dilemma[1]

If Carlyle is not now as widely read as he once was, his work and personality still compel interest, and the existence of the Carlyle Society is itself testimony to their continued significance. Those of us who work in the field of English studies tend to see Carlyle as the first of the great Victorian prophets, and to read him as we read Ruskin, Matthew Arnold, and William Morris in order to increase our understanding of the ways in which the Industrial Revolution and its social and cultural consequences disturbed the moral and the aesthetic imagination of some of the most sensitive characters of the age. Certainly Carlyle's response to the dilemmas posed by a developing industrial democratic society had remarkable influence on a great variety of nineteenth century writers—on John Stuart Mill, on Dickens, on Ruskin, on Morris, among many others—and many who disagreed, or came to diasgree with much that he said nevertheless admitted the power and the relevance of his voice. W. B. Yeats, in "The Trembling of the Veil", recalled that when he asked William Morris "what led up to his movement"—that is, his socialism—Morris replied : "Oh Ruskin and Carlyle, but somebody should have been beside Carlyle and punched his head every five minutes." That sums up very neatly the mixture of admiration and exasperation with which I, for one, still read Carlyle today. We admire him because he was one of the first to see some of the more unpleasant implications of nineteenth century "progress" and because he expressed his insights with such unique vigour, and we are exasperated when vigour turns to mere violence and repetitiveness of expression, and insight gives way to dangerous murk.

Carlyle gave important and influential answers to questions posed by the nature of Victorian society, though the answers themselves

[1] Thomas Green Lecture, Carlyle Society, 1963.

were derived from a pre-Victorian experience. Because Carlyle died in 1881, and produced much of his work in the 1840s and 1850s, we sometimes forget that he was born in 1795 (the same year as Keats) and had written some of his best and most characteristic work before Victoria came to the throne. The powerful and seminal essay, "Signs of the Times", appeared in the *Edinburgh Review* in June 1829. Like so much of Carlyle's writing, especially in the 1820s and 1830s, it attacks the assumptions of a *laissez-faire* society and the principles of Benthamite morality with weapons drawn from German romanticism and transcendentalism. The great enemy is mechanism: "For the wise men, who now appear as Political Philosophers, deal exclusively with the Mechanical province; and occupying themselves in counting-up and estimating men's motives, strive by curious checking and balancing, and other adjustments of Profit and Loss, to guide them to their true advantage: . . ." It is Dynamism, not Mechanism, that man needs for his fullest development; not machines, not "formulas of Profit and Loss", not the panaceas of "our Constitution-builders, Statists, Economists, Mechanists", but the deepest resources of man's "Dynamical nature". He sees tremendous social and political change impending and prophesies "a deep-lying struggle in the whole fabric of society". But true reform must come from within. "To reform a world, to reform a nation, no wise man will undertake; and all but foolish men know that the only solid, though a far slower, reformation, is what each begins and perfects on *himself.*"

This is the voice of Carlyle before he had developed his extra-ordinary idiosyncratic style, made up of Germanisms, English and Scottish colloquialisms, curious diminutives, and other odd tamperings with existing words, all used with the preacher's combination of rhetoric and intimacy, prodding, exhorting, questioning, both leaning towards and thundering at his reader with a remorseless urgency that fascinates, compels, and disturbs. A few years later, in 1833, he was repeating his attack on Benthamism in this way: "Foolish Word-monger and Motivegrinder, who in thy Logic-mill hast an earthly mechanism for the Godlike itself, and wouldst fain grind me out Virtue from the husks of Pleasure,—I tell thee, Nay!" And ten years after that, we hear this:

> It is not to die, or even to die of hunger, that makes a man wretched;
> many men have died; all men must die,—the last exit of us all is in a
> Fire-chariot of Pain. But it is to live miserable we know not why;

to work sore and yet gain nothing: to be heart-worn, weary, yet isolated, unrelated, girt-in with a cold universal Laissez-faire : it is to die slowly all our life long, imprisoned in a deaf, dead, Infinite Injustice, as in the accursed iron belly of a Phalaris' Bull! This is and remains forever intolerable to all men whom God has made.   Do we wonder at French Revolutions, Chartisms, Revolts of Three Days? The times, if we will consider them, are really unexampled.

Carlyle attacked equally Bentham's calculus of pleasure and pain as a basis for ethics and the *laissez-faire* attitude to society and politics which had been so eloquently propounded by Macaulay in 1830, in his review of Southey's *Colloquies*. Here is Macaulay's voice :

> It is not by the intermeddling of Mr Southey's idol, the omniscient and omnipotent State, but by the prudence and energy of the people, that England has hitherto been carried forward in civilisation ; and it is to the same prudence and the same energy that we now look with comfort and good hope. Our rulers will best promote the improve-ment of the nation by strictly confining themselves to their own legitimate duties, by leaving capital to find its most lucrative course, commodities their fair price, industry and intelligence their natural reward, idleness and folly their natural punishment, by maintaining peace, by defending property, by diminishing the price of law, and by observing strict enonomy in every department of the State. Let the Government do this : the People will assuredly do the rest.

It was this doctrine—that the best government was that which governed least, that capital should be left "to find its most lucrative course" and everybody should be left alone to pursue as best he could his own economic self-interest—on which Victorian prosperity was built and which at the same time was responsible for the horrors which the Industrial Revolution and its aftermath brought on England : the blackening of the face of the country, appalling slums, child labour in mines and factories, urban poverty and squalor on an unprecedented scale existing side by side with growing national wealth. The "con-dition of the people" or "the condition of England" question was endemic throughout the greater part of the nineteenth century, and Carlyle was one of the first to ventilate it. This is one aspect of the Victorian dilemma which figures in my title—the ambiguities of pro-gress. John Morley, writing in 1870, saw England as "a paradise for the well-to-do, a purgatory for the able, and a hell for the poor". Twenty-five years earlier Disraeli, in his novel *Sybil*, had seen the country divided into two nations, the working classes and the privileged orders, with their relationship one "of enmity, and therefore of peril". The Great Exhibition of 1851 was a proud monument to the wealth and material progress of Britain, but the cost of this progress was still mounting. The cost was not only the dehumanising of a large section of the population; it was also the "philistinising" of much of the middle class, the development among them of a complacent, insensitive, materialist attitude which Matthew Arnold was to attack cogently and which Carlyle, in a different way and from a different point of view, had seen much earlier and had diagnosed sharply and bitterly.

Belief in the free play of economic forces as the basis for the good society necessarily implied a reluctance to allow government interference even when this free play of economic forces had resulted in the creation of the most appalling human misery. Nowhere are the ambiguities of nineteenth-century progress more clearly evident than in the record of the struggle for legislation to eliminate or at least ameliorate some of the worst abuses of child labour, gross overworking, and similar evils. Bit by bit the legislation was carried, in the teeth of fierce opposition often by highly moral people who believed on principle that to prohibit small children from being worked literally to death by pulling trucks on their hands and knees in mines or to restrict the working of women and youngsters in textile mills to ten hours a day six days a week was to upset the sacred natural working for good of economic forces. Anyone who reads today the Report of the Committee of Factory Children's Labour of 1831, or the two Reports of the Factory Commission of 1833, or the First Report of the Children's Employment Commission on Mines and Manufactures of 1842, will find it hard to believe that men of goodwill tolerated for one day some of the conditions there described, still less that they believed them to be a necessary part of the benevolent working of economic forces. But men's consciences *were* stirred; royal commissions *were* appointed (from whose reports Karl Marx got some of his most powerful ammunition for his attack on the capitalist system) and ameliorating legislation was passed. Even so, Charles Booth, making a detailed investigation of London's poor between 1887 and 1892, "found over thirty per cent of the people of London living in a state of poverty". Indeed, massive poverty, urban slums, and recurring periods of very high unemployment, all co-existing with

vast national wealth, were regarded as part of the nature of things by
most people in Britain throughout the nineteenth century and well
into the twentieth.

The condition of the people ; poverty in the midst of plenty ; complacent philistinism : these represented part of the cost of the industrialisation of Britain and of the immense material and scientific
progress of the nineteenth century, and Carlyle diagnosed these ills
early and pungently.   The other Victorian dilemma was the dilemma
of faith.   Where in the modern world of material and scientific progress
was one to find a dynamic faith?   Where lay the ultimate sources of
value on which a civilisation depended?   To many Victorians of the
middle and late nineteenth century, the geological discoveries of Sir
Charles Lyell and the biological ideas of Darwin, by casting doubt on
the historical accuracy of the biblical account of the creation and of the
origin of man, provoked a crisis of faith which is reflected again and
again in the literature of the period.   But Carlyle's crisis of faith was
provoked by earlier forces.   It was the eighteenth century Enlighten-
ment, not the ideas of Lyell and Darwin, which caused him as a
student at Edinburgh University to lose the stern Calvinist Christian
faith in which he had been brought up, though his mind never lost
its Calvinistic *temper*.   Voltaire and Hume, the sceptical, humanist
thought of the Aufklärung, left him for a time living in a world bereft
of ultimate value, and it was German literature and philosophy of the
late eighteenth and early nineteenth century that enabled him to
provide himself with a new faith.   This new faith was not Christianity,
though he sometimes talked as though it was.   It was a rather vague
belief in the spirituality of the universe and in the moral obligation to
work and achieve self-discipline.   The story of his spiritual emptiness
followed by spiritual recovery is told in that extraordinary book,
Sartor Resartus, which, though ostensibly concerned with the life and
ideas of Professor Teufelsdröckh, is in large part spiritual autobiography.   The Professor reached a point at which

> To me the Universe was all void of Life, of Purpose, of Volition, even
> of Hostility : it was one huge, dead, immeasurable Steam-engine,
> rolling on, in its dead indifference, to grind me limb from limb.   O, the
> vast, gloomy, solitary Golgotha, and Mill of Death !   Why was the
> Living banished thither companionless, conscious?   Why, if there is
> no Devil ; nay, unless the Devil is your God?

At last, while walking in Paris along the "Rue Saint-Thomas de l'Enfer", the Professor faced the Everlasting No and defied it. (The experience was actually the young Carlyle's while walking down Leith Walk.)

> Despicable biped! What is the sum total of the worst that lies before thee? Death? Well, Death; and say the pangs of Tophet too, and all that the Devil and Man may, will, or can do against thee! Hast thou not a heart; canst thou not suffer whatsoever it be; and, as a Child of Freedom, though outcast, trample Tophet itself under thy feet, while it consumes thee? Let it come, then; I will meet it and defy it!

> Thus had the EVERLASTING NO (*das ewige Nein*) pealed authoritatively through all the recesses of my Being, of my ME; and then was it that my whole ME stood up, in native God-created majesty, and with emphasis recorded its Protest. . . . The Everlasting No had said: "Behold, thou art fatherless, outcast, and the Universe is mine (the Devil's);" to which my whole ME now made answer: "I am not thine, but Free, and forever hate thee!"

There follows a movement through the "Centre of Indifference" (where the self is purged of its egotistic concern with its own feelings only) to the realisation, vaguely enough expressed, that the Universe is spiritual and "all that we do springs out of Mystery, Spirit, invisible Force," and finally to the categorical imperative of the Everlasting Yea. First the annihilation of self, then the realisation that "Our Life is compassed round with Necessity; yet is the meaning of Life itself no other than Freedom, than Voluntary Force; thus have we a warfare; in the beginning, especially a hard-fought battle. For the God-given mandate, *Work thou in Welldoing*, lies mysteriously written in Promethean Prophetic Characters, in our hearts; and leaves us no rest, night or day, till it be deciphered and obeyed; till it burn forth in our conduct, a visible, acted Gospel of Freedom." The "greatest happiness principle" of the Benthamites is dismissed contemptuously:

> I asked myself: What is this that, ever since earliest years, thou hast been fretting and fuming, and lamenting and self-tormenting, on account of? Say it in a word: is it not because thou art not HAPPY? Because the THOU (sweet gentleman) is not sufficiently honoured, nourished, soft-bedded, and lovingly cared-for? Foolish soul! What Act of Legislature was there that *thou* shouldst be Happy? A little while ago thou hadst no right to *be* at all. What if thou wert born and predestined not to be Happy, but to be Unhappy! Art thou nothing

other than a Vulture, then, that fliest through the Universe seeking after somewhat to *eat*; and shrieking dolefully because carrion enough is not given thee? Close thy *Byron*; open thy *Goethe*.

The Everlasting Yea asserts : "Love not Pleasure; love God." Yet Carlyle's God is little more than the projection of a feeling of awe at the dynamic forces both within man and in the external universe. He looks at the Schreckhorn during and after a storm and is carried away by the splendour and mystery of Nature :

> How thou fermentest and elaboratest in thy great fermenting vat and laboratory of an atmosphere, of a World, O Nature? Or what is Nature? Ha! why do I not name thee God? Art thou not the "Living Garment of God"? O Heavens, is it, in very deed, HE, then, that ever speaks through thee; that lives and loves in thee, that lives and loves in me?

This is hardly theological argument, but simply a translating of vague feeling into belief. The exclamation "Ha!" covers the logical gap. Nevertheless, though Carlyle's belief in the spirituality and dynamism of the universe and in the wonder and mystery of man's inner resources represented a curious romantic leap in his thought rather than any valid process of reasoning, the belief remained strong and unflinching within him. "The Universe is not dead and demoniacal, a charnel-house with spectres : but godlike and my Father's!" And the consequence of this Carlyle saw as a categorical imperative enjoining work :

> I too could now say to myself : Be no longer a Chaos, but a World, or even Worldkin. Produce! Produce! Were it but the pitifullest in-finitesimal fraction of a Product, produce it, in God's name! 'Tis the utmost thou hast in thee : out with it, then. Up, up! Whatsoever thy hand findeth to do, do it with thy whole might. Work while it is called Today; for the Night cometh, wherein no man can work.

The relation between Puritanism and the gospel of work has more than once been pointed out, and there is little doubt that traces of Carlyle's ancestrial Calvinism can be seen in the religion he worked out for himself. But—in spite of the deliberate ambiguities in the letters to his mother where he used traditional Christian language without intending the traditional Christian meaning, in order not to hurt his mother's feelings—his view of the Christian Church was that it represented an out-moded form which could no longer contain true religious feeling. He mocked Coleridge for thinking he could bring

I

the dead Church back to life, and in *Latter Day Pamphlets* pronounced
that it was "forever forbidden" "to *steal* into Heaven by the modern
method of sticking ostrich-like your head into fallacies on Earth". He
advocated a "speedy end to superstition, . . . locutions, and imaginations which do NOT correspond to fact". The writers of the Enligh-
tenment had done their work all too well, as Professor Teufelsdröckh
admitted :

> "Cease, my much-respected Herr von Voltaire," thus apostrophises
> the Professor : "shut thy sweet voice ; for the task appointed thee
> seems finished. Sufficiently hast thou demonstrated this proposition,
> considerable or otherwise : That the Mythus of the Christian Religion
> looks not in the eighteenth century as it did in the eighth. Alas, were
> thy six-and-thirty quartos, and the six-and-thirty thousand other
> quartos and folios, and flying sheets or reams, printed before and since
> on the same subject, all needed to convince us of so little! But what
> next? Wilt thou help us to embody the divine Spirit of that Religion
> in a new Mythus, in a new vehicle and vesture, that our Souls, other-
> wise too like perishing, may live? What! Thou hast no faculty in
> that kind? Only a torch for burning, no hammer for building? Take
> our thanks, then, and—thyself away."

Carlyle had something of a love-hate relationship with Voltaire. He
never entirely shook off his influence, and accepted permanently the
negative validity of his work : there remained the task of embodying
the divine Spirit of Religion in a new Mythus.

Carlyle's positive creed, then, started from an acceptance of the
validity of the eighteenth-century sceptical critique of the Christian
Church : after moving from here through the suffering scepticism of
the Everlasting No, he learned to accept loss of pride, the necessity
of renunciation and selflessness, and this mitigated his personal anguish
and enabled him to look with new interest on the external forces of
Nature. This led to his discovery that the nature of reality was *geistig*,
spiritual, and this discovery was linked up, not logically but emotionally, with his sense of the infinite within man. "Man's Unhappiness,
as I construe, comes of his Greatness ; it is because there is an Infinite
in him, which with all his cunning he cannot quite bury under the
Finite." At the centre of man is mystery. "Are we not Spirits, that
are shaped into a body, into an Appearance ; and that fade away again
into air and Invisibility? This is no metaphor, it is a simple, scientific
fact : we start out of Nothingness, take figure, and are Apparitions ;

round us, as round the veriest spectre, is Eternity ; and to Eternity minutes are years and æons." As for man's ultimate destiny, "Sense knows not ; Faith knows not ; only that it is through Mystery to Mystery, from God and to God." Already in 1831 he had written : "About the grand Course of Providence, and his final Purposes with us, we can know nothing, or almost nothing : man begins in darkness, ends in darkness ; mystery is everywhere around us and in us, under our feet, among our hands."

A nebulous enough faith, one might say ; yet Carlyle held to it passionately, and made it the basis of the most influential attack ever launched on *laissez-faire* and of a powerful though somewhat less convincing attack on the pleasure principle in ethics. His gospel of work was in a sense a device for eliminating logical gaps in his argument. "Conviction, were it never so excellent, is worthless till it convert itself into Conduct." "Doubt of any sort cannot be removed except by Action." (This is not far removed from the Coleridgean view of proceeding as though a particular religious formulation were true and living the creed into truth by acting it out, so that faith becomes a matter of will and energy.) Carlyle reiterates this position with great force in his long review-article, "Characteristics", which appeared in the *Edinburgh Review* in 1831. "The healthy Understanding . . . is not the Logical, argumentative, but the intuitive ; for the end of Understanding is not to prove and find reasons, but to know and believe." And again : "Man is sent hither not to question but to work." There is a certain anti-intellectual element in Carlyle, an impatience with mere reasoning processes, as though, once having marshalled his insights, he was impatient with any further speculation and wanted to get on with the job.

This position brought Carlyle into head-on collision with what he called "mechanics", a phrase which for him summed up most of the evils of his day—Materialism, Mammonism, Dilettantism, Benthamism, and, of course, *Laissez-faire*. Again, his basic position here was formulated quite early, and is to be seen in "Signs of the Times", which appeared in the *Edinburgh Review* in 1829. First, the attack on the mechanisation of all human activity :

> Were we required to characterise this age of ours by any single epithet, we should be tempted to call it, not an Heroical, Devotional, Philosophical, or Moral Age, but, above all others, the Mechanical Age. It is the Age of Machinery, in every outward and inward sense

of that word ; the age which, with its whole undivided might, forwards, teaches and practises the great art of adapting means to ends. Nothing is done now directly, or by hand ; all is by rule and calculated contrivance. For the simplest operation, some helps and accompaniments, some cunning abbreviating process is in readiness. Our old modes of exertion are all discredited, and thrown aside. On every hand, the living artisan is driven from his workshop, to make room for a speedier, inanimate one. The shuttle drops from the fingers of the weaver, and falls into the iron fingers that ply it faster. The sailor furls his sail, and lays down his oar ; and bids a strong unwearied servant, on vaporous wings, bear him through the waters. Men have crossed oceans by steam ; the Birmingham Fire-king has visited the fabulous East ; and the genius of the Cape, were there any Camoens now to sing it, has again been alarmed, and with far stranger thunders than Gama's. There is no end to machinery.

Carlyle is not here merely indulging in Luddite attacks on machines : he is concerned with the social and moral effects of mechanisation in destroying organic social relationships. As early as 1820 he had written to a friend complaining of the difference between the social order implicit in traditional kinds of work and that produced by modern factories :

> When the machinery was driven by water the Manufacturer had to seek out some sequestered spot where he could obtain a suitable fall of water, and there his workmen form'd the inhabitants of a village around him, and he necessarily bestow'd some attention, more or less, on their morals and on their necessities, had knowledge of their persons and characters, and exercised over them a salutary influence as over men depending on and intimately connected with him and his prospects. This is now quite changed. The manufacturers are transferred to great towns where a man may assemble 500 workmen one week and dismiss the next, without having any further connection with them than to receive a week's work for a week's wage, nor any further solicitude about their future fate than if they were so many shuttles.

This is the "cash nexus" against which Carlyle thundered so eloquently, the impersonal, purely monetary, relationship between human beings, that was implied in "that brutish, God-forgetting Profit-and-Loss philosophy and Life-theory which we hear jangled on all hands". It was this which produced not only appalling slums and hideous poverty, but the state of mind that complacently accepted slums and the dehumanising of human activity and human relationships. This is the side of Carlyle which leads on to Ruskin and to the great radical critiques of *laissez-faire* which lie behind the development of the welfare state in our own time. It was this side of Carlyle which led John Stuart Mill to reconsider his view of *laissez-faire* and to abandon his belief in the uncontrolled forces of the market, and it was this line of thought which led Morris to claim Carlyle as one of the most influential figures in the development of Socialist thought in England. When he talked like this Carlyle held up a mirror to the prospering Victorian middle-classes, to the manufacturers and entrepreneurs and all the others who were busy making nineteenth-century England so great in their eyes and in the eyes of the world, and he made them see some of the awful paradoxes and contradictions in their way of life. If one part of what I have called the Victorian dilemma concerns the ambiguities of progress, then Carlyle can fairly be hailed as the first British man of letters to force a confrontation of that dilemma on to his readers.

Carlyle was much concerned with the fact of poverty. He never romanticised poverty : he had known it himself (though not urban poverty in an industrial slum) and had no illusions about it. "*Die Sache der Armen in Gottes und Teufels Namen*—the cause of the poor in Heaven's name and the —'s" was a toast proposed on a memorable occasion by Professor Teufelsdröchk, and it echoes in a variety of ways through much of Carlyle's later work. His most direct attack came in 1843—in 1842 there was said to be 1·5 million unemployed in England out of a population of 18 million—in *Past and Present*. Yet it is in this remarkable work that we see most clearly an element in Carlyle's thought that was to lead him to some very dubious positions indeed. The attack on *laissez-faire* is, as usual, splendid and vigorous :

> Truly they are strange results to which this of leaving all to "Cash"; of quietly shutting up the God's Temple, with *Laissez-faire*, and Every man for himself,—have led us in these days!

He goes on to concede that "Life was never a May-game for men : in all times the lot of the dumb millions born to toil was defaced with manifold sufferings, injustices, heavy burdens, avoidable and unavoidable ; not play at all, but hard work that made the sinews sore and the heart sore." But though history is full of the records of human suffering, "I will venture to believe that in no time, since the beginnings of Society, was the loss of those same dumb millions of toilers so entirely unbearable as it is even in the days now passing over us." This is because the suffering poor form no real part of any society, unlike the Saxon swineherd who, with all his poverty, nevertheless "had the inexpressible satisfaction of feeling himself related indissolubly, though in a rude brass-collar way, to his fellow-mortals in this Earth". His modern equivalent is "emancipated", he "has what we call 'Liberty'. Liberty, I am told, is a Divine thing. Liberty when it becomes the 'Liberty to die by starvation' is not so divine!"

This is forcefully put, and commands our assent. But note where Carlyle goes from there:

> Liberty? The true liberty of a man, you would say, consisted in his finding out, or being forced to find out, the right path, and to walk thereon, To learn, or to be taught, what work he was actually able for; and then by permission, persuasion, and even compulsion, to set about doing of the same! That is his true blessedness, honour, "liberty" and maximum of wellbeing: if liberty be not that, I for one have small care about liberty. You do not allow a palpable madman to leap over precipices; you violate his liberty, you that are wise; and keep him, were it in strait-waistcoats, away from the precipices! Every stupid, every cowardly and foolish man is but a less palpable madman: his true liberty were that a wiser man, that any and every wiser man, could, by brass collars, or in whatever milder or sharper way, lay hold of him when he was going wrong, and order and compel him to go a little righter. O, if thou really art my *Senior*, Seigneur, my *Elder*, Presbyter or Priest,—if thou art in very deed my *Wiser*, may a beneficent instinct lead and impel thee to "conquer" me, to command me! If thou do know better than I what is good and right, I conjure thee in the name of God, force me to do it; were it by never such brass collars, whips and handcuffs, leave me not to walk over precipices! That I have been called, by all the Newspapers, a "free man" will avail me little, if my pilgrimage have ended in death and wreck. O that the Newspapers had called me slave, coward, fool, or what it pleased their sweet voices to name me, and I had attained not death, but life!—Liberty requires new definitions.

This is the beginning of the road which had already taken Carlyle to his doctrine of hero-worship, to his fierce and continuing attacks on democracy, and was in the end to lead to his defence of every kind of tyranny and cruelty in the name of order and the importance of ordered work. *Laissez-faire* is bad; it means for millions of people simply liberty to die by starvation, and it destroys the traditional sanctities of human relationships (Marx said the same thing). Instead of such liberty, it is clear that "the Toiling Millions of Mankind [are] in most vital need and passionate instinctive desire of Guidance". Where must they turn for this guidance? "The mandate of God to His creature man is: Work!" It must be ordered work, playing its part in an organic society. Order demands subordination:

> Look around you. Your world-hosts are all in mutiny, in confusion, destitution; on the eve of fiery wreck and madness! They will not march farther for you, on the sixpence a day and supply-and-demand principle: they will not; nor ought they, nor can they. Ye shall reduce them to order, begin reducing them. To order, to just sub-ordination; noble loyalty in return for noble guidance. Their souls are driven nigh mad; let yours be sane and ever saner. Not as a be-wildered bewildering mob; but as a firm regimented mass, with real captains over them, will these men march any more, All human in-terests, combined human endeavours, and social growths in this world, have at a certain stage of their development, required reorganising: and Work, the grandest of human interests, does now require it.

Democracy for Carlyle was clearly not the solution. "Democracy, which means despair of finding any heroes to govern you, and con-tented putting-up with the want of them,—alas, thou too, *mein Leiber*, seest well how close it is of kin to *Atheism*, and other sad *Isms*." If men were compelled into self-discipline and ordered work, "all painful tyranny, in that case . . . , were but mild 'surgery' ". Increase in the franchise will only make matters worse:

> The notion that a man's liberty consists in giving his vote at election-hustings, and saying, "Behold, now I too have my twenty-thousandth part of a Talker in our National Palaver; will not all the gods be good to me?"—is one of the pleasantest! Nature nevertheless is kind at present; and puts it into the heads of many, almost of all. The liberty especially which has to purchase itself by social isolation, and each man standing separate from the other, having "no business with him" but a cash-account: this is such a liberty as the Earth seldom saw;—as the Earth will not long put up with, recommend it how you may. This liberty turns out, before it have long continued in action, with all men flinging up their caps round it, to be, for the Working Millions a liberty to die by want of food; for the Idle Thousands and Units, alas, a still more fatal liberty to live in want of work; to have no earnest duty to do in this God's-World any more. What becomes

of a man in such a predicament? Earth's laws are silent; and Heaven's speak in a voice which is not heard.

The puzzle about Carlyle's reaction to *laissez-faire* is that it seems to lead him simultaneously to the political left and to the extreme political right. This may be to some extent a reflection on the ambiguities in our own use of these terms, yet we cannot avoid the conclusion that there were deep ambiguities in Carlyle's position. While he diagnosed clearly and forcefully some of the undesirable implications in both theory and practice of nineteenth century-liberalism, his refusal to concede that even an increasingly educated electorate might have some useful democratic contribution to make to the solution of the problems he exposed so forcefully, led him increasingly to despise all men who were not acting either as leaders or as led.

> Singularly, in the case of human swarms, with what perfection of unanimity and quasi-religious conviction the stupidest absurdities can be received as axioms of Euclid, nay as articles of faith, which you are not only to believe, unless malignantly insane, but are (if you have any honour or morality) to push into practice, and without delay see *done* if your soul would live! Divine commandment *to vote* ("Manhood Suffrage"—Horsehood, Doghood ditto not yet treated of); universal "glorious Liberty" (to Sons of the Devil in overwhelming majority, as would appear); Count of Heads the God-appointed way in this Universe, all other ways Devil-appointed; in one brief word, which includes whatever of palpable incredibility and delirious absurdity, universally believed, can be uttered or imagined on these points, "the equality of men", any man equal to any other; Quashee Nigger to Socrates or Shakespeare: Judas Iscariot to Jesus Christ—and Bedlam and Gehenna equal to the New Jerusalem, shall we say?

There are of course many obvious senses in which men are not equal; but both Christian and Humanist would agree in insisting that in a profound sense it is true to assert that "Quashee Nigger" and Socrates or Shakespeare *are* equal, and if one fails to see this basic equality existing among men *qua* men in the midst of all more obvious inequalities, then one is committed to a doctrine whose implications are frightening. I do not propose here to enter into a discussion of Carlyle's doctrine of heroes and hero-worship, which would require a complete lecture in itself; I can only point to the obvious fact that this doctrine was evolved by Carlyle in an almost desperate attempt to solve the problems posed by his own brilliant analysis of the implications of *laissez-faire*, and it reminds us that the dictatorial solution to the problems of Victorian liberalism is at least as logical, if not at all as humanly adequate, as the democratic.

Carlyle's dismissal of "manhood suffrage" as identical with Horsehood or Doghood is an appalling insult to the humanness in man. The passage comes from *Shooting Niagara: and After?*, Carlyle's last word on "the condition of England question", described by the author himself as "very fierce, exaggerative, ragged, unkempt, and defective". It represented Carlyle's reaction to Disraeli's Reform Bill of 1867, and in it his contempt for man in the mass and for the whole process of democracy rises to a height of fury. Yet in the midst of his scorn for "Parliamentary Eloquences, and Emancipated Niggers ripening towards nothing but destruction", and side by side with his assertions that men must be compelled into virtue by a natural superior or be better hanged, we get his eloquent attack on the "cheap and nasty", his insistence that "if I want an article, let it be genuine, at whatever price", his determination to "annihilate the soot and dirt and squalid horror now defacing this England". In modern industry, he asserts, "nothing but bewilderment, contention, misery, mutual rage, and continually advancing ruin" can dwell. The solution for Carlyle is to call on the Hero to impose wise order and discipline on the nation, so that "with every new Disciplined Man he was widening the arena of *Anti*-Anarchy, of God-appointed *Order* in this world and Nation".

"I found personal sympathy with suffering lay at the root of all his thoughts", wrote Froude of Carlyle, and we know that he fought in the cause of the poor all his life. Yet he vigorously defended the vicious cruelty with which Governor Eyre of Jamaica dealt with the Negroes after their insurrection there in 1861 : Negroes, Carlyle had been told, were lazy and would not willingly work : this offended against his zealous belief in the doctrine of work—anything to Carlyle (especially the later Carlyle) came to be justifiable if it would force work on lazy people. Negroes would be *happier* if forced to work— by whatever terrors. One is reminded of the grim remark made by Stevenson's Weir of Hermiston : "Every man has to work, if it's only at peddling ballants ; to work, or to be wheepit, or to be hangit." For the later Carlyle, this was literally so : "to work or to be wheepit, or to be hangit", and he would justify whipping or hanging if there seemed no other way to compel work.

Carlyle objected to what Ruskin, Matthew Arnold, and William

Morris objected to in nineteenth-century civilisation. He remains one of the great Victorian prophets who saw into the heart of the nine-teenth-century dilemma. But to see a problem clearly is not always to see its solution. It is not Carlyle's diagnosis but his remedies that sometimes appal us. (Though it is only fair to say that we have experience of dictators of a kind that Carlyle had not.) One cannot help feeling that the increasing inadequacy of his remedies, like the growing stridency of his voice and repetitiveness of his arguments, is related in some way to the logical inadequacy of his positive creed. Carlyle's journey from the Everlasting No to the Everlasting Yea was curiously jerky and subjective and involved many leaps across logical chasms, so that often he substituted rhetoric for logic. Time and again he appeals with increasing loudness to a God whose existence he intuited in a transient moment of Nature mysticism and whose psychological and logical meaning he never looked into very closely. If one aspect of the Victorian dilemma concerns the bases of faith and sources of value in the modern world, then I think that it can be fairly said that Carlyle thought he had solved it while in fact he had not solved it at all. In other words, I suggest that one might be able to relate the inadequacy of Carlyle's positive thought—of his remedies for the problems he described so accurately and vividly—to the in-adequate intellectual foundations of his faith.

In these remarks I have had to leave out any discussion of Carlyle the artist, of his remarkable use of language and those special rhetorical devices which he invented that give his writings their characteristic pungency and power. It was fashionable not so very long ago to dismiss Carlyle entirely as a thinker and to comment on him as an "artist in words" only. This is largely the view expressed by Logan Pearsall Smith in his essay, "Thomas Carlyle: the Rembrandt of English Prose". Pearsall Smith refers with approval to Henry James the elder's view of Carlyle as "not a moralist at all, but an artist; picturesqueness in man and nature was what he cared for above all things; he was, in fact, a painter who valued the good and evil of the world as a painter does his pigments, for the opportunities they give for the display of his pictorial powers". But one cannot really divorce art from vision and imagination as simply as this. That great prose-poem, as it has been called, *The French Revolution*, is not simply a piece of fancy playing about with words : Carlyle's vision of a great retributive force at the heart of things finally breaking out to manifest its stern justice in human history and then rounding on its own ministers when they in turn showed themselves incapable of the heroism and morality which the historical moment demanded—this vision, as John Holloway has shown in his careful analysis of Carlyle's style in this work, is bound up with the very fabric of Carlyle's language. It arises from the very heart of Carlyle's moral imagination. One cannot discuss the style, the art, in the book without discussing the moral imagination at work in it. The extraordinary vitality, the characteristic combination of violence and intimacy, of the colloquial and the rhetorical, the remarkable ability to rub the reader's nose in what is being described, to plunge him with unsparing violence in the very feel and smell sound and texture of it all, is an astonishing achievement—and not merely as a piece of verbal virtuosity, but as the emanation of an incandescent historico-moral imagination.

However much one may be offended by the violence and the arbitrariness of Carlyle's social and political thought in the latter part of his career, one returns again and again to the living strength of the record of his responses to the problems of men and society in his time. Most of all, I think, we find this vitality in his letters and other informal writings, which often capture with a special kind of impromptu brilliance the impression of a personality or a situation. He can be unfair, of course, as in his picture of Charles Lamb as a "pitiful, ricketty, staggering, stammering Tom fool". (Though even here we are grateful for the vivid record of Lamb's conversation: "He said: There are just two things I regret in English history; first that Guy Faux's plot did not take effect (there would have been so glorious an *explosion*); second that the Royalists did not hang Milton (then we might have laughed at them).") There are some wonderful character sketches in his *Reminiscences*, like that account of Wordsworth in old age silently, slowly, and steadily gnawing at some raisins after dinner. And the account of the fifty-three-year-old Coleridge which he gives us in his *Life of Sterling* (the most intimate and revealing of his major works) is now classic:

> The deep eyes, of a light hazel, were as full of sorrow as of inspiration; confused pain looked mildly from them, as in a kind of mild astonishment. The whole figure and air, good and amiable otherwise, might be called flabby and irresolute; expressive of weakness under possibility of strength. He hung loosely on his limbs, with knees bent, and stooping attitude; in walking, he rather shuffled than decisively

stept ; and a lady once remarked, he never could fix which side of the
garden walk would suit him best, but continually shifted, corkscrew
fashion, and kept trying both. A heavy-laden, high-aspiring and
surely much-suffering man. His voice, natually soft and good, had
contracted itself into a plaintive snuffle and singsong ; he spoke as if
preaching,—you would have said, preaching earnestly and also hopelessly the weightiest things. I still recollect his "object" and "subject",
terms of continual recurrence in the Kanteen province ; and how he
sang and snuffled them into "om-m-mject" and "sum-m-mject", with
a kind of solemn shake or quaver, as he rolled along,

But Carlyle the observer of his fellow men is rather a different
Carlyle from Carlyle the confronter of the Victorian dilemma. What
Carlyle made of that confrontation has been my main theme and, if I
have not minimised its deficencies, I hope I have also made clear its
abiding value.

7

Yeats's Earlier Poems: Some Themes and Patterns[1]

The greatness and originality of Yeats's middle and later poems have led to the dismissal of his earlier poetry, by most critics, as of merely biographical interest, illustrating the morass of late nineteenth-century romanticism from which the poet's developing genius eventually rescued him. There is of course some justification for this. The moaning self-indulgence of such a poem as "The Sad Shepherd", the meretricious orientalism of "Anashuya and Vijaya", and what he himself later called "all that overcharged colour inherited from the romantic movement" found in so many of the poems in his first three collections, are not really worth serious critical attention. Nevertheless, there is much of interest in these early poems, some of which at least are of value in their own right. It is true that when we find ourselves arrested by a particular early poem it will generally turn out to be a drastically revised version that we are looking at, and if we turn to the original version in an early volume or in *Poems and Ballads of Young Ireland* or in the indispensable Allt-Alspach variorum edition we may well find something much vaguer in expression and much less striking in imagery. Even so, the original version sometimes achieves a sufficiently arresting presentation of a theme to make clear that a real poet is at work here. And even where it does not, there may be in the nature of the theme itself or in the occasional line of phrase something that stirs the reader to attention. I do not want to make too great a claim for the quality and interest of Yeats's earlier poetry; but I believe that a fair amount of it is of real interest, not simply to the pedant interested in charting a map of development, or a researcher

[1] Originally published in *In Excited Reverie : A Centenary Tribute to W. B. Yeats*, ed. A. N. Jeffares and K. G. W. Cross. London (Macmillan) 1965. Pp. 48–67.

133

trying to classify themes and techniques, but to the reader and critic concerned with the kinds of imagination and the uses of language out of which poetry develops and indeed to (dare I use such an old-fashioned phrase?) the lover of poetry.

As I have already suggested, we are not very interested in the "inarticulate moan" of "The Sad Shepherd", which when originally published in the *Dublin University Review* in October 1886 bore the unpromising title "Miserrimus". Nevertheless, the theme of the poem is worth some attention. The sad shepherd tries in vain to arouse the sympathy of nature, but the natural world is unconcerned with him and makes no response :

> Then cried the man whom Sorrow named his friend :
> 'Oh sea, old sea, hear thou my piteous story ;'
> The sea swept on and cried her old cry still,
> Rolling along in dreams from hill to hill ;
> And from the persecution of her glory
> He fled, . . .
>
> (Original version)

The poet here is not employing the conventional romantic device of allowing nature to become a sounding board for human feeling. Man fools himself if he thinks that nature exists to respond to his emotional needs. The poet, said Wordsworth, "considers man and nature as essentially adapted to each other, and the mind of man as naturally the mirror of the fairest and most interesting properties of nature". So for Wordsworth, the key word is *relationship*. But for Yeats, even in his early romantic phase, it was a conviction of the essential dichotomy between man and nature that most possessed him. Not relationship but difference was what haunted Yeats. Further, a sense of this difference can become intolerable. The shepherd fled "from the persecution of her glory" (he tightened the line up in a later version, but kept this phrase unchanged). Now "persecution" is an interesting and indeed arresting word in this context. Nature persecutes man by giving him the expectations of its sympathy—because of its beauty and its mood-creating role—only in order to withold it. Wordsworth held that "Nature never did betray the heart that loved her", but Yeats knew better : for him, at least in his early phase, nature's continual betrayal of man's expectations of it was part of the pattern of reality. And that pattern was built of opposites, to be captured in poems whose structure involves a two-term dialectic.

Nothing is more striking in Yeats's development as a poet than his gradual replacement of a two-term by a three-term dialectic. His early poems are full of simple contrasts between pairs, and such contrasts often provide the basic structure : man versus nature, the domesticated versus the wild, the human versus the fairy, the temporal versus the changeless, the modern versus the ancient, the familiar versus the remote, and so on. In his later poetry he resolves these "antinomies of day and night", achieving a resolution of opposites either in a *tertium quid* or else in a sense of the interpenetration of opposites—

"Fair and foul are near of kin,
And fair needs foul," I cried.

But the two-term dialectic has its own poetic possibilities, as the word "persecution" in "The Sad Shepherd" suggests.

This is not to claim that Yeats consistently explored these possibilities in his early poetry. Sometimes he was content with the more traditional romantic mood-creating use of a natural background :

The woods were round them, and the yellow leaves
Fell like faint meteors in the gloom, and once
A rabbit old and lame limped down the path ;
Autumn was over him : . . .

This is well enough done in its way, which is the Tennysonian elegiac way, but less interesting than what Yeats does in, say, "The Madness of King Goll", where he elaborates the implications of the "persecution" of the sad shepherd in a highly original manner. It is a disturbing sense of the essential *otherness* of the natural world that derives King Goll mad, his madness being indicated by the refrain with which each stanza ends :

They will not hush, the leaves a-flutter round me, the beech leaves old.

The poem itself has a narrative base, the king describing what he was before he went mad and the circumstances under which he went mad, with the refrain reminding us that at the time of the telling he actually *is* mad. Man cannot come to terms with nature, which haunts, distracts, and finally maddens him. And if you have been brought up to believe that man and nature are one, and that the function of nature is to serve man, then the realisation of the falsity of this, the discovery of the uncanny otherness of nature, will make your mind snap. It is interesting that in later revisions—and this is a poem whose final text is much changed from the original form—Yeats altered the imagery in order to bring out this theme, which in the first version was almost lost amid the lushness of the detail, though it was very much present in the underlying structure. In revising, Yeats brought structure and imagery into closer unity, and the result is a genuinely impressive poem. Let us look briefly at the final version.

The poem opens with King Goll before his madness, the successful ruler of his kingdom :

> I sat on cushioned otter-skin :
> My word was law from Ith to Emain,
> And shook at Inver Amergin
> The hearts of the world-troubling seamen,
> And drove tumult and war away
> From girl and boy and man and beast ;
> The fields grew fatter day by day,
> The wild fowl of the air increased ;
> And every ancient Ollave said,
> While he bent down his fading head,
> "He drives away the Northern cold."
> *They will not hush, the leaves a-flutter round me,*
>   *the beech leaves old.*

He sat on a cushioned otter-skin, thus using wild nature for his comfort and prestige. His victories gave peace to "girl and boy and man and beast"—with beasts casually included in the world of men. He had power over men and animals : the fields grew fatter, "the wild fowl of the air increased". And the wise men flattered him by telling him that he had dominion even over the weather. Only in the refrain at the end are we shaken into realisation that the king is now mad, and that he realises that nature, far from being the servant and comforter of man, is something alien and haunting.

It was while he was playing his expected role of warrior and military saviour of his country that a sense of the appalling alienation of nature from man overcame him. Here is the third stanza :

> But slowly, as I shouting slew
> And trampled in the bubbling mire,
> In my most secret spirit grew
> A whirling and a wandering fire :

I stood : keen stars above me shone,
Around me shone keen eyes of men :
I laughed aloud and hurried on
By rocky shore and rushy fen ;
I laughed because birds fluttered by,
And starlight gleamed, and clouds flew high,
And rushes waved and waters tolled.
They will not hush, the leaves a-flutter round me,
    the beech leaves old.

The point is made by a simple juxtaposition of imagery : the "keen
stars" were above him and the "keen eyes of men" were around him.
A sense of the utter difference between the two overcame him, and he
broke into mad laughter : "I laughed *because* birds fluttered by, and
starlight gleamed, and clouds flew high." That "because" is lunatic
logic, and brilliantly establishes the point of the stanza, bringing the
imagery into focus (this does not happen in the original version, which
is differently worded). As a result of this strange epiphany, King Goll
now wanders aimlessly through the countryside, trying to establish
contact with that other world of nature. In the process, he becomes
alienated from human interests :

I came upon a little town
That slumbered in the harvest moon, . . .

He can make no contact with the sleeping town, but finds an "old
tympan" lying "deserted on a doorway seat" and takes it away with
him to the woods, where, to its accompaniment, he sings "of some
inhuman misery". The tympan—like the Aeolian harp of the earlier
romantics—belongs to the word of both man and nature, and King
Goll removes it from the former to the latter. His song, which begins
as though it might be about the human world ("when day's toil is
done"), is in fact about the world of nature ; in any case, the suggestion
that he might have been using the tympan to bridge the two worlds
and to bring himself back into some knowledge of a specifically human
emotion destroys the instrument, and he is left at the end with "the
kind wires torn and gone", howling meaninglessly like an animal,
condemned to wander through nature but now part of neither man's
nor nature's world, only crazily aware of their perpetual difference.

The limitations of a poem of this sort are obvious : the presentation,
however hauntingly, of a sense of the dichotomy between the human

K

and the natural world is in itself more of an emotional exercise than a fully realised poem dealing with some genuine centre of human experience. But the poem teases and disturbs and impresses, even if in a somewhat too self-consciously "poetic" way, and clearly represents—even in its original form—something more than the faded romanticism which is the only quality now ascribed by most critics to the early Yeats.

The poem which follows "King Goll" in the *Collected Poems*, written about the same time, is "The Stolen Child", and here too we find that the whole structure and meaning are based on a sense of irreconcilable difference between two worlds. Once again, we have a refrain, but used somewhat differently this time, in order to represent the call of wild nature to the human infant still new enough to the human world to be able to renounce it and move over to the other world, this time not simply the world of nature but the world of faery, which is part of the inhuman world of herons, water-rats, berries, moonlight, and "dim grey sands". The changes made in later revisions are here much less significant than in "King Goll" and the poem is in any case simpler in both language and structure. The siren call of the faery world (which significantly changes in rhythmic pattern from the body of the stanza) simply summons the child to come away and join the faery band, leaving a world "more full of weeping than you can understand". The first three stanzas of the four-stanza poem build up a picture of the faery world of nature with all the traditional romantic appeal, and it seems that the poem is throwing its weight on the side of the seduction ; but when we come to the final stanza the imagery suddenly changes in tone and implication, and the warm, familiar, human world—the "calves on the warm hillside" (not wild animals but animals bred for human use), "the kettle on the hob" (presented as an image of peace) and the "brown mice" which "bob round and round the oatmeal-chest" (images of domesticity and the friendly humanising of natural objects) —is presented as something rashly given up in exchange for something cold and inhuman. The point is made very delicately, and the meaning is carried largely by the imagery. As in "King Goll", there is developed a sense of the mystery and terror of that other world of the natural elements, of beauty untouched by human desire, human need, or human familiarity, that derives some of its force from folklore. It is perhaps worth noting that both these poems have a background in

Irish myth and legend : it was his use of Irish material that, at a very early stage, redeemed Yeats from the merely picturesque use of exotic detail. The terror of nature has nothing to do with any moral feeling, such as that which led Wordsworth to feel that nature was after him because he had stolen a boat. The moral is a purely human category, a category to which wild nature, in these poems of Yeats, is an utter stranger. One might say that these poems, for all their use of some traditional romantic properties, contain implicit criticisms of the falsity and sentimentality of at least one romantic attitude to nature.

A similar theme can be recognised in such a simple and even trivial-seeming poem as "To an Isle in the Water", which at first sight seems to be a conventional invitation to the poet's beloved to fly with him "to an isle in the water". But the thought of the poem is in fact more interesting than this. The girl is a "shy one", and shyness is a characteristic of wild creatures ; when the poet sees her in a domestic setting, or engaged in domestic duties, he feels that she does not belong there, and this feeling prompts him to suggest that he carry her off to where she does belong—the world of wild nature.

> Shy one, shy one,
> Shy one of my heart,
> She moves in the firelight
> Pensively apart.
>
> She carries in the dishes,
> And lays them in a row.
> To an isle in the water
> With her would I go . . .

She moves "apart" in the firelight—and there can be no doubt that firelight has the same force in the poem as the warm hillside and the oatmeal-chest have in "The Stolen Child". The domestic precision of the first two lines of the second stanza keep a careful balance between a suggestion of the comfortable and familiar on the one hand, and the mechanical and boring on the other. The theme of escape from domesticity to wild nature is thus given a new dimension : the girl herself, because of her shyness, seems to the poet to belong to the wild, and so to be unfitted for the domestic routine which she carries out, and that is why he proposes to carry her off to what seems to him to be her proper element. When "she carries in the candles and lights the curtained room", this may seem at first sight as though she is being admirably domestic, so much so as to provoke in the poet a desire to carry her off to a home which they can share together. But this is not what the poem's true meaning seems to be. The poet wishes to go off with her to where she seems really to belong. It is true that the irreconcilable difference between the human and the natural world, which is suggested in "King Goll", is here modulated into a gap across which there can be bridges, so that there can be girls who, though living in a domestic setting, belong by temperament to the other side. But the dialectic of the poem remains a two-term one.

There are many variations on this theme in Yeats's early poems. "Who Goes with Fergus?"—quoted by Buck Mulligan in Joyce's *Ulysses*—suggests that the world of ancient heroic legend, which Yeats first learned about in the pages of Standish O'Grady, is divorced from the normal passions of the human world and associated with the impersonal world of nature :

> Who will go drive with Fergus now,
> And pierce the deep wood's woven shade,
> And dance upon the level shore?
> Young man, lift up your russet brow,
> And lift your tender eyelids, maid,
> And brood on hopes and fears no more.
>
> And no more turn aside and brood
> Upon love's bitter mystery ;
> For Fergus rules the brazen cars,
> And rules the shadows of the wood,
> And the white breast of the dim sea
> And all dishevelled wandering stars.

The "For" which opens the third line of the second stanza is the pivot of the poem, and a rather puzzling one. "Go with Fergus and don't bother about ordinary human hopes and fears, for Fergus rules both the heroic and the natural world." It is odd to have the heroic world associated with "shadows", the "dim sea", and the "dishevelled wandering stars", but Yeats's imagination was always liable to do the unexpected, even in the early 1890s (the poem originally appeared in the second act of *The Countess Kathleen*). Further, we must remember who Fergus was. In Yeats's words, "he was the poet of the Red Branch cycle [who was] once king of all Ireland, but gave up his throne that he might live at peace hunting in the woods". Yeats made his own uses of Irish heroic story, as he did of Irish popular folklore ;

from both he extracted ways of playing variations on the two-term
pattern that he was so fond of in his early phases.

A more interesting example than either of the preceding two of
Yeats's working with pairs of contraries is "The Man Who Dreamed
of Faeryland", a poem of considerable power and originality in spite
of a title calculated to scare off most modern readers.   A man involved
in ordinary human emotions and ordinary human affairs is made aware,
on suddenly confronting objects from the natural world like fishes
and worms, of the strange otherness of that world, and after that he
can know no peace.   Though Yeats made a number of verbal changes
in later editions, the poem as it now appears in the *Collected Poems* is
not significantly different from the original version which appeared
in *The National Observer* in February 1891 and one is not in any way
distorting its nature and meaning if one uses the later and more
accessible text.   The first stanza sets the basic pattern :

> He stood among a crowd at Dromahair ;
> His heart hung all upon a silken dress,
> And he had known at last some tenderness,
> Before earth took him to her stony care ;
> But when a man poured fish into a pile,
> It seemed they raised their little silver heads,
> And sang what gold morning or evening sheds
> Upon a woven world-forgotten isle
> Where people love beside the ravelled seas ;
> That Time can never mar a lover's vows
> Under that woven changeless roof of boughs :
> The singing shook him out of his new ease.

In the first stanza it is "some tenderness" that he had known ; in the
second stanza it is "some prudent years" ; in the third stanza it is
"vengeance" that he "might have known" and in the final stanza it is
"unhaunted sleep" that he might have known.   Love, money-making,
anger, and finally rest, represent the normal human lot.   The hero of
the poem had known something of the first and second, but was
prevented from venting his anger on those that mocked him by a
sudden revival of his awareness of the alien world of nature, and that
awareness has since prevented him from finding peace in the grave.

The poem pivots on the single conjunction "but", which opens the
fifth line of each stanza except the last, which employs a slightly
different construction with the same logical pattern.   He was buying

a silk dress for his girl, like any other man, but—. He was worrying about money like any other man, but—. He would have revenged himself on those that mocked him, but—. He might have rested in peace in the grave, but—. This seems an odd way in which to build up a poem, but in fact it succeeds remarkably well. The "but" in each stanza introduces the result of the man's confrontation with nature. The results are disturbing. They do not involve the realisation that nature is utterly different from the world of human emotions and plans ; rather, they suggest the existence of a world in which Time does not destroy and where all activity is part of the cosmic dance of life. Indeed, there is an anticipation here both of Yeats's later conception of Byzantium and of his later use of the idea of the Plotinian dance of life—though it was to be many years before he would read the books to which modern scholars have attributed his interest in these ideas. Here is the final stanza :

> He slept under the hill of Lugnagall ;
> And might have known at last unhaunted sleep
> Under that cold and vapour-turbaned steep,
> Now that the earth had taken man and all :
> Did not the worms that spired about his bones
> Proclaim with that unwearied, reedy cry
> That God has laid His fingers on the sky,
> That from those fingers glittering summer runs
> Upon the dancer by the dreamless wave.
> Why should those lovers that no lovers miss
> Dream, until God burn Nature with a kiss?
> The man has found no comfort in the grave.

Yeats is here combining with his earlier recurring idea of the dichotomy between man and nature a view of the destructive consequences of being possessed by a vision. The vision comes through nature, and it is not entirely consistent, nor is it fully apprehended by the hero ; but its partial and confused character is a guarantee of its genuineness. There is nothing simple or comfortable or utopian about the vision man gets from nature : it may contain glimpses of Byzantium, but it does not give the peace and wholeness of Byzantium ; it disturbs and distracts, unfitting man for his place in the normal human world while not fitting him for any other. This is a very Irish poem, and the material comes from Irish folklore, but Yeats is here using Irish folklore for his own uncanny purposes. It is interesting to see how far he can go in this direction without using any of the apparatus he was later to develop for himself in *A Vision*. There is a curious deadpan tone in the poem which belies the strangeness of its content and adds to its power. The movement from the first four lines of each stanza through the essential "but" to the distracting vision is achieved with extraordinary calm ; the rhythms of the poems are steady and even throughout. And the final line— "The man has found no comfort in the grave"—is done almost with a shrug, an anti-climactic climax. In the second stanza the disturbing knowledge comes to him from

> A lug-worm with its grey and muddy mouth.

This is not simply the nature imagery of an Irish poet brought up on the Pre-Raphaelites. There is an anti-romantic use of romanticism here which with our hindsight we can see was surely going to lead to something even more interesting.

What one might pedantically call the mutations of the two-term dialectic thus represent something of real interest in the early Yeats, and one could follow them much further than I have here done. I should like now to discuss another theme or attitude (it is sometimes one and sometimes the other and sometimes both) that can be traced in the very earliest poems, and which later becomes a distinguishing quality of much of his greatest poetry. To turn once more to "The Sad Shepherd" (not an especially good but nonetheless an interesting poem) : we find in the second line the phrase "high comrade" (origin-ally "high kinsmen"), and we may perhaps say to ourselves that this use of the adjective "high" comes from Yeats's preoccupation with Irish heroic legend and has something to do with the sense of lineage, of heroic manners, and of exhibitionist courtesy which belongs to such literature. This is true enough, but there are other things at work here as well. Here is the first stanza of "The Rose of the World" :

> Who dreamed that beauty passes like a dream?
> For these red lips, with all their mournful pride,
> Mournful that no new wonder may betide,
> Troy passed away in one high funeral gleam,
> And Usna's children died.

This poem dates from 1891. Some nineteen years later, writing of Maud Gonne in "No Second Troy", he talked of her beauty as

> Being high and solitary and most stern.

In "Adam's Curse" (1902), also referring to Maud Gonne, he wrote

> I had a thought for no one's but your ears :
> That you were beautiful, and that I strove
> To love you in the old high way of love ; . . .

These three examples will suffice. I want to draw attention to the early stage at which Yeats began to use the word "high" to indicate the kind of aristocratic courtesy which he was later to associate with the life of the Great House, with art patrons of the Italian Renaissance, with "innocence and beauty", with "traditional sanctity and loveliness", with the tragic gaiety of Hamlet and Lear, and with the horseman who is enjoined to cast a cold eye on life and on death. There are many elements compounded here, but they can all be related, however circuitously, to Yeats's early admiration of the Irish heroic mode. It is difficult to over-estimate the influence on Yeats of Standish O'Grady's *History of Ireland, Heroic Period* (published in 1878). To O'Grady, wrote Yeats in 1914, "every Irish imaginative writer owed a portion of his soul". He went on : "In his imaginative *History of Ireland* he had made the old Irish heroes, Fion, and Oisin, and Cuchullan, alive again, taking them, for I think he knew no Gaelic, from the dry pages of O'Curry and his school, and condensing and arranging, as he thought Homer would have arranged and condensed. Lady Gregory has told the same tales, . . . but O'Grady was the first, and we read him in our 'teens."[2] Beside O'Grady's *History* must be set the influence of the character of John O'Leary. "O'Leary had joined the Fenian movement", wrote Yeats in 1907, "with no hope of success, as we know, but because he believed such a movement good for the moral character of the people ; and had taken his long imprisonment without complaining. Even to the very end, while often speaking of his prison life, he would have thought it took from his Roman courage to describe its hardship. The worth of a man's acts in the moral memory, a continual height of mind in the doing of them, seemed more to him than their immediate result. . . . A man was not to lie, or even to give up his dignity, on any patriotic plea, and I have heard him say, 'I have but one religion, the old Persian : to bend the bow and tell the truth', and again, 'There are things a man must not do to save a nation', and again 'A man must not cry in public to save a nation' . . ."[3] We must bear this passage in mind when we read

[2] *The Autobiography of William Butler Yeats*, New York, 1938, pp. 189–90.
[3] *Essays and Introductions*, London, 1961, p. 247.

Romantic Ireland's dead and gone,
It's with O'Leary in the grave,

if we want to be sure that we know what Yeats meant by "Romantic".

In the same essay as that in which he described O'Leary's character, Yeats wrote : "Three types of men have made all beautiful things, Aristocracies have made beautiful manners, because their place in the world puts them above the fear of life, and the countrymen have made beautiful stories and beliefs, because they have nothing to lose and so do not fear, and the artists have made all the rest, because Providence has filled them with recklessness."[4] Later in this essay he declared that "in life courtesy and self-possession, and in the arts style, are the sensible impressions of the free mind, for both arise out of a deliberate shaping of all things, and from never being swept away, whatever the emotion, into confusion or dullness".[5] And one could quote again and again from Yeats's prose writings to show his admiration for traditional courtesy, his belief in the *gesture* (both in life and in art), his view that heroism, sternness, and joy are related in both art and life. "We will not forget how to be stern, but we will remember always that the highest life unites, as in one fire, the greatest passion and the greatest courtesy."

The "high funeral gleam" with which Troy passed away is thus an expression of heroic tragedy, of tragedy done with *style*, an idea that from a very early stage possessed Yeats's mind and continued to possess it until the end : we can set the line "Gaiety transfiguring all that dread" from "Lapiz Lazuli" beside this line from "The Rose of the World" as representing the final version of this idea. In his early poetry it is related to Irish heroic legend and history, and though later it becomes involved with many other sources this should not lead us to ignore the importance of the Irish elements in this characteristic Yeatsian notion. Yeats's admiration of the Great House tradition, which he came to see as standing for a way of life which converted chaos into order by custom and ceremony, is generally ascribed to the influence on him of Coole Park : but in fact his view of the Irish past had already conditioned him to respond in this way, just as it later helped him to construct his own myth of a great eighteenth-century Anglo-Irish civilisation which took in Swift, Berkeley, Sheridan, Goldsmith, Burke, and Grattan.

[4] *Op. cit.*, p. 251.   [5] *Op. cit.*, p. 253.

Again and again in Yeats's early poetry we find Irish folklore, Irish heroic story, Irish history, and even Irish landscape working in his imagination to mitigate the excesses of a self-indulgent romanticism, of mere dreaminess and decorativeness. Long before he knew Pound or became interested in Japanese No plays or came under any of those other influences which strengthened his belief in the importance of stylisation in art, he had found Irish reasons for moving in the direction he was to sum up towards the end of his life in the lines beginning

> Irish poets, learn your trade,
> Sing whatever is well made.

Even the association of classical and Celtic myth in "The Rose of the World"—

> Troy passed away in one high funeral gleam
> And Usna's children died—

helps to prevent the image of Helen of Troy from operating as a vague literary reference, concentrating it into a symbol of doomed heroic passion which stands in sharp contrast to the "cloudy glamour" of other of his early poems. His long-continued hopeless love for Maud Gonne also helped to concentrate his conception of the heroic relationship between beauty, dignity, and destruction :

> What could have made her peaceful with a mind
> That nobleness made simple as a fire,
> With beauty like a tightened bow, a kind
> That is not natural in an age like this,
> Being high and solitary and most stern?
> Why, what could she have done, being what she is?
> Was there another Troy for her to burn?

These lines come somewhat later. We can see in the earlier poems more clearly the struggle between the vaguely plangent and the stylised heroic. In "The Rose of Battle" we find :

> Rose of all Roses, Rose of all the World!
> You, too, have come where the dim tides are hurled
> Upon the wharves of sorrow, and heard ring
> The bell that calls us on ; the sweet far thing.
> Beauty grown sad with its eternity
> Made you of us, and of the dim grey sea.

This is the early dream style, and adjectives like "sweet", "sad", and "dim" and phrases such as "the wharves of sorrow" proclaim very plainly to what literary world *this* poem belongs. Sometimes Yeats went over these early poems to change the romantic melancholy into heroic mourning, and the alteration is instructive. Thus the second stanza of "The Sorrow of Love" originally read :

> And when you came with these red mournful lips,
> And with you came the whole of the world's tears,
> And all the sorrows of her labouring ships,
> And all the burden of her myriad years.

This was later changed to

> A girl arose that had red mournful lips
> And seemed the greatness of the world in tears,
> Doomed like Odysseus and the labouring ships
> And proud as Priam murdered with his peers ; . . .

The association of Homeric with Irish themes seems to have done Yeats nothing but good. The Helen-Dierdre identification provided him with many effective poetic attitudes, and sometimes we find even in his more plangent and melancholy lines something that reminds us of Homer in that mood of his that especially pleased Matthew Arnold—what one might call the more Virgilian Homer. It may be mere personal fancy to see in these lines from "The Secret Rose" (1896)

> Who met Fand walking among flaming dew
> By a grey shore where the wind never blew

the same kind of tone achieved by Homer in the twenty-third book of the *Iliad* when he describes the grieving Achilles after the death of Patroclus lying alone

ἐν καθαρῷ, ὅθι κύματ᾽ ἐπ᾽ ἠϊόνος κλύζεσκον

(in a lonely place where the waves splashed upon the shore),

but it is certainly true that Yeats in the 1890s was seeking and finding ways of associating the elegiac and the heroic so as simultaneously to discipline the former and humanise the latter.

The attempts are not of course always successful. Even the revised version of "He Remembers Forgotten Beauty" (originally written in

1896) moves from sighing and kissing and "white Beauty" to the high
and the lonely in a way that does not really unite them :

> And when you sigh from kiss to kiss
> I hear white Beauty sighing, too,
> For hours when all must fade like dew,
> But flame on flame, and deep on deep,
> Throne over throne where in half sleep,
> Their swords upon their iron knees,
> Brood her high lonely mysteries.

But the association of the high and the lonely is interesting : we think
of the line from "No Second Troy", "Being high and solitary and
most stern" and his description of the Irish genius as "distinguished
and lonely". And we know where this association will take Yeats
eventually.

The dreamy and the disciplined are but two of the pairs of opposites
that form the patterns of so many of Yeats's early poems, and it would
be inaccurate to suggest that the former came from the "companions of
the Cheshire Cheese" and the latter from Irish heroic story. For one
of the companions, Lionel Johnson, who much influenced Yeats, had
from the beginning emphasised the importance of ritual and ceremony ;
Yeats later talked about the "austere nobility" of Johnson's verse
and recalled his favourite adjective "marmorean". Later, the contrast
between self-indulgent dream and heroic self-discipline gave way to
profounder contrasts and complex resolutions—the contrast between
"the foul rag and bone shop of the heart" and the timeless world of
art and artifice represented by Byzantium being only one modulation
of the later pattern. But much of what is often regarded as uniquely
belonging to the later Yeats can be found struggling to find expression
in the earlier and occasionally succeeding. And even where this is not
so, the simpler two-term dialectic of the earlier poems can yield something impressive and memorable more often than recent critics, with
their eyes fixed almost solely on the later poems, are prepared to admit.
As for what one might call the "middle poems"—notably those in
The Green Helmet and *Responsibilities*—they include "No Second
Troy", "September 1913", and "To a Shade", all admirable, as well as
one of the most important statements of his heroic aesthetics, "Upon
a House Shaken by the Land Agitation". Irish politics, too, (as his
Senate speeches show) stimulated Yeats's imagination to further work

on the relation between good art and the good life.   From the beginning he differed from most other members of the Rhymers' Club in
rejecting the escapist view of art represented by the fin-de-siècle ideal.
His question

> How should the world be luckier if this house
> Where passion and precision have been one
> Time out of mind, became too ruinous
> To breed the lidless eye that loves the sun?
> And the sweet laughing eagle thoughts that grow
> Where wings have memory of wings, and all
> That comes of the best knit to the best?

is a question about life, about civilisation, about the relation between
tradition and the present, as well as about art.   The "written speech /
Wrought of high laughter, loveliness and ease" that he prescribed for
citizens as well as writers may sound a utopian prescription in these
days of mass media.   But it represents something deeply pondered and
deeply imagined, something that lay close to the core of Yeats's
imagination, something that we can see developing in his poetry from
a very early stage.

8

Sir Herbert Grierson[1]
1866–1960

Herbert John Clifford Grierson—"Professor Grierson" to generations of students—was born on 16 Jan. 1866 in Lerwick, Shetland, second son of Andrew John Grierson and Alice Geraldine
(Clifford) his wife. The Griersons had been in Shetland since the beginning of the eighteenth century, becoming lairds with the purchase in 1765
of the Shetland estate of Quendale which consisted of the south-west
corner of the mainland. Here, on his father's property, Herbert
Grierson spent most of his childhood summers. His education began
with a governess at home, but he was soon sent for a short period to
the Anderson Institute in Lerwick. Of the Lerwick period of his
education he later remarked : "I acquired the Lerwick dialect and also
some swear-words." His memories of this time later centred on
fishing from the pier, boating, cliff climbing, and playing in the streets.

In August 1875 Grierson's father sent him to Cheltenham, to a
school run by two sisters of his mother. Here his real education began,
and he received a good grounding in Latin, French, and Geometry.
After spending the summer holidays of 1877 at Quendale, he was sent
to the Gymnasium in Aberdeen, a school founded in the 1840s on the
German model with the intention of providing a wider education than
that given by the city grammar schools. These latter schools had as
their objective the Aberdeen University Bursary Competition, for
which Latin, a little Greek, Mathematics, and English Grammar were
required. The "Gym" offered a wider course—Greek, Latin, Mathematics, English (which included History and Geography), French,
and even some German, its objective being less the University Bursary

[1] Originally published in *Proceedings of the British Academy*, Vol. XLVI, pp.
319–32.

Competition than the Indian Civil Service. But the school was already in decline when Grierson attended, though its standards remained reasonably high. In his own words, he "drifted up through the various classes, acquiring very little solid knowledge, either classical or mathematical"—he found mathematics increasingly uncongenial—but reading on his own a great deal of fiction and poetry.

The idea of going on from school to Aberdeen University was casually suggested to him by a fellow pupil one day in his last year at the Gym : the notion had never occurred either to him or to his father before. His father agreed with the suggestion ("having nothing better to suggest", as Grierson much later remarked) and he spent the following summer in Lerwick preparing for the Bursary Competition. He should in fact have spent another year at school working for this ; as it was, only the fortunate introduction of a new regulation enabling a candidate to offer Higher English (with prescribed books) and French instead of the single difficult Latin prose paper enabled him to do moderately well. He entered King's College, Aberdeen, in October 1883.

A few months after Grierson's ninetieth birthday, when we were talking together and he was reminiscing about his youth, I asked him whether his interest in English literature had first been stimulated at school. "At school?" he replied. "Why, the only English we ever did at the Gym was to memorise Dr Bain's Grammar". Dr Bain was Professor of Logic and Rhetoric at Aberdeen ; in his time literary studies there were still associated with logic, and the medieval *trivium* of grammar, logic, and rhetoric still determined in some degree the context in which English literature was approached and the limitations under which it was studied. Bain's successor, Professor Minto, was relieved of the logic and was expected to confine himself to rhetoric and to some rudimentary courses in English literary history. It was under Minto that Grierson studied English at King's College. "I remember", he told me, "he gave us some lectures on the French predecessors of Chaucer and on the early miracle plays. The last word in my notebook is 'Marlowe'. He got as far as mentioning Marlowe, but he never discussed the plays." There was, of course, no English School in any proper sense of the term at Aberdeen at that time. Students taking an Arts degree had to take Latin, Greek, Mathematics, and Physics as their main subjects, with a certain amount of logic, rhetoric, and metaphysics. One could read extra philosophy if one wanted "philosophy honours", and this, after a period of pleasant drifting in which he did little real work but read a great deal of poetry, he eventually decided to do, on the prompting of a friend. This meant reading Plato and Kant on his own—there were no lectures for honours candidates—and Grierson did so, having been warned that he had better not tackle Kant without also having read Locke and Hume. He could have taken "classical honours" instead of "philosophy honours", but the hard work at compulsory mathematics, his weakest subject, left him insufficient time for the detailed work on Latin and Greek texts. Curiously, for one who was to prove himself so gifted in literature, he was never able to translate *into* a classical language, and the prospect of writing a Latin prose, both at Aberdeen and later at Oxford, filled him with dread.

At the end of his third year he obtained a temporary position as second house-master at his old school, the Gym; this required no teaching, only some general supervision of discipline after teaching hours, and it left him plenty of time for study. But a breakdown in health forced him to give up his intention of reading for honours in both Classics and Philosophy; he dropped Classics, and did well enough in Philosophy to win the Bain gold medal. (At that time the Honours course in a Scots university was a fourth year added to the old seven subject Ordinary degree course.) He also won the Seafield medal in English, for which one had to sit a special paper. This was in 1887, when he graduated at Aberdeen with still no clear idea of where he was going.

The two years between his graduating at Aberdeen and proceeding to Oxford were confused and unsettled. He was unsuccessful in his attempt to obtain the Fullerton Scholarship at Aberdeen. He taught for a while at a girls' school (the Gym had by now closed down), tutored, and marked essays for Professor Minto. "At the end of 1888," he has written, "I seemed to be doomed to become an inferior school-teacher." But once again a friend came to his help with advice that proved decisive. This friend was himself a friend of J. A. Stewart, at that time Student of Christ Church (later White's Professor of Moral Philosophy), and had spoken to Stewart of Grierson. Stewart told Grierson's friend that the Holford Exhibition at Christ Church, generally confined to candidates from Charterhouse, would be open *pro hac vice*, as there was no suitable candidate from the school. So Grierson went to Oxford and sat for the Holford, which he won on the strength of his essay (on "Fanaticism"), which impressed D. B. Monro, Provost of Oriel, the Homeric scholar.

At Oxford Grierson made something of a reputation as a talker (on political and theological rather than on specifically literary topics). "The Griersons had a' a great volubility of speech", an old Shetland peasant woman once remarked. Much of his talking was done with Balliol men, fellow Scots among whom he made more friends than with men at his own college. He was very conscious of English class distinctions and sensitive about his relative poverty and lack of English social connexions. Though he could be voluble, Grierson was all his life essentially a shy man, and was easily rebuffed. Yet he made good friends at Oxford, one of the most intimate being Patrick Duncan, later Sir Patrick Duncan, Governor-General of South Africa.

He got a Second in Mods, and turned with relief to the work for Greats, which he found much more congenial. His careful reading of Plato had a permanent influence on his thought, the *Republic* freeing him, as he was later to put it, from Sidgwick's *Ethics*. "The *Republic* implanted in my mind the conviction that righteousness, justice (*dikaiosunē*) had its roots in our social nature, that no voice from Sinai or any other mountain would be intelligible or carry conviction unless something in ourselves gave assent willingly or unwillingly." It was only in his final year at Oxford that he pulled himself together and did his best work (the same pattern he had followed at Aberdeen) ; he was staying with a friend in Aberdeen when, as he used to recall in later years, the telegram from his scout arrived with the words "First Class". His telling of this incident used almost always to be accompanied by a recollection of himself walking across Tom Quad after taking his degree wondering what on earth he was going to do for a living. He wanted to take up an academic career, but he knew he was not a good enough classic to be a classics don, and there seemed no other appropriate subject.

Fortunately, changes were afoot which were to offer him precisely the kind of career that would afford most scope to his talents. A Royal Commission on the Scottish Universities, at work in 1889–92, reconstituted the entire curriculum and among other innovations made English Language and Literature a full degree subject. At the same time, a Mr John Gray Chalmers had given money to establish a Chair of English at Aberdeen, the patronage to lie with the Crown (in effect, with the Secretary of State for Scotland). In Aberdeen, shortly before

L

his final examinations at Oxford, Grierson had heard of these changes, and talked about their significance with Principal Geddes of Aberdeen University. From Geddes he learned that an interim lecturership in English would be established until the ordinance founding the Chair had gone through ; if he got a First in Greats, Geddes told him, he would propose him to the Senatus for the lecturership. In due course he applied, with influential backing from Sidgwick in Oxford (who had been impressed by Grierson's knowledge of the poet Cowper, about whom Sidgwick was enthusiastic) as well as from Geddes, and on 30 Sept. 1893 he received a letter from Geddes announcing his appointment as Lecturer in English for the coming session, "with the full knowledge that you are to be in the field for the Chair".

So, almost by accident, Grierson was launched on his long and fruitful career as a university teacher of English. He was very conscious of the limitations of his knowledge in this field. Chaucer, Shakespeare, Milton, Cowper, Scott, Byron, Shelley, Keats, Tennyson, Browning, Arnold, Morris, Rossetti, and Swinburne constituted at this time the bulk of his reading in English literature. But his study of Aristotle's *Ethics* at Oxford led him, when meditating on how he might organise his first lectures on Rhetoric, to look at Aristotle's *Rhetoric*, and it was in the study of this book and its careful application to the general problem of literary style that he developed those views on "rhetoric and English composition" which he expressed so vividly in his lectures first at Aberdeen and later at Edinburgh and which, after his retirement, he published in 1944. He had to deliver his inaugural lecture as Lecturer in English at Aberdeen before he had completed his work on the *Rhetoric* ; his subject was "Style", and he drew heavily not on Aristotle but on Pater, to the disgust of the second Mrs Bain who sent him an anonymous letter saying : "Why Oxford? Why Pater? when everything was so much better at Aberdeen. All you need will be found in Bain's books and better."

His first year at Aberdeen was tough. In addition to the Rhetoric lectures he worked up a historical course on English literature which began with Anglo-Saxon poetry and went on through French romance and allegory to Chaucer and then on to the more modern writers. He tried to arrange that the more difficult authors came on a Monday so that he could have the week-end to read them up in. He has described a lecture on Pope, prepared in a week-end of continuous reading and writing, which elicited the comment from an older student, who was attending the class for his own amusement : "Well, we fairly took the guts out of Pope!"

All this time Grierson was canvassing for support in his application for the new Chair. He did not really expect to get it, as he was young and inexperienced, and there were known scholars of English, such as Oliver Elton, in for it. But he had good supporters—the two members of Parliament for Aberdeen, the M.P. for Kincardineshire, and some influential voices in Oxford—and to his own surprise, gratification, and, one might almost say, trepidation, he was successful, and was duly appointed the first Chalmers Professor of English at Aberdeen in 1894, at the age of twenty-eight. No one knew better than he did how ill prepared he was to be a Professor of English : his great ambition was to prove his fitness for the position by doing something impressive in English studies.

Grierson's career from now on became a triumphant vindication of his appointment to the Aberdeen Chair. He set himself with immense energy to master the whole field of English literature and to produce scholary and critical work that would not only justify his appointment but also justify the academic study of English, which was viewed with considerable suspicion by the conservative. By the time of his appointment to the Regius Chair of Rhetoric and English Literature at Edinburgh in 1915, as the successor to George Saintsbury, he had won a great reputation for himself in the field of English studies and had also contributed significantly to the pioneer task of making English literature a central "liberal arts" subject at university level. In large measure, Grierson's taking up English literature had been a matter of accident ; but soon after he started lecturing it became clear that the subject was peculiarly his own, and that his combination of critical sensitivity, philosophical understanding, scholarly thoroughness, literary imagination, and appreciation of technical craftsmanship in words was exactly what was required to make a great Professor of English. His tenure of the Chairs at Aberdeen and at Edinburgh marked an epoch in the history of the Scottish universities and of the study of English literature in Britain.

In September 1896 Grierson married Mary Letitia, daughter of Sir Alexander Ogston, then president of the surgical section of the British Medical Association. Being wife of a young Professor of English who had still his academic reputation to make was no sinecure, and Grierson has drawn a picture of his wife sitting for hours alone in the dining-room or drawing-room, sewing, while he sat alone in the study reading and writing.   Grierson himself had no head for practical matters, and it was his wife who managed the financial affairs of the house (at least, after the occasion, early in his marriage, when he allowed himself to be defrauded of £200 by a dishonest lawyer, and so had to take on extra examining and some school-inspecting to help make good the loss) ; she also read and criticised everything he wrote, as well as performing the more regular duties of a housewife and (eventually) of the mother of five daughters.   She was a devoted help-meet, up to her death in October 1937.

George Saintsbury was appointed to the Chair of English at Edinburgh in 1895, with a high reputation as critic and literary histor-ian, and Grierson, feeling very much his position as a junior, called on him in Edinburgh soon afterwards.   There followed a visit by Saints-bury to Aberdeen, where he stayed with the Griersons (and gently pointed out at a dinner party that the maid was serving whisky under the impression that it was sherry : "It doesn't at all trouble me, but it may trouble the ladies", he added).   The result was that Grierson was enlisted by Saintsbury to write a book in the series "Periods of European Literature" that Sainstbury was editing.   Edmund Gosse had undertaken to do the first half of the seventeenth century, and had subsequently backed out, so now Grierson was to do it.   He seized the opportunity of having a book published in an established series. Conscious of his lack of original scholarship in the field, and anxious not to serve up a mere re-hash of what had been done before, he determined to be thoroughly original and scholarly in at least one aspect of his subject.   He had been told by Oliver Elton that Dutch literature was of the highest importance in the seventeenth century ; he would therefore learn Dutch and do especial justice to the chapters on Dutch literature.   This he did, and the Dutch chapters are the most original and impressive in the book, which appeared after much hard work in 1906.   Grierson maintained his interest in and knowledge of Dutch throughout the rest of his long life, and was several times in Holland.

Grierson's next work was the result of a meeting with Professor Macneile Dixon when they were both on holiday in Lossiemouth in 1907.   Together they planned an anthology of longer English poems read or suitable to be read at the universities, and it was published under their joint editorship in 1909 as *The English Parnassus*, a book which has held its place in school and university teaching for fifty years. But Grierson was already at work on a much more important project, which grew directly out of his work on the seventeenth century for Saintsbury. This led to his being asked to write the chapter on John Donne in the *Cambridge History of English Literature* which in turn led to the greatest of all his academic achievements, his monumental edition of John Donne's poems for the Clarendon Press, which appeared in two volumes in 1912. His work with Stewart in Oxford on the text of Aristotle had introduced him to textual criticism of manuscripts, and as almost none of Donne's poems had been printed during his lifetime the problems involved in settling Donne's text were not substantially different in kind. His task was to settle both text and canon, and in addition to provide a commentary elucidating a notoriously difficult poet. It was I suppose a coincidence—or perhaps some obscure working of the *Zeitgeist*—that Grierson should have devoted so much critical and scholarly attention to Donne at a time when a major shift in English poetic taste and in the creative impulse in English poetry, closely related to a new interest in and admiration for Donne's poetry, was on the point of taking place. Coincidence or not, it is not easy to find a happier linking of the scholarly and the creative aspects of a literary culture: Grierson's Donne proved to be not only a masterly piece of textual editing but also an exciting event in the history of English poetry. And when, in 1921, he produced his anthology of *Metaphysical Lyrics and Poems of the Seventeenth Century*, with an introductory critical essay which defined and explained the nature of that "metaphysical" poetry that was coming so rapidly into favour and was having such an important effect on the younger poets, he put into his debt a whole generation of poets, critics, and students. It is worth noting that T. S. Eliot's influential and often reprinted essay on metaphysical poetry was written as a review of Grierson's anthology.

Looking back in old age on his years as an Aberdeen professor, Grierson used to say that they included the happiest years of his life. In spite of immensely hard work and periods of nervous strain and almost breakdown, he was working in a community in which he felt at home (though a community which was always critical, especially of a professor of such a newfangled subject as English), and in which he was visibly making his reputation. He and his wife had numerous friends in the city and the county, and they felt that they belonged.

His appointment to the Regius Chair of English at Edinburgh in 1915 was generally regarded (though not by Aberdonians) as a step up-wards, and he welcomed it as such as well as a wider arena for his activities. But he also felt the greater coldness of the Edinburgh people ('East wind-y and West End-y', as he used often to quote), the greater formality of their entertaining and their greater sense of the numerous factors, including the locality of his house, which determined a man's social position.

By the time of his appointment to Edinburgh Grierson had made himself master of a very wide field of English literature, and the magisterial survey of the whole field which he gave there to his First Ordinary English class was a remarkable presentation of the develop-ment of English literary history in the context both of the history of ideas and of literary forms and standards. The Scottish university practice of having the professor give a massive introductory survey of his subject sometimes has unhappy results, but for Grierson it was an opportunity to display not only the vast scope of his scholarship, and his ability to order an enormous amount of complicated material, but also that combination of authority and inquiry, of assured know-ledge and humane speculation, that was one of his main characteristics as scholar and critic. For him the history of literature was bound up with the history of thought as well as with the history of sensibility. It was bound up also with changes in the way words have been used, in the shifting suggestions which give words what he called their "colour" and thus help to make both poetry and rhetoric possible. Though this latter interest was mostly developed in his Friday lectures on Rhetoric, it also played its part among others in his general course on the history of English literature. Catching sight of an observation or reminder on the left-hand page of his large folio notebook (he kept the left side free for the jotting down of additional ideas), or perhaps suddenly thinking of some illustration or amplification or modification of what he had been saying, he would go off into an illuminating digression. Sometimes his students would wonder how he would find his way back to the main line of his discourse ; but he always did ; he would return, sometimes with great syntactical ingenuity, to the point from which he had taken off to digress, and then continue with the central argument.

There must be many of his former students who remember how, during these moments of digression, he used to turn slightly to the

right, so that he was almost at right angles to his audience, and gently
tug at his right ear lobe with his right hand. As one of his students
during the latter part of his tenure of the Edinburgh Chair, I always
thought that this ear-tugging was a sign that he was sharing a train of
thought with his audience—thinking aloud, almost—and it indicated
a certain shyness which was in curious contrast with his formal professorial manner. We thought him then—even his honours students,
whom he met in smaller classes and with whom he would indulge
more freely in these controlled digressions—very professorial, very
stern, and very much above us all. And yet he had this oddly shy
manner of almost apologetically withdrawing into his own speculations. He did not seem very approachable. When, as a fourth-year
honours student, I first knocked at the door of his retiring room to ask
him about something, the voice from within sounded sharp, even testy.
"Yes? What is it?" Many years later, when I had got to know him
well, he confided to me that he was always shy of his students and that
his apparent sharpness of manner was the result of an uncertainty
about what to say to them when they approached him in private.
The annual party he gave for his honours students was, he told me,
preceded by desperate attempts to memorise topics of conversation
appropriate to particular students. He told me, too, something that I
think few of his students would ever have guessed—that he never got
over being nervous before giving a lecture and that he could never
settle down to any writing before his day's lecturing was done. His
predecessor, Professor Saintsbury, used to give his lectures in the
afternoon, leaving the morning for his writing. But as soon as
Grierson got a classroom of his own (at first he shared one with the
Professor of Latin) he rearranged the timetable so that he lectured in
the morning ; otherwise his mornings would have been wasted, for
he would have been too nervous to concentrate on writing in the
morning when faced with the prospect of lecturing in the afternoon.

    Another thing that all his former students must remember was his
characteristically sing-song way of reading poetry. He would sustain
an almost even pitch for several lines and then, at the first real pause in
the sense, do a sort of audible loop, heightening and then lowering
the pitch of his voice to come to rest always on the same cadence. No
one who heard him read from *Paradise Lost* can have ever forgotten
this highly individual quality in his reading of poetry. Some people did
not like it—he once told me sadly that on a few occasions the students

shuffled their feet in disapproval when he read a passage of poetry—but many others found it very impressive. He never changed his way of reading poetry—for which, incidentally, he had a remarkable memory. A few weeks after his 94th birthday, and only just over a week before his death, I was talking to him about the Burns Cult and he started to recite some of Burns's songs, all in exactly that same old cadence. It was a cadence more appropriate to Milton than to Burns, but still, it was a pleasure to hear the tones ring out in the old familiar way : I imagined myself back in Minto House in 1930.

Grierson's twenty years in the Edinburgh Chair of English were busy and fruitful. In 1915 appeared an important article on Milton in Hastings's *Encyclopaedia of Religion and Ethics*; in 1921 he brought out his influential anthology of metaphysical poetry ; in 1923 he gave the Leslie Stephen lecture on "Classical and Romantic" (published with other essays and addresses in *The Background of English Literature*, 1924) ; in 1925 he published an edition of Milton in two volumes. Meanwhile, his growing international reputation led to his being invited to lecture on the Continent and in America. He gave the Messenger Lectures at Cornell University in 1926–7 ; they were published in 1929 as *Cross-Currents in English Literature of the XVIIth Century*, a contribution to the history of ideas as well as to the understanding of literature, with a characteristic interweaving of historical, philosophical, psychological, and aesthetic elements. It has remained one of his most popular works, and has recently appeared in an American paperback series. In 1929 he gave a course of lectures at the University of Heidelberg, and it was while he was there that Cambridge University invited him to accept the degree of Doctor of Letters ; he crossed over from Heidelberg in order to receive it. He spent the academic year 1932–3 lecturing at Columbia University, while J. C. Smith took over his classes in Edinburgh during his absence. On his return from America in 1933 he began his last two years as Edinburgh professor, resigning the chair in 1935. By this time he was well advanced in the elaborate twelve-volume edition of Scott's letters, in which he had the assistance of Davidson Cook, W. M. Parker, and others : the first volume came out in 1932 and the last in 1937. It was the new knowledge about Scott gained from editing these letters than enabled Grierson to write his biography of Scott, supplementing and correcting Lockhart, *Sir Walter Scott, Bart.*, 1938. Among his other publications during his Edinburgh period were *Lyrical Poetry from Blake to Hardy*, 1928 (in the "Hogarth Lectures" series) and *Milton and Wordsworth, Prophets and Poets*, 1937.

Shortly after retiring, Grierson was greatly surprised and flattered at being asked to stand as candidate for the position of Rector, traditionally a signal mark of esteem by the students, but very rarely bestowed on professors. He was duly elected, and served from 1936 to 1939. He was knighted in 1936, and his wife lived long enough to become Lady Grierson and to see him elected Rector : she died in October 1937, and for the remaining twenty-three years of his long life Grierson was always threatened with loneliness, which sometimes afflicted him with a great sense of desolation But until the outbreak of war in 1939 he was kept busy. He was in America again in 1938–9, lecturing at Smith College and elsewhere, and war started soon after his return. For the next ten years he lived on at his old house in Edinburgh, 12 Regent Terrace, taking in boarders sometimes to help with the expense and employing a housekeeper whom he described as "efficient but *not* very economical". Here he was visited occasionally by fellow scholars and by former pupils, but the lack of mobility imposed by the war restricted the number of his visitors. It was in large measure to keep himself from brooding during these difficult years that he wrote, together with J. C. Smith, *A Critical History of English Poetry*, published in 1944—not one of his best works, for he was writing, as it were, from memory and simply setting down what he had worked out many years before. But the writing of it was a pleasure to him ; among other things, it gave him the intellectual companionship of his old friend J. C. Smith. Smith's death in 1946 and the departure for London in 1947 of another old friend, Joan Sergeant, left him very much alone. The decision to move to Cambridge, where his daughter and his son-in-law Professor Bruce Dickins (once one of his lecturers at Edinburgh) were living, was in the circumstances inevitable.

Grierson suffered for the last twenty-five years of his life and perhaps longer from arthritis, which made walking more and more difficult for him. Already in the early 1930s he had to sit down while lecturing. The last ten years of his life, spent at Cambridge, were made extremely troublesome by the fact that, while physically perfectly well in all other respects, he grew steadily less able to move about and was often in considerable pain. Eventually he had to move to a nursing home,

Hope House in Brooklands Avenue, but he never really reconciled himself to this necessity. For a while he was able to make brief excursions from Hope House, hobbling on two sticks, but eventually he had to give these up. He was able to attend a party at the Garden House Hotel to celebrate his 90th birthday, and occasionally after that used to go out to dine or for a drive with a friend. I used to take him for a drive into the country on Saturday mornings, and I remember the shock to both of us when we realised one day that his increased stiffness and lameness made it impossible for him to get into the car. The last phase was, inevitably, sad ; he was very conscious of having outlived all his contemporaries. Yet until the week before his death on 19 Feb. 1960 he could exhibit liveliness and humour, and was in particularly good form when talking about his early life. Much of what I have written here I got from his own lips during the regular visits I paid him during his last eight years.

Grierson's work on Donne and the metaphysical poets has made him an important figure in the history of modern poetic theory and practice. Yet this was partly accidental. There is a sense in which he was not modern at all. He was one of the last professors of English to come to his subject through classics and philosophy, with no formal academic study of English behind him. He developed his own approach to English studies—indeed, as the first Chalmers Professor of English at Aberdeen he had, so far as that university was concerned, to *invent* English studies. For him, literary criticism was not a technical exercise but a mature placing of a given work within the whole field of human thought and expression. He had nothing of the modern critic's view of a work of literature as a timeless structure of meaning. Literature was written by and for men in a given historical situation, and, while always sensitive to literary artistry and to the formal aspects of poems, novels, and plays, he always saw them in the context of their time and place. Ultimately, for Grierson as for Coleridge, human knowledge was one. He objected to every kind of fragmentation and every kind of narrowness. His books, like his lectures, have the note of shared experience ; they were the communications of a man who had something to report on the nature and meaning of works of literature he had both enjoyed and pondered. There is no trace of the exhibitionist in anything he ever wrote : there may be areas where his critical mind was less sensitive than we might have expected or hoped, but even here we cannot help responding to the integrity of the utterance. He never falsified his own literary experience, never played tricks on the reader or audience. And he always assumed that his audience was intelligent and interested. I remember once talking to him of my experience as a professor of English in America and remarking on how cunningly some American academic teachers managed to arouse an interest in literature among students who arrived in a mood of indifference or hostility. His reply was characteristic. "If any one comes to me and asks, 'Why should I read Shakespeare?' I always reply : 'If you're not interested, don't.' " And he barked out that *don't* almost contemptuously. Grierson was no evangelist : he always assumed an interest in those to whom he talked. He was no pedant, either, and did not believe in mere erudition for its own sake. Literature provided insights into the human situation and criticism and scholarship provided insights into literature. Understanding and appreciation were always the end.

He was a modest man, always a little surprised at the fame he acquired, and in his later years sometimes reciting with incredulous and half-amused wonder his long list of honorary degrees. "Do you think", he asked me only a few weeks before his death, "that any of my books will live? Perhaps the Donne? And the *Cross-Currents*?" He seemed to be asking for reassurance that his life's work had not been in vain. That reassurance was not difficult to give. Grierson's work on Donne and on the seventeenth century will certainly live : not only does it combine important textual, critical, interpretative, and historical scholarship ; it also heralded one of the great critical revaluations of English literary history, which played its part in creation as well as in criticism. And so long as any members of the generations whom he taught survive, Professor Grierson will live in their memories as a great personality and a great teacher.

9

The Identity of Burns[1]

Robert Burns is not merely the national poet of Scotland ; he is a
world-wide symbol, a universal excuse for celebration and sentimentality. Further, the Burns cult developed soon after the poet's
death and has been maintained at a steady level of irrational enthusiasm
ever since. It is a cult participated in by people who do not normally
have any interest in poetry and indeed by not a few who do not even
read Burns's poetry but who cherish his memory, adore his furniture,
his snuffbox, his masonic apron, and his wife's pinkie-ring, memorise
the names of the girls he made love to, and fiercely challenge anybody
who denies that Burns was the greatest poet who ever lived anywhere
in the world. Who was Burns and what was his relation to the
Scotland of his day? What kinds of poems did he write and how good
are they and why? What is there about his character and achievement
that can throw light on the way in which he is remembered and celebrated?

Burns was the son of an Ayrshire tenant farmer who had migrated
to this part of Scotland from his native Kincardineshire in order to
improve his prospects. A pious, hard-working, stern but fundamen-
tally kindly man, the elder Burns strove desperately but in the end
vainly to establish himself as a prosperous farmer. This was a bad time
for Scottish farming. Farm rents were grossly inflated, and agricultural methods had not yet properly assimilated the new ideas that were
coming in from England ; it was a difficult transitional period, when
increased productivity had not yet caught up with increased expense.
The result was that Burns's father, dogged continually by ill-luck
first on one farm and then on another, died worn out and bankrupt
in 1784. It was a hard struggle for the whole family : it was excessive

---

[1] Originally published in *Restoration and Eighteenth Century Literature*, ed. Carroll
Camden, Chicago, 1963, pp. 323–400.

physical work at the plough as a boy, together with considerable periods of undernourishment, that laid the foundations of that rheumatic heart disease which plagued Burns as a young man and finally caused his death at the early eage of thirty-seven.

If the elder Burns's economic ambitions failed, his educational ambitions for his children were more successful. He joined with other farmers in the neighbourhood in hiring a schoolmaster, who lived at different farmhouses in rotation and taught the farm children. The teacher, John Murdoch, was a rather priggish young man of eighteen, who instructed his pupils with pedantic thoroughness in English grammar and syntax, in turning verse into "its natural prose order", and in the genteel English literary taste of the day. It must be emphasised that Burns's formal education was wholly English. The principal textbook used by Murdoch was Arthur Masson's *Collection of Prose and Verse*, which was a purely English compilation, containing passages from the eighteenth-century English poets, including Thomson, Gray, and Shenstone, as well as extracts from Shakespeare, Milton, and Dryden, and prose selections from Addison and from the *Letters Moral and Entertaining* of Elizabeth Rowe. (Thomson, of course, was a Scot, but he had sought his literary fortune in London and made his name as an English poet writing in standard English.) Young Robert also learned the merest rudiments of Latin and acquired a smattering of French. His father managed to borrow other books to round out his children's education. Thus Burns read Salmon's *Geographical Grammar* and William Derham's *Physico-Theology* and *Astro-Theology*, two books that presented the facts and theories of physics and astronomy as evidence for the existence of a beneficent Divine Designer; John Ray's *The Wisdom of God Manifested in the Works of the Creation* also treated science as part of the "argument from design" and helped to lay the foundations of that somewhat genial Deism which was Burns's religion in adult life. From Thomas Stackhouse's *New History of the Holy Bible*, to which the elder Burns subscribed, Burns learned biblical history and geography. His maternal uncle brought home by mistake (he was looking for a different sort of book) "a collection of letters by the Wits of Queen Anne's reign", from which Burns learned to write letters in the formal style of the English Augustans. Gradually, Burns extended his reading, devouring everything he could lay his hands on. He read Pope, Shakespeare, John Locke, as well as theological and agricultural works and—the only books read in his young days that could show him something of a Scottish instead of an English literary tradition— Allan Ramsay's poems and anthologies. His knowledge of Greek and Roman mythology he got from Andrew Tooke's *Pantheon*. Later, in his early twenties, he discovered that archsentimental novel, Henry Mackenzie's *Man of Feeling* ("a book", he once wrote, "I prize next to the Bible"), as well as Sterne's *Tristram Shandy* and that remarkable rhetorical-sentimental compendium of pseudo-Gaelic poetry, Macpherson's Ossian.

Burns's formal education was sporadic and in some measure fragmentary, but he did have a formal education, and he knew Shakespeare, Milton, Pope, and the Bible much better than the ordinary educated man of today knows them. But it was in many respects an artificial education, having little to do with the world he lived in, and the result was that Burns's taste was never certain in English literature. He fell heavily for the sentimental movement that was all the rage at that time, and he read even such a poet as Gray— "the elegantly melting Gray", he called him—for what we would consider the wrong reasons. Indeed, Burns read the later eighteenth-century poets as his age read them, for their tender feeling and proneness to emotional overflow. This really represented something quite alien to Burns's genius, something that every now and again was to come in and corrupt his poetry and falsify his vision. Such writers as Shakespeare and Pope could do him nothing but good—the former helped him to see the potentialities of the poetic use of language and the workings of the poetic imagination, and the latter taught him much about the craft of verse. But Shenstone and Henry Mackenzie did him nothing but harm, and even Gray and Collins were used by him as food for emotional self-indulgence.

If Burns had never broken out of the genteel English education provided by Murdoch, he might have become at best a minor Scottish Shenstone, writing derivative poems in an English he had learned solely from books. But throughout his childhood and youth, he received another kind of literary education, quite different from the formal one he learned from his teacher. The folk tales of the Ayrshire countryside and the Scottish folk songs he heard sung in field and in kitchen represented another tradition altogether from that represented in Masson's anthology. Then there were the poems of Allan Ramsay, and—last and greatest influence of all, which finally revealed to him the possibilities of a poetry that was both Scottish and regional and at the same time universal—the poems of Robert Fergusson, who had died at the age of twenty-four in the public Bedlam of Edinburgh when Burns was a lad of fifteen. The development of Burns as a poet represented the interaction of these Scottish literary forces with the English literature he had studied more formally.

Why should a son of an Ayrshire tenant farmer in the late eighteenth century have been brought up on Gray and Shenstone rather than on the poets of his own country? The answer to this question is a complex one, but is worth trying to give, however briefly, because it concerns the heart of the problem faced by Burns as a poet and faced by us in trying to understand what he was and how he became what he was.

In the Middle Ages, Scotland was an independent country with a literature and a literary language of its own. That language, which we now know as Middle Scots, was originally the same as the Anglian speech of Northumbria, but eventually, as Scotland matured as a nation, this northern form of English became a language in its own right, with its own relation to Latin and to French and its own characteristic idioms and formations. The great Scottish poets of the fourteenth and early fifteenth centuries, notably Robert Henryson and William Dunbar, developed a rich and complex Scots literary language, which, while arising ultimately out of the ordinary spoken language of the people, reached far beyond it by a consciously artful moulding of style and enlargement of vocabulary. It was a language in which thought and emotion could both find expression, in which the full range of utterance from the casual and colloquial to the formal and "aureate" was possible, in which the whole man could speak. In 1603, James VI of Scotland inherited the throne of England and went south to becomes James I, taking with him many of his Court poets, who henceforth were to write artificial and derivative poems in English. Thus Scottish culture lost at a blow the Court patronage of the arts, which, in an age before commercial publishing and in a country too poor to support lavish private patronage, was essential if a native poetry and music were to flourish. Many other factors—the breakup of the Auld Alliance with France and the turning of a now Protestant Scotland toward England, the prestige of Elizabethan English literature, among others—combined with the loss of a Court centre for the Scottish arts to turn Scottish writers' eyes toward England. By 1707, when the Scottish Parliament ceased to exist after having voted an "incorporating union" between England and Scotland, the cultural situation in Scotland had become desperately confused. The language of even educated Scotsmen remained Scots, but more and more the written language was coming to be English. Scotsmen who wanted literary publication wrote in English and sought an English audience. Even David Hume, the great Scottish philosopher and historian, who spoke a broader Scots than Burns did, used to send his manuscripts to an English friend for the removal of Scotticisms ; and indeed, in 1761, a visiting Irishman lectured to large Edinburgh audiences on the proper pronunciation of southern English. In 1787, the Aberdeen professor and minor poet James Beattie produced a list of *Scotticisms, arranged in Alphabetical Order, designed to correct Improprieties of Speech and Writing.* Everywhere people were imitating English speech and English style. The Edinburgh critics and leaders of taste, the literati, as they liked to call themselves, considered themselves patriotic Scotsmen, but they felt that Scotland could only vindicate its culture to the world by absorbing English and European culture and beating the English in their own language. They thought of Scots, which in spite of everything most of them continued to speak, as a corrupt dialect of English.

If a nation's literature is written in one language while its daily conversation is conducted in another, then the written language tends to become highly formal and conventional—often well suited for philosophical or historical discourse but less suited for the complex of thought and feeling required by poetry—and the spoken language degenerates into a series of regional dialects. Where there is no national literary language, the national speech will inevitably degenerate into regional dialects, to be transcribed phonetically by local humorists or with antiquarian zeal by backward-looking patriots. Literature in Scots after about the middle of the seventeenth century became more and more literature of low life, the patronising exhibiting of national customs, or the mock-archaisms of playful scholars. From the early eighteenth century on, the imitation of older Scottish songs and poems became a favourite drawing-room sport, and at the same time editors and anthologists collected for patriotic reasons not only the remnants of traditional Scottish songs but also specimens of older Scottish poetry dating from the time when Scottish literature had a genuine and full literary language of its own. But the élite—the professors and leaders of taste—looked to English and the genteel English tradition. Thus there was no language in which the whole man could express himself; men's public and private selves spoke in different accents, thought and emotion sought different languages, and there was as a result no speech for true contemporary poetry. Allan Ramsay tried hard to use elements of the Scots spoken language in poems descriptive of urban low life and of pastoral activity, and he achieved a limited success. Robert Fergusson made a much more remarkable effort to re-create a genuine Scots poetic tongue and in his Edinburgh poems succeeded in using Scots with a wholeness that had not been seen for generations, but his early death left his work unfinished. It was only when Burns as a young man discovered Fergusson's poems that he was led to continue where Fergusson had left off. But it was natural—indeed, inevitable—that insofar as Burns received a formal education it should have been oriented toward England, not Scotland. Was a true Scottish poetry still possible in Burns's day, or was it the fate of every Scottish poet to become either a rustic purveyor of regional humour, an antiquarian writer of *pastiches*, or to turn south and achieve at best the status of a minor English poet working with only part of his creative self?

Burns, after some hesitation, chose the Scottish rustic mode, refined and enriched by a knowledge of such older Scottish poetry as had been made available by eighteenth-century anthologists and by his study of Ramsay and, more especially, Fergusson—and enriched also by his knowledge of English poetry and his appreciation of poetic craftsmanship in English. Synthesising his native Ayrshire dialect with literary elements from older Scots, and with elements from literary English, he produced a poetic language of surprising flexibility, ranging all the way from neo-classic English to local Scots vernacular and varying continually in the degree to which it drew on each. Burns could of course also write wholly in standard English, and while it would not be accurate to say that when he did so he invariably produced bad poetry, it *is* true to say that his worst poems are sentimental English poems that he wrote with an eye on the genteel Edinburgh audience. Burns's Edinburgh admirers wanted him to be sentimental, edifying, and respectably rustic in an English idiom. His own genius ran to satire, iconoclasm, and a kind of passionate lyrical poetry that seizes the realised moment of experience and renders it without regard for the moral or philosophical consequences. He sometimes allowed

M

himself to be deflected from his true modes of writing by the demands
of his audience ; but on the whole it is astonishing how this young
Ayrshire farmer stuck to his guns in the face of well-meant but
thoroughly misguided criticism from friends and well-wishers in high
places.

It must be remembered that at the time when Burns published his
first volumes of poems at Kilmarnock in 1786, there was in educated
circles in Edinburgh and beyond a strong cult of the primitive.
Edinburgh critics developed theories of poetry based on notions of
how primitive man first expressed his passions. Macpherson's Ossian
was supposed to show the natural simplicity and high emotional quality
of primitive man's experience and expression. Interest in primitive
poetry—the term covered an enormous range, from the Bible to the
alleged oral literature of Peruvian Indians—had been developing
throughout Britain for a considerable time : Percy's *Reliques* and
Gray's interest in Norse and Welsh poetry are only the better known
aspects of a complex and widespread movement. In Edinburgh this
movement was mixed up with the cult of the sentimental as represented
by Mackenzie's *Man of Feeling*. Thus when Burns presented a volume
of poems "chiefly in the Scottish dialect" to the educated public of
Scotland, he was careful to pose as a genuine primitive and to arouse
the interest of the literati in the poetry of a supposedly illiterate peasant.
In his Preface he emphasised his lack of education. He overstated the
case deliberately. The literati took the bait he offered them with
delight. "Whoever will read his lighter and more humorous poems",
wrote Mackenzie in reviewing the volume in the *Lounger* of 9 Dec.
1786, ". . . will perceive with what uncommon penetration and
sagacity this Heaven-taught ploughman, from his humble and un-
lettered station, has looked upon men and manners". This was hardly
fair to John Murdoch, to Burns's father, and to the other sources that
had contributed to Burns's not inconsiderable education, but if Burns
was misunderstood it was in some degree because of the part he
deliberately chose to play before the literati.

Not that Burns appeared in anything like a deferential pose before
the Edinburgh critics when he paid his extended visit to that city
after the publication of his poems. Pride and passion, as he once
wrote, were the two main elements in his make-up, and he demanded
from nobleman and peasant alike recognition of his genius and treatment as in every respect an equal. He frequently gave offence in

Edinburgh by resenting the patronising condescension of well-born
ladies and gentlemen. From his earliest years, he had resented the facts
of class difference in the Scotland of his day, and when as a small boy he
had played with the sons of local landowners, he nursed the bitter
grievance that when he and they grew up they would move in different
spheres, and he would be expected to touch his cap to people whom
he considered no better than himself simply because they happened to
own land. Burns was never a man to suffer fools gladly, whatever
their rank or profession. So if he paraded himself as an uneducated
ploughman in Edinburgh, it was not out of humility, but to emphasise
the authenticity of his poetic genius and inspiration. He knew, too,
that formal education was no guarantee of wisdom :

> What's a' your jargon o' your schools,
> Your Latin names for horns an' stools ;
> If honest nature made you fools,
>   What sairs your grammars?
> Ye'd better ta'en up spades and shools,
>   Or knappin'-hammers.

In verse like this, the true democratic instinct of Burns finds adequate
expression : neither rank nor learning can make a natural fool appear
any less a fool—not, at least, in the eyes of Rabbie Burns.

The answer, then, to my first question—"Who was Burns?"—is
that he was the proud and ambitious son of a struggling Scottish tenant
farmer, born into a Scotland whose culture was deeply divided between
a superficial genteel tradition and a half submerged and attenuated
national tradition, who captured an audience for his Scots poetry
among the educated classes of his day by cashing in on contemporary
interest in the primitive sources of poetry and the virtues of the
"natural man", and who in considerable degree, but not wholly or
consistently, resisted the demands of that audience that he should play
up to their sentimental expectations of the ideal peasant poet. The
sources on which he drew were the oral folk tradition of his own people,
such older Scottish poetry (and it was a fairly small segment) as was
available to him in contemporary collections, the Scottish poems of
Ramsay and Fergusson, and a variety of anthologies of songs and
ballads, all this stiffened by a sense of craftmanship he learned partly
from his study of older English poetry and intermittently threatened by
his immersion in the late eighteenth-century sentimental movement.

Though Burns began his poetic career as a song writer (under the joint influence of love, music, and the desire to emulate the son of a local laird who had written a song for *his* girl), it was in the latter part of his life that he wrote most of his songs : his earliest real successes were satirical poems dealing with local church politics, poems projecting with vivid particularisation aspects of experience in a farming community, and verse epistles, a traditional Scottish form in which Burns rapidly acquired remarkable skill. His satirical poems— "The Holy Fair", "Holy Willie's Prayer", "The Ordination", among others—show a high technical virtuosity and indicate that Burns had learned his trade from a variety of sources both Scottish and English. Most of them derive from his taking sides with those who believed that the essence of religion was a good heart, against the extreme Calvinists who stressed original sin, the inability of good works to save man, the predestined damnation of the vast majority of all men as a result of Adam's fall and the similarily predestined salvation of a tiny minority not through any virtuous acts of their own but through the arbitrary bestowal of God's grace. "Holy Willie's Prayer" is a dramatic monologue in which the speaker all unconsciously damns the creed he professes by revealing the sanctimoniousness and hypocrisy that it inevitably breeds : it is one of the great verse satires of all time. "The Holy Fair" gives an account, in an old Scottish stanza-form, of an outdoor communion celebration, then a feature of Scottish religious life, mischieviously using accepted biblical and religious phraseology to stress the contrast between what really goes on and what is supposed to go on. The whole thing is done in a mood not of bitterness but of joyful exposure of the indomitable claims of the flesh. The brilliance of the ambiguous imagery, the adroit intermingling of the carnal and the spiritual meanings of the same word, the variations of tempo and the manipulation of levels of suggestiveness show a high art : here is no spontaneous bubbling-up of simple peasant emotion but a conscious use of the multiple resources of a complex verse form. On a simpler level, but in its own way equally impressive, is such a poem as "To a Louse", where with affectionately ironic humour Burns reduces to her proper size the proud country lass, masquerading as a fine lady in church because of her new bonnet, by the way he contemplates the louse crawling on the bonnet, visible to the poet as he sits beside her though unknown to the girl herself. It is a perfect little poem, dealing with loving particularisation with an aspect of a subject that is the theme of many of Burns's poems, especially of his satires—the relation between appearance and reality, between what is pretended and what really is.

Burns's greatest poetic achievement is his satires. These show a command of a greater variety of poetic skills, a subtler and more complex use of the medium of poetry, than any other kind of poetry he wrote. They are not, however, the poems quoted by orators at Burns suppers. Indeed, such orators generally quote the worst of Burns, the platitudinous or sentimental or jingling or crudely rhetorical Burns. Another important group are his verse letters. This is not a kind of poetry that has ever been popular in England. But in Scotland it had been a tradition since the beginning of the eighteenth century, and Burns learned of the tradition from Ramsay. It represented a handling of language peculiarly suited to his genius, counterpointing the formal and the colloquial, moving out from the carefully localised picture of the poet in a specific time and place to his reflexions as they arise naturally from the given situation to a progressively widening circle of comment that culminates in a series of clinching epigrams before the poet returns to himself and his correspondent to sign off in an adroitly turned conclusion. These verse letters show remarkable skill in combining a colloquial ease with a formal pattern in such a way that each brings out new significance in the other.

To Burns the satirist, and Burns the writer of masterly verse letters, I would add Burns the narrative poet. Even though he wrote only one narrative poem, "Tam o' Shanter", it is enough to enable us to list narrative poetry among his claims to high poetic distinction. This rendering in octosyllabic couplets of a local folk story is a triumph of *pace* ; the variations in tempo are handled with the utmost adroitness to achieve not only a narrative style that follows the curve of the action most cunningly but also a wealth of humorously ironic comment on human frailty and human imagination. The opening sets the scene in the local pub where the hero sits happily boozing in a cosy interior while outside the storm rises. This contrast between the cosy interior and the harsh weather outside is an old tradition in Scottish poetry : it can be found as far back as the opening of Henryson's *Testament of Crisseid*, perhaps the first medieval narrative poem to tell the truth about the weather in these islands. (Even Chaucer has his eye on the French rose garden, which in turn derives from the Mediterranean centre of secular medieval poetry ; his Canterbury pilgrims have no meteorological problems, even in an English April ; and when it rains in his *Troilus and Criseyde*, it is only in order to give the hero the opportunity of spending the night with the heroine.) Tam's climax of conviviality is soon reached, and splendidly described. There follows a mock-serious passage in pulpit-English describing the evanescence of pleasure, culminating in a sudden switch back to Scots, this time in a tone of homely proverbial wisdom. Then comes the description of the storm, growing ever more rapid in movement until it has reached the point at which the name of the Devil can be appropriately introduced. The superstitious and drunken imagination of Tam is built up by a remarkable progression of comically horrible images until at last he reaches Alloway Kirk, sees the Devil and the dance of the witches, and, his fancy caught by a "winsome wench and wawlie" dancing in a particularly short shift, he calls out to her in approval and thus betrays his presence. In a flash the witches are after him, and he gallops madly along on his faithful mare Maggie. It looks as though the end has come. But Maggie escapes by crossing a running stream (which witches cannot cross) just as the leader is on her. Her tail, however, has been seized and plucked off. Tam arrives home with a tailless mare. The poem ends with a mock-solemn warning against drink and girls, in language that is a parody of Scottish pulpit moralising. The whole story can of course be explained by the fact that Tam was drunk and only imagined the witches. But how do we explain Maggie's loss of her tail? Every incident *except one* can be rationally explained. This is a formula for supernatural tales told to a modern sceptical audience that has been followed ever since, notably in Scott's "Wandering Willie's Tale".

So I think we can grant Burns's skill as a narrative poet even though we have only one example to judge by. "Tam o' Shanter" was written in 1790 when Burns was combining farming at Ellisland with his duties as a recently appointed excise officer. He had returned reluctantly to farming after his prolonged visit to Edinburgh—reluctantly, because he knew from experience that the back-breaking work and economic risks of farming at that time would seriously cut down his opportunities of writing poetry. He wanted some sort of government job to enable him to have the leisure for writing and the opportunity for meeting and talking with interesting people that were so important for him. Even after he gave up his farm and settled in Dumfries as a full-time exciseman, he never had the leisure a poet really requires.

"Tam o' Shanter" makes us realise what Burns might have done had he had time and opportunity to cultivate all his poetic faculties properly. One single poem in a vein of which he was clearly a past master —it is a tantalising glimpse of what we might have had if Burns had had health, leisure, and a more congenial environment for poetic creation.

By a more congenial environment, I do not simply mean more educated friends, though it is true that Burns was hampered by the fact that the people he could talk to as intellectual equals (and he found few if any) tended to patronise him socially. I mean a society that did not condemn him to be a performing peasant poet as an illustration of primitivist theories of poetry. I have already suggested that Burns's admirers did him harm, or did their unconscious best to do so. Though Burns resisted the advice that many of them gave him to abandon the Scottish tradition in language and form, he was often content to give them the kind of attitudinising they wanted. His duty poem in praise of Edinburgh, "Edina, Scotia's Darling Seat!", is a shocking bad performance in a neo-classic English idiom that he was never really able to handle, though some aspects of eighteenth-century English poetic idiom he could use with real skill. If we want to see the real Burns side by side with the bogus Burns, we have only to set "To a Mouse" beside "To a Mountain Daisy". The former recognises with wry humour the fellow feeling that joins the poet and the little creature and skilfully turns the theme round at the end to project his own unhappy situation. The unsentimental use of diminutives to strengthen the note of friendly concern ("Thy wee-bit housie, too, in ruin!"), the effective introduction of a rustic proverbial idiom that both bridges the worlds of mice and men and sounds an appealing note of rueful wisdom ("The best-laid schemes o' Mice an' Men, / Gang aft a-gley"), the mastery of tone and movement throughout—these show Burns working with a fine assurance in a medium of which he was complete master. But "To a Mountain Daisy" is an exercise in sentimental attitudinising for the benefit of the tender feelings of his genteel readers. The poetic device known as the pathetic fallacy—the attribution of human thought and feeling to an inanimate object—is a dangerous one at best, and Burns's use of it here, in addressing the daisy, is clumsy and histrionic. In particular, the comparison of the daisy to a country maid betrayed by a rustic seducer—the betrayed maiden is a standard property in sentimental fiction of the period—is grotesquely inappropriate. We know that Burns was attitudinising when he wrote this poem. He enclosed a copy in a letter to a friend with the remark : "I am a good deal pleased with some sentiments myself, as they are just the native querulous feelings of a heart which, as the elegantly melting Gray says, 'Melancholy has marked for her own.' "

We can see familiar defects in parts of "The Cotter's Saturday Night", an attempt to improve on Robert Fergusson's poem on the same theme, "The Farmer's Ingle". But Fergusson's poem remains the more successful, a shrewdly affectionate account of an evening in a farm kitchen set against a sense of the underlying rhythm of the seasons and of agricultural labour. Burns opens the "Cotter" with a monstrous stanza addressed to the prosperous Ayr lawyer Bob Aiken : "My lov'd, my honor'd much respected friend!" And the stanza ends with the suggestion that this bustling and prosperous townsman would be happier in a humble rustic cottage than in his comfortable house in Ayr :

> What Aiken in a Cottage would have been ;
> Ah! tho' his worth unknown, far happier there, I ween!

This is sentimental nonsense, and Burns knew it ; even the verse echoes dully and mechanically to such forced sentiments. The real opening of the poem is the fine second stanza, setting the time and place with an intimate sense of the quality of living that is involved here, and adding just a suggestion of controlled melancholy in the observation of rustic rest after rustic toil that he got from Gray's *Elegy*. There are other stanzas equally fine ; but at intervals Burns the professional sentimentalist showing off his ideal rustics to a genteel Edinburgh audience steps in and wrecks the poem.

I am not maintaining that Burns wrote good poems only when he wrote in Scots and not in English. Many of his finest poems are in an English tipped with Scots, and many of his best songs contain only an occasional Scots word. The linguistic situation in Burns's Scotland was so confused that only by creating a synthetic language of his own, out of his native spoken dialect, standard southern English, and Scots of other times and regions, could Burns have achieved any flexibility in operation at all : this language was in the nature of things neither consistent nor arbitrary, but varied according to the demands of particular kinds of poetic situations. I *am* maintaining, however, that when Burns kept his eye on the literary fashions of educated Scotsmen of his day and wrote for the taste of the literati instead of in one of the ways that he knew suited his own genius, his poetry is generally bad. And there is no doubt that in English literature of his own time his taste was very uncertain. But he was not alone in that. He learned much, however, from English poetry, whose influence we can trace in his work in all sorts of ways. He used what he learned, of course, for his purposes in his own way, sometimes, for example, transforming an elegant piece of Augustan wit into the idiom of Scottish folk song. In the Second Epistle of Pope's "Moral Essays" occur the lines

> Heaven, when it strives to polish all it can
> Its last best work, but forms a softer Man.

Burns gave this thought a completely different kind of expression in the last stanza of "Green grow the rashes O":

> Auld Nature swears, the lively Dears
>   Her noblest work she classes, O :
> Her prentice han' she try'd on man,
>   An' then she made the lasses, O.

I have claimed Burns as a great poet in virtue of his satire, his verse letters, and his one narrative poem. There remain, of course, his songs. In April 1787, Burns met in Edinburgh James Johnson, a self-educated lover of Scottish songs, who had invented a cheap process for printing by using stamped pewter plates, a combination that led him to project a series of volumes of songs. He enlisted Burns's assistance, and gradually, as Burns became more and more the dominant partner in the project, the original character of the enterprise changed : it became a vast six-volume anthology of Scottish songs, old and new. Later, Burns was approached by George Thomson, a more educated and genteel publisher of Scottish songs, for help in *his* collection. Burns responded to both requests avidly, with the result that the great majority of his own songs were written for and first appeared in either Johnson's *Scots Musical Museum* or Thomson's *Select Scottish Airs*. It is important to understand exactly what Burns did for Scottish song. He found Scottish folk song in a confused and fragmentary state. The decay of the courtly musical tradition after 1603, Presbyterian disapproval of popular secular song, and indeed the whole confused condition of Scottish culture all contributed to this. Scottish airs had been popular since the latter part of the seventeenth century, and many collections of Scottish songs and song tunes appeared both in Edinburgh and London in the eighteenth century. But the great majority of older songs survived only in fragments, as an odd chorus or a few garbled lines. One of the favourite sports of Scottish ladies and gentlemen of the period was writing new words to old airs, and these words were generally frigid and derivative. Burns's aim was to recover as many airs and sets of words as he could and, where the existing words were fragmentary or impossibly coarse or equally impossibly genteel, to re-create the song in the true spirit of the folk tradition. It was a staggering programme, nothing less than a single-handed re-creation of the whole body of Scottish folk song. Further, Burns undertook to provide words to tunes which, though they may originally have had words, now existed only as dance tunes. He was anxious that all Scotland should be represented, and in his journeys in Scotland scrupulously collected such songs and fragments as he could find, to rework them into complete songs. We can trace his journeys by the provenance of the songs—a fisherman's song from Fife, an old Aberdeen folk song, a song about an alehouse keeper on the Moray Firth, innumerable love songs connected with particular hills, valleys, streams, and woods in Perthshire, Stirlingshire, Dunbartonshire, Ayrshire, Dumfriesshire, and other Scottish counties. If Burns had not been uncannily in tune with the folk spirit in Scottish song, he would be execrated today for having spoiled the original fragments by bogus improvements. But in fact he did not spoil them ; he saved them from total corruption and disappearance and gave them new life and meaning and popularity.

The greater part of Burns's poetic activity in the last years of his life was taken up with these songs. He collected, revised, completed, rewrote, and re-created hundreds of songs, devoting an immense amount of energy to the task and refusing all payment from Johnson or Thomson, declaring that he did it for Scotland's sake. And this was no theatrical gesture : it was true. He regarded this vast work as a contribution to the preservation and renewal of his country's culture. The amount of work he did on a particular song would vary in accordance with the state of the original and the amount of time at his disposal. If only a chorus or a few fragments of verse survived, he might substantially rewrite the whole song. Often the first verse and the chorus survived, and Burns provided more verses. Sometimes he rewrote an old bawdy song as a tender and passionate love song or, as in the case of "John Anderson My Jo", as a poem of married affection. On many occasions, he took a popular dance tune, slowed down the tempo to bring out musical qualities obscured by the fast dancing pace, and wrote a song for it. Burns, though no singer, had an acute ear for melody and a genius for fitting words to music such as few poets have possessed. His correspondence with Thomson about the words and the music of the songs he sent him is full of technical discussions of prosody and of musical rhythm and time.

Burns wrote all his songs to known tunes, sometimes writing several sets of words to the same air in an endeavour to find the most apt poem for a given melody. Roughly speaking, we can divide Burns's songs into three categories : those he rewrote from old fragments, completely new songs he wrote to old tunes, and new songs he wrote for dance tunes which, though they may originally have been song tunes, did not exist as such in Burns's day. But the categories are not always separate and sometimes fade into one another. Many songs that we know from a variety of evidence must have been substantially written by Burns he never claimed as his. He never claimed "Auld Lang Syne", for example, which he described simply as an old fragment he had discovered, but the song as we have it is almost certainly his, though the chorus and probably the first stanza are old. (Incidentally, Burns wrote it for a simple and moving old air, which is *not* the tune to which it is now sung, as Thomson set it to another tune.) Sometimes Burns sent Johnson snatches and fragments, unimproved, sufficient to fit the tune. At other times he hastily produced some provisional words, which, as he explained apologetically, might do to keep the tune alive until better words could be produced. Many of the songs are extremely slight and trivial. But many others are splendid examples of the embodiment of passionate experience in art.

It is the uncanny ability to speak with the great anonymous voice of the Scottish people that must be part of the explanation for the special feeling Burns arouses. But his songs are not all in a simple folk idiom, though most of them have that air of simplicity (whatever the subtleties below the surface) so necessary to a sung poem. There is the symbolic colour and imagery of "Open the Door to Me Oh!" which so impressed W. B. Yeats :

> The wan moon is setting ayont the white wave,
>   And time is setting with me, oh!

There is that wonderful mixture of tenderness and swagger—so characteristic of the male in love—in "A Red, Red Rose", Burns's rewriting of an old fragment. There is the magnificent abandonment to the moment of experience in "Yestreen I Had a Pint o' Wine" :

> The kirk and state may gae to hell,
>   And I'll gae to my Anna.

There is the controlled historical melancholy of the Jacobite songs where Burns gives this romantic lost cause a new meaning in terms of human emotion :

> Now a' is done that men can do,
>   And a' is done in vain :
> My Love and Native Land fareweel,
>   For I maun cross the main, my dear,
>   For I maun cross the main.

There is that splendid drinking song, "Willie Brew'd a Peck o' Maut", with its rollicking chorus :

> We are na fou, We're nae that fou,
>   But just a drappie in our e'e ; . . .

There is a wonderful counterpointing of folk feeling and high cere-mony, of simple emotion and pageantry, in "Go, Fetch to Me a Pint o' Wine", where the whole atmosphere of medieval romance and ballad is concentrated in two stanzas. There is the magical tenderness of "O Lay Thy Loof in Mine, Lass"—though here I would particularly emphasise the importance of taking the words with the tune : it is the tune that lights up the words. There is the lilting love song he com-posed to one of his wife's favourite airs, "The Posie" :

> O Luve will venture in, where it daurna weel be seen,
> O luve will venture in, where wisdom ance has been. . . .

(Again, it is lost without the music.) There is that sprightly piece of ironic self-compliment, "There Was a Lad Was Born in Kyle". There is the moving benedictory cadence, so perfectly wrought together with the music, in "Ca' the Yowes to the Knowes" :

Ghaist nor bogle shalt thou fear ;
Thou'rt to love and Heaven sae dear,
Nocht of ill may come thee near,
    My bonnie dearie.

A final word on Burns as a man. He was a man of great intellectual
energy and force of character who in a class-ridden sociery never
found an environment in which he could fully exercise his personality.
After his death, the lively literary lady Maria Riddell wrote a character
sketch of him in the *Dumfries Journal* in which she said that his
powers of conversation, his impromptu wit, his ability to grasp new
ideas, his intolerance of stupidity and arrogance, his capacity for
devastating ironic comment, were in her opinion even more impressive
than his poetry. "I believe no man was ever gifted with a larger
portion of the *vivida vis animi*", she wrote. But it was not only the
class structure of his society, which led to his being alternately patronised and sentimentalised over, that constricted him. Coming to
Edinburgh between the age of Hume and the age of Scott, Burns
found no one really worthy of his mettle. The problem was, however,
more than one of personalities. The only substitute for the rejected
Calvanism available to Burns in the Scotland of his day was a sentimental Deism, a facile belief in the good heart as all, which though
also part of late eighteenth-century English culture, was in England
likely to be involved with other and more profound currents of
thought. Let us be clear on one point. In spite of the annual Burns
orators, the truth is that Burns in his adult life was not a Christian. He
was in a vague sort of way a Deist, who believed in a benevolent
designer of the universe and who believed in good-heartedness,
generosity, and openness as the supreme virtues. He was also an
egalitarian in politics, a sympathiser with the French Revolution, and
an unremitting opponent of the class system of his time. He was at
the same time a shrewd and penetrating observer of contemporary
politics and of human psychology as he found it in the ladies and
gentlemen who entertained and patronised him. As for his famous
amours, the fact here is that Burns was unable to be on terms of sexual
equality with his intellectual equals (or near-equals) : the result was
that he could only flirt with the well-born ladies, while he sought
physical satisfaction with country lasses. His sex life is part of the
schizophrenia of the Scottish culture of his time and of the split
personality that this forced on him.

I have tried to answer the questions I began with. Who was Burns
and what was his relation to the Scotland of his day? What kind of
poems did he write and how good are they and why? It remains for
me to try and relate what I have said to the Burns cult, which I began
by referring to. How can this be explained? I think, very roughly,
there are three reasons for the Burns cult. One is the fact that Burns
was a humble peasant who stood up for human worth regardless of
rank or possessions : he is the most spectacular example in our literature
of a humble rustic who really made good in the literary world. Another is that in his songs he identified himself with the folk tradition
and spoke with moving authenticity for the daily experiences of men
and women as they are encountered in ordinary life. The third reason,
which is bound up with the second, is his ability to speak for man's
"unofficial self", his total lack—in his best and most characteristic
poems—of any idealising haze or of anything that the reader not pro-
fessionally interested in literature might regard as pretentious expansion of significance. His love songs are worlds apart from, say,
Shelley's *Epipsychidion*, and Shelley is not a poet normally celebrated
in country pubs or city clubs. I am not now talking of degrees of
poetic merit, but differences in poetic *kind*. The odd thing is that in
spite of the fact that the popular feeling about Burns—on which, after
all, the Burns cult is based—derives from a true insight into the nature
of one side at least of his poetry, the kind of thing spouted annually at
Burns suppers does not : it derives from and seeks inspiration in the
sentimental-rhetorical Burns, who is not the real Burns at all.

The poet, wrote Wordsworth, is "a man speaking to men". I think
we feel this about Burns more than we feel it about any other poet.
His voice, when it is his genuine voice, is not the voice of a prophet or
a seer or of one who wishes to elevate or edify ; it is the voice of man
as he is, at work and at play, in love and in hate, sounded with a
vibrant clarity it is hard to match elsewhere. Soon after Burns's death,
the Industrial Revolution changed the face of much of the part of
Scotland he knew best, and later generations looked back from black
cities and slag heaps to Burns and saw him through the mists of
nostalgia for a lost rustic way of life as the singer of a sentimentalised
countryside, the "wee hoose amang the heather" sort of thing. This
vulgarisation of Burns in the nineteenth century led to his having a
bad influence on subsequent Scottish poetry. But that was not Burns's
fault. And if we go back, not to what is said about his poetry, but to

the poems themselves, especially the great satires, the verse letters, "Tam o' Shanter", and the songs, we shall hear that disturbingly human voice, in mockery, in gaiety, or in passion, laying bare the essence of the human condition as it is known to daily living. It is a voice that compels assent; and we respond, as Joyce's Molly Bloom responded to life at the end of *Ulysses*, with acquiescence and affirmation: "Yes", we say, "Yes . . . yes".

10

Hugh MacDiarmid:
The Early Poems[1]

The long overdue collected edition of Hugh MacDiarmid's poetry recently published by Macmillan in New York (it is Scotland's bitter shame that she has had to wait for America to produce a collected edition of her greatest modern poet) opens with the poem "A Moment in Eternity", which originally appeared in his *Annals of the Five Senses* (1923) and was later included in *To Circumjack Cencrastus* (1930). Anyone who comes to this poem from the Scots lyrics in *Sangschaw* or *Penny Wheep* might well be surprised at what at first sight looks like its conventional English romantic imagery. The poem is frankly mystical, an account in terms of imagery largely of light of an intimate revelation of God and Eternity.

> And again the wind came
> Blowing me afar
> In fair fantastic fires,
> —Ivies and irises invading
> The upland garths of ivory ;
> Queen daisies growing
> In the tall red grass
> By pools of perfect peace ;
> And bluebells tossing
> In transparent fields ;
> And silver airs
> Lifting the crystal sources in dim hills
> And swinging them far out like bells of glass
> Pealing pellucidly
> And quivering in faery flights of chimes ;

[1] First published in *MacDiarmid : A Festschrift*, ed. K. D. Duval and Sydney Goodsir Smith. Edinburgh, 1962, pp. 21–47.

Shivers of wings bewildered
In alleys of virgin dream ;
Floral dances and revels of radiance
Whirling in stainless sanctuaries ;
And eyes of Seraphim,
Shining like sunbeams on eternal ice,
Lifted toward the unexplored
Summits of Paradise.

"Transparent", "dim", "crystal", "faery", "virgin dream", "radiance", "stainless", "Seraphim", "eternal ice"—this seems like a curious combination of Vaughan and Blake and Shelley and even Milton, worlds apart from, say,

An' the roarin' o' oceans noo'
Is peerieweerie to me :
Thunner's a tinklin' bell : an' Time
Whuds like a flee.

Yet this early poem of MacDiarmid's is not as far removed from his later works as one might imagine. The difference lies in the degree of verbal realisation of the subject, not in the nature of the subject itself. In "A Moment in Eternity" MacDiarmid is seeking for words to contain an experience whose reality is wholly independent of the poem ; the poem attempts to clothe the experience, and the comparatively facile eloquence which results is an eloquence of expression— the poet wears his words as indications of the nature and importance of his experience, as a high-ranking officer wears appropriate uniform and insignia or as peers wear robes at a coronation. The result is not ineffective, yet not wholly satisfactory either, because the imagery is not *special* enough, it does not fully contain the utter individuality of that complex of thought and feeling which prompted the poem.

Take, by contrast, the little "Ex Vermibus" from *Sangschaw* :

Gape, gape, gorlin',
For I ha'e a worm
That'll gi'e ye a slee and sliggy sang
Wi' mony a whuram.

Syne i' the lift
Byous spatrils you'll mak',
For a gorlin' wi' worms like this in its wame
Nae airels sall lack.

N

> But owre the tree-taps
> Maun flee like a sperk,
> Till it hes the haill o' the Heavens alunt
> Frae dawin' to derk.

What explodes this poem into its unique comic-yet-serious meaning is the brilliant transition from the visual to the aural to the visual again by means of which the wriggling worm becomes in the bird the actual trills of song first as expressed in splendidly turned crotchets and quavers ("mony a whuram", "byous spatrils"), then as notes to the ear, and finally as light-giving sounds that illumine Heaven. This, too, is in its way a mystical poem, but here MacDiarmid has found the appropriate kind of language for his kind of mysticism—or perhaps we might say that he has by now developed that kind of response to language which enables him to see the experience potential in the words. He wrote in *Lucky Poet* of "the act of poetry being the reverse of what it is usually thought to be, not an idea gradually shaping itself in words, but deriving entirely from words". This is a deliberate oversimplification, but it provides an important clue to what is going on in this poem. The vision, which moves from worm to bird-with-worm to note to sound to illuminated Heaven, is not an "idea" clothed in language : it is the total realisation in language of what cannot exist outside this particular realisation.

Of course, something of this sort can be said of any successful poem. But the process of verbal realisation in MacDiarmid demands special attention, for he has created his own language as few other poets have done—not invented it, but out of English and Scots, out of modern Scots dialects and medieval Scots literary vocabulary, created a language which, at its best, is at one with his version of experience. "Ex Vermibus" begins with an almost casual familiarity, the poet addressing the bird as he approaches it with a special worm :

> Gape, gape, gorlin',
> For I ha'e a worm
> That'll gi'e ye a slee and sliggy sang
> Wi' mony a whuram.

"Now there's a fine worm for you, birdie", one might say. The tone is familiar, humorous, interested. "I ha'e a worm / That'll g'ie ye a slee and sliggy sang." "Now *that*'ll really make you sing", is the rough prose equivalent, but then what becomes of the splendid "slee and sliggy sang" with its *conspiratorial* suggestion—the poet and the bird are now working together to produce something quite remarkable. We are prepared now for something more than the poet approaching the bird with a fine wriggling worm hoping that the worm will make the bird sing particularly well. We are prepared not only for that translation of the wriggling of the worm into the wriggling of the notes and the trilling of the sound (*quavering* quavers, one might say), but also for that odd mixture of comradeship and impersonality in the poet's relation to the bird, quite different from Burns's attitude to the mouse or from anything in the Scottish animal-poetry tradition. The poet's involvement in the bird's singing success grows out of the language. It seems at first that the little poem is simply going to play some tricks with language, assimilating the worm to the song through the intermediary of the wriggle. (The place played in the poem by the progression "slee and sliggy sang"—"mony a whuram"—"byous spatrils"—"airels" warrants a long discussion in itself: if only all discussion of the possibilities of Lallans in modern Scottish poetry were linked to concrete examples like this!) But the linking of the material and the spiritual, of a greedy bird and a vision of Heaven, is much more than a trick of language. It is an aspect of the mystic's habit of seeing eternity in a grain of sand, of refusing to accept the normal categories that isolate the material from the spiritual and the trivial from the overwhelmingly important. The worm become song turns into a spark that sets Heaven ablaze—and it is not a flash in the pan, but a blaze that lasts "frae dawin' to derk". A verbal joke becomes a striking poem : I can think of no more immediately convincing illustration of how MacDiarmid makes language work in his Scots poems from *Sangschaw* to *A Drunk Man Looks at the Thistle* than this wonderful little lyric.

Something like this happens in nearly all of MacDiarmid's early short poems in Scots. It is misleading to talk simply, as so many critics have done, of the beauty and tenderness and delicacy of these poems and then proceed to wonder what happened to these qualities in MacDiarmid's later poetry. These poems properly read will take us to the heart of MacDiarmid as a poet and enable us to see both the achievement of this early phase of his career and his later need to make a different kind of verbal attack upon experience. The shortest poems are often the most revealing. Consider "The Bonnie Broukit Bairn",

with its deliberate bringing together of astronomical myth, colloquial
violence, and sudden flash of impatient insight :

> Mars is braw in crammasy,
> Venus in a green silk goun,
> The auld mune shak's her gowden feathers,
> Their starry talk's a wheen o' blethers,
> Nane for thee a thochtie sparin',
> Earth, thou bonnie broukit bairn!
> —*But greet, an' in your tears ye'll droun*
> *The haill clanjamfrie!*

The modulation of the language more than corresponds to the progression of the mood and the emergence of the insight—it positively
creates them.   The phrase "a wheen o' blethers" suddenly transmutes
the splendidly dressed planets to a group of stairhead gossips, and the
turning away from them towards the earth, humanised by the diminu-
tive in "thochtie" and by the rising tenderness of the apostrophe,
"Earth, thou bonnie broukit bairn", leads at last to that wonderful
putting of the other planets in their place that is achieved by that
splendid phrase, "the haill clanjamfrie".   Or consider the choice of
Scots words in "The Watergaw" through which a sense of wonder and
foreboding is distilled and observe how the colloquial and proverbial
"there was nae reek i' the laverock's hoose" mediates between the
strangeness of nature and strangeness of human relations.   Or take
"Au Clair de la Lune", that uncanny sequence of lyrics where once
again (and this is particularly noticeable in "Moonstruck") the strangeness, the reality, and the power of the experience are determined by the
vocabulary and by the manipulation of the movement, speed, and
length of the lines.   Perhaps the most remarkable example of all is
"The Eemis Stane" :

> I' the how-dumb-deid o' the cauld hairst nicht
> The warl' like an eemis stane
> Wags i' the lift ;
> An' my eerie memories fa'
> Like a yowdendrift.
>
> Like a yowdendrift so's I couldna read
> The words cut oot i' the stane
> Had the fug o' fame
> An' history's hazelraw
> No' yirdit thaim.

Criticism stands powerless before this miracle of verbal choice and placing. The unexpectedness yet, once expressed, the extraordinary *rightness* of the comparison of the world in the cold harvest night to an "eemis stane" wagging in the sky (and how much is lost by translating the phrase "wags i' the lift", how uniquely expressive is "how-dumb-deid o' the cauld hairst nicht", and how pallidly rendered by "insecure stone" is "eemis stane"!) makes the poem almost a miraculous work of nature rather than a contrived work of art. The beautifully controlled rise of emotion caught by the repetition of "like a yowendrift" leads the poem effortless to a new and strangely moving use of the image of the eemis stane, which now becomes a worn tombstone with its inscription obliterated by moss and lichen, "the fug o' fame an' history's hazelraw".

If we say that there is a mystical centre in these poems and point out that time and again MacDiarmid shows himself to be obsessed with attitudes to time and eternity, this does not mean that this is an "other worldly" poetry which soars off into the Empyrean and leaves all common dailiness of human life behind. Far from it : there is nothing of Shelley but quite a bit of Blake in MacDiarmid, and his vision comes from proper realisation of the ordinary. The little poem "Country Life", with its contrast between the life of nature outside and the homely domestic interior (an old Scottish tradition this, but here used in a new way), is really made of the same materials as his more visionary poems, the only difference being that it doesn't push through to the vision but is content to state the contrast with a compelling simplicity, the very precision of the contrasting images suggesting, though not developing, some of the implications of the contrast :

> OOTSIDE! . . . Ootside!
> There's dooks that try tae fly
> An' bum-clocks bizzin' by,
> A corn-skriech an' a cay
> An' guissay i' the cray.
>
> Inside! . . . Inside!
> There's golochs on the wa',
> A cradle on the ca',
> A muckle breeze o' cones
> An' mither fochin' scones.

This, I think, for all its brevity and simplicity, is a better poem than

"I heard Christ Sing", with its more lax vocabulary and its echoes of the 'nineties.

God, Christ, and Eternity figure frequently in these poems, but though the traditional themes of Christian religious poetry can be found here again and again there is at work in the treatment of them a rock-like apprehension of the sheer stubbornness of life and indeed of the whole universe—what I can only describe as an inspired *coorseness*—that is bound up both with MacDiarmid's sensibility and with his language. One sees it in "The Sauchs in the Reuch Heuch Hauch" with its deadly last stanza :

> There's no' a licht that the Heavens let loose
> Can calm them a hanlawhile,
> Nor frae their ancient amplefeyst
> Sall God's ain sel' them wile.

One sees it, too, in the end of "Crowdieknowe" :

> Fain the weemun-folk'll seek
> To mak' them haud their row
> —*Fegs, God's no blate gin he stirs up*
> *The men o' Crowdieknowe!*

and in "The Frightened Bride" :

> Seil o' yer face! Ye needna seek
> For comfort gin ye show yer plight.
> To Gods an' men, coorse callants baith,
> A fleggit bride's the seilfu' sicht.

The poems in *Penny Wheep* continue many of the same methods and themes. In a poem such as "Cloudburst and Soaring Moon" we see that ability to use natural scenery in order to give meaning to a human situation while at the same time (as in Chinese classical poetry and the economical Japanese verse forms of the *tanka* and *hokku*) doing it all by simple juxtaposition, that is such a characteristic part of MacDiarmid's early talent :

> Cloodburst an' soarin' mune
> And 'twixt tha twa a taed
> That loupit oot upon me
> As doon the loan I gaed.

Noo I gang white an' lanely
But hoo I'm wishin', faith,
A clood ance mair cam' ower me
Wi' Jock the byreman's braith.

This is one of the simpler examples of this particular technique; one
can see clearly just what is going on here. A more complex welding
of nature, mood, and glint of insight that transcends both, is in that
brief but finely wrought poem "Somersault", where the Scots words
achieve an effect of enormous precision and at the same time of
enormous suggestiveness:

I lo'e the stishie
O' Earth in space
Breengin' by
At a haliket pace.

A wecht o' hills
Gangs wallopin' owre,
Syne a whummlin' sea
Wi' a gallus glower.

The West whuds doon
Like the pigs at Gadara,
But the East's aye there
Like a sow at the farrow.

The similes of the last stanza startle us by their apparent incongruity,
and the shock of attention that results provides that combination of
cosmic geography and a sense of the earthiness of physical life—the
midden heap linked to the stars, and *both equally there*—that is at the
core of so much of MacDiarmid's poetry.

Sometimes the fusion of language and experience fails and Mac-
Diarmid has to fall back on a tame gnomic remark, as at the end of
"Parley of Beasts":

It's fain I'd mell wi' tiger and tit,
Wi' elephant and eel,
But noo-a-days e'en wi' ain's sel
At hame it's hard to feel.

These last two lines, with the inversion having no other function than
to assist the rhyme, fall curiously flat (there is no question here of the
idea of the poem "deriving entirely from words"). In his later poetry

MacDiarmid develops a quite different way of handling the discursive poem of ideas, pushing past words towards the total rhythm of the meaning, oblivious of any incidental bathos or awkwardness, because he knows where he is going, the power of the whole deriving not from an instantaneous fusion of words and experience but from the cumulative pressure of thought and feeling in action. Until he developed this, he found difficulty in crossing from the visionary to the didactic; that interesting but not wholly successful poem "Sea-Serpent" gives clear evidence of this. Yet that deservedly popular short lyric, "Wheesht, Wheesht", which is not one of the visionary lyrics but a coolly objective statement of a situation, has the beautiful clarity and concentration, as well as the uncanny rightness in the choice of Scots words, that we find in what I call the visionary lyrics. A comparison of this poem with Robert Graves' "Down, Wanton, Down" will show MacDiarmid's extraordinary delicacy of feeling and language.

At the very time when he seemed to be resisting the urge to write longer poems—*Penny Wheep* includes the little poem, "To One Who Urges More Ambitious Flights", which contains the line "Wee bit sangs are a' I need"—MacDiarmid was working out a technique of the long poem considered as a poem-sequence in which incidental short lyrics could take their place enriched by their context. In 1926, the same year that saw the publication of *Penny Wheep*, appeared *A Drunk Man Looks at the Thistle*, his masterpiece in a *genre* which, if he did not actually invent, he certainly developed in a new way.

> I amna' fou' sae muckle as tired—deid dune.
> It's gey and hard wark coupin' gless for gless
> Wi' Cruivie and Gilsanquhar and the like,
> And I'm no' juist as bauld as aince I wes.
>
> The elbuck fankles in the coorse o' time,
> The sheckle's no' sae souple, and the thrapple
> Grows deef and dour : nae langer up and doun
> Gleg as a squirrel speils the Adam's apple.
>
> Forbye, the stuffie's no' the real Mackay . . .

This is the opening of *A Drunk Man*, with its splendid rendering of fatigue and a sense of the passing of time anchored to the realities of contemporary Scottish life both by its setting and by the sudden increase in the colloquial tone in "Forbye, the stuffie's no' the real Mackay". The slow movement of the first line, with the dead fall of its last two words, captures the moment of utter tiredness that invites drunkenness, and this is both personal to the speaker and symbolic of the state of Scotland. But it does more than this: it is the precise equivalent, in terms of the placing and meaning of this line in the poem, of Dante's

Nel mezzo del cammin di nostra vita
Mi ritrovai per una selva oscura,
Che la diritta via era smarrita.

But in MacDiarmid's lines the allegorical and symbolic elements are totally subsumed in a real contemporary world of commonplace experience. MacDiarmid, too, was "nel mezzo del cammin" when *A Drunk Man* appeared, and the poem is something of a testament. It is not, however, presented as a formal vision, but is allowed suddenly to open out before us as though we have pushed open the door of a pub and found ourselves inside with the speaker. This *placing* of the reader in the poem is achieved partly by the quietly conversational opening in which the writer confronts the reader as though the two had always been together. And then the matter-of-fact reference to "Cruivie and Gilsanquhar and the like" shrugs the social context into the poem in a way which takes for granted our knowledge and accept-ance of it. The last line of the opening stanza gives the first casual suggestion of the speaker's resigned awareness that he has lost his youth—"And I'm no juist as bauld as aince I wes". This leads into the next stanza, where a rising elegiac note is brilliantly developed in a colloquial Scots language with reference to the tiring of the drinker's elbow and the stiffening of his wrist in the course of years of boozing. Who but MacDiarmid could have sounded the true medieval "ubi sunt" plangency in such everyday—indeed, such "low"—imagery?

The elbuck fankles in the coorse o' time,
The sheckle's no' sae souple, and the thrapple
Grows deef and dour: nae langer up and doun
Gleg as a squirrel speils the Adam's apple.

Note, too, how the poet will not allow himself the self-indulgence of remaining long in this elegiac mood, the brisk and humorous imagery of

nae langer up and doun
Gleg as a squirrel speils the Adam's apple

breaking in to suggest a short ironic laugh—ironic, yet amused (there
is an engaging suggestion of the poet being amused by his own simile
here). This in turn leads to reflexions on the price of whisky having
gone up and the quality gone down, which provide the introduction
of one of the poem's main themes—the state of Scottish civilisation :

> It's robbin' Peter to pey Paul at least . . .
> And a' that's Scotch aboot it is the name,
> Like a' thing else ca'd Scottish nooadays
> —A' destitute o' speerit juist the same.

The pun on "speerit" links the state of Scotch whisky to the state of
Scotland.

Thus in five beautifully manœuvred stanzas MacDiarmid has moved
us from confronting a tired man in a pub to confronting questions
about civilisation. A wry parenthesis follows, in which he justifies
this method : now for the first time he appears as a poet confronting
the reader, no longer simply as a drinking companion drawing the
reader into a pub conversation :

> (To prove my saul is Scots I maun begin
> Wi' what's still deemed Scots and the folk expect,
> And spire up syne by visible degrees
> To heichts whereo' the fules ha'e never recked.

> But aince I get them there I'll whummle them
> And souse the craturs in the nether deeps,
> —For it's nae choice, and ony man s'ud wish
> To dree the goat's weird tae as weel's the sheep's!)

There is now an "I" and a "they". The poet has clearly emerged as
the satirist. But where does the reader stand at this point? Is he
with the poet, or is he one of "them"? MacDiarmid wants to keep
the reader's position uncertain for as long as possible, for it is only by
allowing the reader to feel that he makes a "we" with the author and
then suddenly shocking him into seeing himself as one of "them"
that he can achieve the special kind of shock treatment which is an
important part of his satirical method. Is the poet enlisting the
emotional support of professional Scotsmen in deploring the decline
of things Scottish? If the reader is fooled into thinking this, he has
not long to wait before being disillusioned, for the attack on the professional Scots flashes out in the immediately following stanzas and

we are startled into the realisation that all the standard and respectable
Scottish attitudes are part of the decline that has been talked about.
This technique of getting the reader (as he thinks) on the poet's side
and then hitting out hard and suddenly at the position the reader thinks
he now shares with the poet is very common in MacDiarmid's poetry ;
it is a satirical device he has made peculiarly his own—a new twist to
Baudelaire's "hypocrite lecteur", who becomes not "mon semblable,
mon frère", but "*leur* semblable, *leur* frère".

The Burns cult is the symbol of the false Scottish feeling that is
such a central target for MacDiarmid, and the relatively broad satire
of its handling is an indication of how natural a target it is :

> Croose London Scotties wi' their braw shirt fronts
> And a' their fancy freen's, rejoicin'
> That similah gatherings in Timbuctoo,
> Bagdad—and Hell, nae doot—are voicin'
>
> Burns' sentiments o' universal love,
> In pidgin' English or in wild-fowl Scots, . . .

The attack, of course, is not on the sentiments themselves, but on
the sentimentality, hypocrisy, and routine platitudinousness of these
proceedings.   Similarly the comic-satiric treatment of the international
aspect of these gatherings—

> You canna gang to a Burns supper even
> Wi'oot some wizened scrunt o' a knock-knee
> Chinee turns roon to say "Him Haggis—velly goot!"—

is not of course aimed at the Chinese or any other foreign nation ; the
target is the bogus internationalism associated with annual spoutings
about "A man's a man for a' that".

The speaker in the poem, it must be remembered, is both dead tired
and somewhat drunk.   This device serves a similar purpose to the
dream allegory in medieval literature ; a drunk man, like a dreaming
man, has his own logic, and his thoughts and feelings can be developed
in a sense of sequence which may at first sight appear totally disordered
but which in fact has a true order of its own which is part of the poetic
pattern of the whole.   Thoughts about the Burns cult lead to reflexions
on hypocrisy in modern life and comparisons of Burns's fate to Christ's
before the poet pulls himself up by recalling his own state :

But that's aside the point! I've got fair waun'ert.
It's no' that I'm sae fou' as just deid dune,
And dinna ken as muckle's whar I am
Or hoo I've come to sprawl here 'neth the mune.

That's it! It isna me that's fou' at a',
But the fu' mune, the doited jade, that's led
Me fer agley, or 'mogrified the warld.
—For a' I ken I'm safe in my ain bed.

Jean! Jean! Gin she's no' here it's no' *oor* bed,
Or else I'm dreamin' deep and canna wauken,
But it's a fell queer dream if this is no'
A real hillside—and thae things thistles and bracken!

This interesting transitional passage reveals the poet as now outside
the pub—on a moonlit hillside—and provides the first knowledge of
his wife back at home, that Jean whose name and presence act as a
kind of anchor, bringing the poet back again and again from fancy to
the homely realities of everyday life until the remarkable ending,
where, after the beautiful concluding lyric on silence ("yet ha'e I
Silence left, the croon o' a' ") with the poet's last rising cry, "O I ha'e
Silence left", her dry realism rounds the poem off:

—"And weel ye micht,"
Sae Jean'll say, "efter sic a nicht!"

It is Jean's words echoing in his mind, not her physical entry into the
poem, that provides this comment, for the poet's sense of his wife is a
force in the poem that breaks through intermittently to provide a
variety of effects.

But this is to anticipate. After the moment of half-waking on the
hillside, as it were (and what a host of archetypical associations *that*
brings in!), the poet proceeds to develop his earlier train of thought,
still rather staggeringly, for

It's hard wark haud'n by a thocht worth ha'en'
And harder speakin't, and no' for ilka man ;
Maist Thocht's like whisky—a thoosan' under proof,
And a sair price is pitten on't even than.

But the weaving quality of the thought is necessary for this kind of
poem ; it enables the poet to move easily between the commonplace
realities of modern Scotland and of his own daily life and varying
kinds of speculative reaching out or of sudden lyrical intensity. The

sharpness of the satire can be set against the moments of self-doubt.
Most satirical poets (Pope, for example) feel the necessity of maintaining the pose of complete confidence in their own rightness and moral
superiority if they are to have a position from which their satire can be
effectively launched. MacDiarmid does something more difficult : he
allows the objects of his scorn to destroy themselves by the way they
appear in his lines, and then at intervals shows us himself groping
towards a philosophy. This visible process brings the reader into a
special kind of relationship with the poet, quite different from the kind
of relationship which, say, Pope establishes in the "Epistle to Dr
Arbuthnot" by enabling the reader to identify himself with the recipient of the letter, Pope's intimate friend and thus one of the elect.
In MacDiarmid's case the poet commands further assent by the
integrity with which he displays his own uncertainties :

> I'll ha'e nae hauf-way hoose, but aye be whaur
> Extremes meet—it's the only way I ken
> To dodge the curst conceit o' bein' richt
> That damns the vast majority o' men.
>
> I'll bury nae heid like an ostrich's,
> Nor yet believe my een and naething else.
> My senses may advise me, but I'll be
> Mysel' nae maitter what they tell's. . . .
>
> I ha'e nae doot some foreign philosopher
> Has wrocht a system oot to justify
> A' this : but I'm a Scot wha blin'ly follows
> Auld Scottish instincts, and I winna try.
>
> For I've nae faith in ocht I can explain,
> And stert whaur the philosophers leave aff,
> Content to glimpse its loops I dinna ettle
> To land the sea serpent's sel' wi' ony gaff.

This leads to a cry for water (has he stumbled into a stream, or is his
mouth dry from too much alcohol, or does he want to water the
Waste Land of modern Scotland?) which at once modulates down to
the matter-of-fact and the domestic again :

> Water! Water! There was owre muckle o't
> In yonder whisky, sae I'm in deep water
> (And gin I could wun hame I'd be in het,
> For even Jean maun natter, natter, natter). . . .

(That "*even* Jean" is deft : it prevents the reference from being surly and from in any way endangering the solidity of this relationship : she is clearly a very special woman, but *even* she natters.)   The domestic imagery of this stanza moves naturally to thoughts of "the toon that I belang tae", which shares in the common drouth :

> And in the toon that I belang tae
> —What tho'ts Montrose or Nazareth?—
> Helplessly the folk continue
> To lead their livin' death! . . .

"What tho'ts Montrose or Nazareth?"   This links up with the preceding references to Christ, and at the same time provides one of those periodic expansions of context by means of which MacDiarmid links Scotland to the world and makes his poem a poem about civilisation and about the whole question of the possibilities of redemption in the world past and present as well as a poem about the state of his own country.   There follows the first of the inset lyrics, a finely localised account of the poet in the pub based on the Russian of Alexander Blok.   Though this was obviously written separately, its insertion into *A Drunk Man* at this point provides a moment of lyrical concentration which lights up the whole context.   It is about the relation of drink and the Muse, about the poet's necessity to seek for something beyond common experience in the very midst of common experience.   The pub itself is situated in the midst of all the symbols of domestic routine :

> And heich abune the vennel's pokiness,
> Whaur a' the white-weshed cottons lie ;
> The Inn's sign blinters in the mochiness,
> And lood and shrill the bairnies cry.

But there is also moonlight on the lochan :

> And on the lochan there, hauf-herted
> Wee screams and creakin' oar-locks soon'
> And in the lift, heich, hauf-averted,
> The mune looks owre the yirdly roon'.

The pub mediates between domesticity and moonlight, as it were, and itself provides both rough society and private mystery : on the note of private mystery the lyric ends :

My soul stores up this wealth unspent,
The key is safe and nane's but mine.
You're richt, auld drunk impenitent,
I ken it tae—the truth's in wine!

We then turn to the poet again, staggering about among the thistles on the Scottish hillside under a Scottish moon :

The munelicht's like a lookin'-glass,
The thistle's like mysel',
But whaur ye've gane, my bonnie lass,
Is mair than I can tell.

This has almost parodic overtones of the conventional Scottish song in the Burns tradition ("my bonnie lass"). But in fact MacDiarmid is taking up the theme of the preceding lyric—the vision seen in the glass of whisky—and developing it into a search for identity :

A man's a clean contrairy sicht
Turned this way in-ootside,
And, fegs, I feel like Dr. Jekyll
Tak'n guid tent o' Mr Hyde. . . .

The thistle seems to threaten him, he is aware of his own unshaven and semi-drunken condition, there is a roaring in his ears—then suddenly the poet falls into another lyric (again "freely adapted" from Alexander Blok) in which feelings of foreboding and even of terror are turned to another anticipation of the coming of the Muse, the "strange Goddess" both "forekent" and unimaginable. Then he turns on her in a violent colloquial outburst :

Or dost thou mak' a thistle o' me, wumman? But for thee
I were as happy as the munelicht, . . .

Moonlight plays on the next few stanzas, which slowly settle down into a more regular (but never wholly regular) metrical beat as the poet reflects on "the need to wark, the need to think, the need to be" that constrain a man ; and now he can use the thistle and moon images in a new way :

For ilka thing a man can be or dae
Aye leaves a million mair unbeen, unthocht, undune,
Till his puir warped performance is,
To a' that micht ha' been, a thistle to the mune.

The immediate scene now weaves in and out of the lines—the
hillside, the thistles, and bracken, the moonlight—as the poet tries to
force it into a meaning by contemplation ("And yet I feel this muckle
thistle's staun'in' / Atween me and the mune as pairt o' a Plan") and
as he does so the very quiddity of the thistle takes hold of him and
provokes new insight :

> I never saw afore a thistle quite
> Sae intimately, or at sic an 'oor.
> There's something in the fickle licht that gi'es
> A different life to't and an unco poo'er.

A short lyric on "the Gothic thistle", from the Belgian poet George
Ramaekers, effectively concentrates this moment of vision before the
poet shrugs it off with

> But that's a Belgian refugee, of coorse.
> *This* Freudian complex has somehoo slunken
> Frae Scotland's soul— . . .

The Scottish thistle is wilder than Ramaekers', and in any case "To
meddle wi' the thistle and to pluck / The figs frae't is *my* métier". An
adaptation of a poem on the octopus from the Russian of Zinaida
Hippius presents the thistle-octopus as a monstrous threat and at the
same time the poet's own soul, and the notion temporarily unhinges
him, so that he is lost on the ebb and flow of his own thoughts—

> The munelicht ebbs and flows and wi't my thocht.

Then, cutting across this ebb and flow, comes the sudden awareness
that there are many people who have no doubts or hesitances, who
know what is important to them, and write about it. It is a great
splash of comic irony :

> And O! to think that there are members o'
> St. Andrew's Societies sleepin' soon',
> Wha to the papers wrote afore they bedded
> On regimental buttons or buckled shoon,
>
> Or use o' England whaur the U.K.'s meent,
> Or this or that anent the Blue Saltire,
> Recruitin', pedigrees, and Gude kens what,
> Filled wi' a proper patriotic fire!

These people, so confident in their routine reactions, have in a sense
chosen a better part :

> Nae doot they're sober, as a Scot ne'er was,
> Each tethered to a punctual-snorin' missus,
> Whilst I, puir fule, owre continents unkent
> And wine-dark oceans waunder like Ulysses. . . .

The poet then breaks into a short lyric ("suggested by the German
of Else Lasker-Schüler") in which moonlight, the thistle, and the
poet's soul are presented as in complex and disturbing counterpoint.
A shift in rhythms and stanza form then brings in a passage which
makes a transition from the thistle to the bagpipes—

> Your leafs
> Mind me o' the pipes' lood drone
> —And a' your purple tops
> Are the pirly-wirly notes
> That gang staggerin' owre them as they groan.

The language and the thought, moving faster as it were to the music
of the pipes, present a brief version of the Caledonian Antisyzygy
with comic anecdote and comic ideas side by side ("Grinnin' gargoyle
by a saint") before we reach four stanzas which reflect briefly on the
Scottish educational system (explaining how a village drunk can
bring in so many "foreign references") and then break down in temporary confusion :

> Guid sakes I'm in a dreidfu' state.
> I'll ha'e nae inklin' sune
> Gin I'm the drinker or the drink,
> The thistle or the mune.

The moments of semi-drunken confusion in the poem serve as
effective transitions; when the image on the screen comes back into
focus, as it were, we are somewhere else—but where we are is always
related to the main theme and purpose of the work as a whole. We
move then to a short section in two-line stanzas on celebration in
Scotland :

> Drums in the Walligate, pipes in the air,
> Come and hear the cryin' o' the Fair.
> A' as it used to be, when I was a loon
> On Common-Ridin' Day in the Muckle Toon.

o

Things are different now ; yet the poet's vision of some splendid celebration has grown stronger and wilder :

> But I'll dance the nicht wi' the stars o' Heaven
> In the Mairket Place as shair's I'm livin'.

But the cosmos is too grandoise : the nostalgic mood with which the section opens returns at the close of it in a more limited human context :

> Devil the star ! It's Jean I'll ha'e
> Again as she was on her weddin' day . . .

This moving to and fro between the cosmos and the particularised moment of individual experience—between Blake and Burns, one might say—is an important feature of the poem, and one of Mac-Diarmid's characteristic devices. This note rises in the powerful lyrical interlude that follows :

> Nerves in stounds o' delight,
> Muscles in pride o' power,
> Bluid as wi' roses dight
> Life's toppin' pinnacles owre,
> The thistle yet'll unite
> Man and the Infinite!

The individual is a microcosm of the universe :

> Lay haud o' my hert and feel
> Fountains ootloupin' the starns
> Or see the Universe reel
> Set gaen' by my eident harns, . . .

This vision is linked with the thistle ; yet another look shows that "the howes o' Man's hert are bare, / The Dragon's left them for good" ; the thistle has fled to become, "rootless and radiant", a Phoenix in Paradise, and we are left gaping at vacancy :

> There's nocht but naethingness there,
> The hole whaur the Thistle stood, . . .

A shift of rhythms helps to modulate from elegy into self-mockery, as the poet addresses himself as a "thistleless fule", and then another shift brings three stanzas of deliberately self-conscious speculation

about what poets and artists can achieve in such a world. The wildness
that always lies near the surface in this poem breaks out for a moment
in the poet's half-ironic, half-defiant assumption of a pose of traditional
bardic dignity (the language is in fine contrast to Milton's account of
the poet "with all his singing robes about him") :

> —Crockats up, hair kaimed to the lift,
> And no' to cree legs wi' !

The wildness then swings the poem into an almost hysterical short
lyric of departure and discovery—"We're ootward boond frae
Scotland. / Guid-bye, fare-ye-weel ; guid-bye, fare-ye-weel" which
comes near to dissolving everything in "coutribat and ganien" before
the screen clears again and we see the poet meditating on the relation
between mind and body. Jean here plays her mediating part, anchoring the poem again in a physical relationship which is at the same time
more than physical. This leads in to a group of related lyrics on love
and sex and the combined lusts, fears, jealousies, and mysteries that
are involved in marriage, to culminate in the brilliant and well-known
"O wha's been here afore me, lass". A pause after the striking conclusion of this lyric is followed by some wry reflexions on women
and child-birth, which brings the poet round to the birth of Christ,
touched on first with a shrugging irony :

> Wull ever a wumman be big again
> Wi's muckle's a Christ? Yech, there's nae sayin'.

The Christ child is all very well, but ordinary births and ordinary
bairns are different :

> Christ had never toothick,
> Christ was never seeck,
> But Man's a fiky bairn
> Wi' bellythraw, ripples, and worm-i'-the-cheek ! . . .

Moonlight, thistle, child-birth combine in the poet's mind in tor-
mented speculation which dissolves in a wild jig :

> O Scotland is
> THE barren fig.
> Up, carles, up
> And roond it jig. . . .

> A miracle's
> Oor only chance.
> Up, carles, up
> And let us dance!

But Burns has degenerated into the kailyard, Dunbar has been discarded; Scotland had taken the wrong road. A four-line stanza with five-stressed lines brings in this sterner tone, moving with a deliberate tiredness. The lesson is—and the poet's voice turns momentarily to that of the preacher now—

>   to be yersel's,
> Ye needna fash gin it's to be ocht else.
> To be yersel's—and to mak' that worth bein', . . .

Whatever Scotland is, she is not England; with implicit echoes of the Rose as used in so much English poetry (such as "Go, lovely rose") the poet turns to explain his quarrel with England:

> I micht ha'e been contentit wi' the rose . . .

The quarrel is in fact less with England than with the Scots for grovelling before the richer country and for ignoring the strengths of their own culture. The movement of the verse becomes less bland:

> I micht ha'e been contentit—gin the feck
> O' my ain folk had grovelled wi' less respec', . . .

This leads to an attack on the "drumlie clood o' crudity and cant" and to another lament over Scotland:

> Eneuch! For noo I'm in the mood,
> Scotland, responsive to my thoughts,
> Lichts mile by mile, as my ain nerves,
> Frae Maidenkirk to John o' Groats!

He turns again to Cruivie and Gilsanquhar in the pub: inquire as to what are the prophets and priests and kings of Scotland "and Cruivie'll goam at you, Gilsanquhar jalouse you're dottlin'!" The lines shorten as he contrasts his own concern with his country with their complacency, their rude health with his "gnawin' canker". The language becomes bitter and colloquial—

> Guid sakes, ye dinna need to pass
> Ony exam. to dee. . . .

The poet's predicament is the theme of the succeeding group of lyric passages which move, as so often in *A Drunk Man,* between metaphysical speculation and the familiar realities of daily experience. The thistle in the moonlight takes on ever changing shapes and meanings :

> The munelicht is my knowledge o' mysel',
> Mysel' the thistle in the munelicht seen, . . .

Gropings after self-knowledge, speculations on the relation between love and lust (Jean flits in and out again), thoughts on human destiny, lead back to the thistle, on whose significance the poet muses in a grave and slow-moving passage in six-line stanzas before turning to a ballad measure in which, giving now a quite new significance to the Rose, he writes a symbolic lyric on the General Strike :

> I saw a rose come loupin' oot
> Frae a camsteerie plant. . . .

This is the precise equivalent of Yeats's "A terrible beauty is born", but quite differently done. Scotland's self-torture is both beautiful and bitter : the Devils admire the technique of crucifixion of this silly Christ :

> Like connoisseurs the Deils gang roond
> And praise its attitude,
> Till on the Cross the silly Christ
> To fidge fu' fain's begood!

The unexpected word "connoisseurs" breaks into the colloquial Scots here with extraordinary effect, and the word is repeated with increasing irony in the next two stanzas.

What, then, is the Thistle? The long passage in fast moving octosyllabic verse that follows wrests all possible meanings out of the Scottish national plant, and as the meanings proliferate the poet's drunkenness is used as a means of explaining the ever expanding images :

> Gin I was sober I micht think
> It was like something drunk men see!

Whisky and theology move together with sex and mystical vision in a drunken dance of moods and ideas which bring together most of the

recurring motifs in the poem.   This sequence ends with a sudden
sobering :

> Aye, this is Calvary—to bear
> Your Cross wi'in you frae the seed,
> And feel it grow by slow degrees
> Until it rends your flesh apairt,
> And turn, and see your fellow-men
> In similar case but sufferin' less
> Thro' bein' mair wudden frae the stert!

A wild focussing of the poet's fiercely colloquial language and a
mingling of religious and domestic imagery provides a startling two-
stanza interlude :

> I'm fu' o' a sticket God.
> THAT's what's the maitter wi' me.
> Jean has stuck sic a fork in the wa'
> That I row in agonie. . . .

The poet then returns to his meditations on Scotland's destiny which
in turn flows into a "Letter to Dostoevski" in which Scotland appears
both as a particular region of the world with its own special history
and topography and a symbol of something universal and eternal :

> And as at sicna times am I,
> I wad ha'e Scotland to my eye
> Until I saw a timeless flame
> Tak' Auchtermuchty for a name,
> And kent that Ecclefechan stood
> As pairt o' an eternal mood. . . .

The Russian-Scottish juxtaposition is employed as a catalyst to project
this counterpointing of time and eternity, locality and universality,
which is at bottom a poetic testament of MacDiarmid's kind of Scottish
nationalism.

The lyric which follows is a moving appeal to Jean to illuminate
through her love his own identity and the true nature of his Scottish-
ness, after which the poet returns to brooding over the thistle and its
possible meanings.   The verse now becomes ever more flexible, the
lines contracting or expanding as the thought and emotion demand.
As the emotion steadies the verse jells again, as it were, so that we get
a section in neatly turned four-line stanzas in which the irony is

relatively straightforward : this includes the parody of the famous lines
from Home's *Douglas* :

> My name is Norval. On the Grampian Hills
> It is forgotten, and deserves to be. . . .

The poet then returns to Dostoevski in a lyric whose rising elegiac
rhythms draw the whole poem into a plangent sense of loss which yet,
somehow, is related to a sense of hope :

> The wan leafs shak' atour us like the snaw.
> Here is the cavaburd in which Earth's tint.
> There's naebody but Oblivion and us,
> Puir gangrel buddies, waunderin' hameless in't.
>
> The stars are larochs o' auld cottages,
> And a' Time's glen is fu' o' blinnin' stew.
> Nae freen'ly lozen skimmers : and the wund
> Rises and separates even me and you.
>
> I ken nae Russian and you ken nae Scots.
> We canna tell oor voices frae the wund.
> The snaw is seekin' everywhere : oor herts
> At last like roofless ingles it has f'und.
>
> And gethers there in drift on endless drift,
> Oor broken herts that it can never fill ;
> And still—its leafs like snaw, its growth like wund—
> The thistle rises and forever will ! . . .

This seems to me to be the true emotional centre of *A Drunk Man*.
Yet MacDiarmid cannot allow himself such a simple slogan as "The
thistle rises and forever will" without raising the counter-statement.
His nationalism does not go in for crude sloganising. So :

> The thistle rises and forever will,
> Getherin' the generations under't.
> This is the monument o' a' they were,
> And a' they hoped and wondered.

Here the thistle is a gravestone as well as a symbol of hope, and we
are left to make what we will of the conflicting meanings. The poem
then plunges into another lively ironic account of the barren civilisation
of modern Scotland.

    The Scots are as good as anybody else at laying flattering unctions to their souls. "Fier comme un Ecossais" is a description they like to cherish. MacDiarmid exposes it by repeating it three times in the midst of a short ironic lyric which reveals the hollow centre of the modern Scot—and of much more than the Scot—as Eliot does in "The Hollow Men" but more succinctly :

> The wee reliefs we hae' in booze,
> Or wun at times in carnal states,
> May hide frae us but canna cheenge
> The silly horrors o' oor fates.

The poet returns to the thistle, pursuing its twisted snakeshape to a host of further implications. And the rose? Whatever his quarrel with the thistle, it is not to the rose that he will turn :

> And let me pit in guid set terms
> My quarrel wi' th'owre sonsy rose, . . .

Good or bad, the rose "ootside me lies". The final dismissal of the rose precedes a final endeavour to *place* Scotland :

> He canna Scotland see wha yet
> Canna see the Infinite,
> And Scotland in true scale to it.

All very well, but as images of Scotsmen crowd in, from John Knox to Harry Lauder, the poet is moved to protest :

> Mercy o' Gode, I canna thole
> Wi' sic an orra mob to roll.

The poet now conducts a "dialogue of one". His other voice refuses to allow him to repudiate "this huge ineducable / Heterogeneous hotch and rabble". It tells him somewhat portentously :

> A Scottish poet maun assume
> The burden o' his people's doom,
> And dee to brak' their livin' tomb.

The ironic voice replies :

> And I look at a' the random
> Band the wheel leaves whaur it fand 'em.
>   "Auch, to Hell,
> I'll tak' it to avizandum." . . .

The poet will go back to Jean, anyway—

> She'll ope her airms in welcome true,
> And clack nae mair aboot it.

In the coda (as it might be called) the poet looks up in wonder at the stars and feels his heart and brain "toomed". In the superb concluding lyric he falls back on silence, the ultimate eloquence :

> Yet ha' I silence left, the croon o' a'.

> No' her, wha on the hills langsyne I saw
> Liftin' a foreheid o' perpetual snaw.

> No' her, wha in the how-dumb-deid o' nicht
> Kyths, like Eternity in Time's despite.

> No' her, withooten shape, wha's name is Daith,
> No' Him, unkennable abies to faith

> —God whom, gin e'er He saw a Man, 'ud be
> E'en mair dumfooner'd at the sicht than he.

> —But Him, whom nocht in man or Deity,
> Or Daith or Dreid or Laneliness can touch,
> *Wha's deed owre often and has seen owre much.*

> O I ha'e Silence left,

>   —"And weel ye micht."
> Sae Jean'll say, "efter sic a nicht!"

We are left in the end with the forthright voice of womanly common sense, anchoring the whole poem in that domestic reality that it has kept returning to.

I make no apology for having devoted most of my space to *A Drunk Man*. It is not only MacDiarmid's finest sustained performance but also the greatest long poem (or poem-sequence) in Scottish literature and one of the greatest in any literature. It is hardly less than miraculous that in an age when Scottish culture is so confused and adulterated a poem with this kind of originality, this kind of integrity, and this kind of technical brilliance has been written. It would be pleasant indeed to think that this extraordinary achievement marks the opening of new creative possibilities for Scottish literature, but it would be quite unrealistic to make the claim. It is over thirty-five years since *A Drunk Man* was written, and what other Scottish poet has come within a hundred miles of this kind of greatness? MacDiarmid created his own Scottish Renaissance by sheer force of creative personality. His particular brand of what I can only call trans-humanism, which cuts across all accepted political, social, and moral attitudes in its almost mystical search for whatever is fully realised, truly itself, whether it is a community or a stone, is the clue to the apparent contradictions in his thought and, more significantly, to the way he uses language. MacDiarmid's synthetic Scots works in his poetry as no other language could work because his imagination works linguistically; for him, the proper naming of things is the revelation of their real meaning in experience. He is first and foremost a poet, and he is always less effective when he adopts any other role. His greatest work was produced in the 1920s and 1930s. I know he does not like people to say this, and I know too that some of his more recent work has remarkable qualities. But after one has re-read carefully all his published poetry, one is left in little doubt that (as with Wordsworth, though without anything like such a definite decline) the greatest is on the whole the earlier. Such a judgment sounds, however, grudging in the face of such real genius. Let us remember that when we talk about MacDiarmid's "greatest" work we are using the word in its proper sense, not journalistically. Dunbar, Burns, and MacDiarmid are the great Scottish trio. Let pedants wrangle over which of these deserves the precedence; there can be little doubt that MacDiarmid is the greatest miracle.

Lincoln and Whitman[1]

Early in July 1855 Walt Whitman published the first edition of his *Leaves of Grass*, that extraordinary manifestation of a new kind of poetic energy in America which he was to re-work, amplify, and enlarge throughout the rest of his life. Country schoolmaster, printer, carpenter, house-builder, and more continuously journalist, the thirty-six-year-old Whitman had led a curiously sloppy existence before belatedly discovering himself as America's new poet. That self-discovery was bound up with his adoption of a new *persona*. Hitherto he had been Walter Whitman Jr; now he was "Walt Whitman, an American, one of the roughs, a kosmos". He had been described in his early twenties as "tall and graceful in appearance, neat in attire. He usually wore a frock coat and a high hat, carried a small cane, and the lapel of his coat was almost invariably ornamented with a boutonnière". But there was nothing of the dandy in the famous portrait of himself which he set opposite the title-page of his revolutionary volume : as we all know, this shows the bearded poet in a pose of studied virility and informality, his open shirt revealing the under-shirt beneath, his large soft hat at an angle, his right hand on his hip and his left in his pocket : a sort of combination of Garibaldi and Adam Bede.

Had this pose any political significance? To answer that question we must go of course to his poetry, but also to his earlier life. He had been brought up in what might loosely be called a radical atmosphere. His father had known and admired Tom Paine and had been a friend of the dissident Quaker, Elias Hicks, whom Walt as a child had heard preach and whose doctrine of the inner light was to influence the poet's development of his doctrine of a democracy of individuals combining

---

[1] Delivered at a Conference of the German Association of American Studies, Berlin, June 1965.

emphasis on the self with emphasis on the unity of American society. The elder Whitman had christened three other of his sons George Washington, Thomas Jefferson, and Andrew Jackson, and seems to have professed a Jeffersonian cum Jacksonian democracy. The young Walt Whitman read Tom Paine and also found "daily food" (as he later wrote) for years in the writings of Fanny Wright, the Scottish-born free-thinker, reformer, feminist, and abolitionist. It is therefore no surprise to find him, when editor of the Brooklyn *Daily Eagle* in 1846–8, championing such progressive causes as the abolition of capital punishment, and of flogging in schools, and supporting the Free Soil movement. The *Eagle* was a Democratic paper, and Walt Whitman's editorials offended the conservative Democrats of New York state, with the result that he lost the editorship. In the many slap-dash reviews he wrote at this time he expressed literary judgments in which we can trace his political radicalism. Walter Scott, whose novels he enjoyed, was nevertheless suspect as "a Tory and a High Church and State man" and Dr Johnson was "a sycophant of power and rank" with his head better educated than his heart.

Whitman's brief and unsuccessful career as a journalist in New Orleans in 1848 was followed by his founding and editing the Brooklyn *Freeman*, which supported the Free Soil cause ; after a year his embroiling himself once again with the conservative Democrats resulted in his resignation. But his journey to New Orleans and back had produced in him a vision of a wider and still widening America, so that he was now able to combine his democratic individualism with a vision of American expansiveness and variety. During the years when the poems which were to make up the first edition of *Leaves of Grass* were gestating—years in which he was engaged in a variety of journalistic and other activities—this counterpointing of American individuality and American space must have been developing steadily in his thought. At the same time, under the influence of the classic American radical suspicion of the feudal and decadent Old World as well as of Emerson's plea for an indigenous American literature, free from dependence on Europe—"We have listened too long to the courtly muses of Europe"—he was searching for a national American idiom, a personal voice which could nevertheless speak uniquely for his great, diverse, and troubled country.

In the Preface to *Leaves of Grass* Whitman wrote : "The Americans of all nations at any time upon the earth have probably the fullest poetical nature. The United States themselves are essentially the greatest poem. In the history of the earth hitherto the largest and most stirring appear tame and orderly to their ample largeness and stir. Here at last is something in the doings of man which corresponds with the broadcast doings of the day and night. Here is not merely a nation but a teeming nation of nations. Here is action untied from strings necessarily blind to particulars and details magnificently moving in vast masses. Here is the hospitality which forever indicates heroes. . . . Here are the roughs and beards and space and ruggedness and nonchalance that the soul loves."

"Here are the roughs and beards and space and ruggedness and nonchalance that the soul loves." This is certainly one clue to "Walt Whitman, an American, one of the roughs, a kosmos", one clue to the bearded, open-shirted figure of the frontispiece. But let us quote a little more from the 1855 Preface :

> The American poets are to enclose old and new for America is the race of races. Of them a bard is to be commensurate with a people. To him the other continents arrive as contributions . . . he gives them reception for their sake and his own sake. His spirit responds to his country's spirit . . . he incarnates his geography and natural life and rivers and lakes. Mississippi with annual freshets and changing chutes, Missouri and Columbia and Ohio and Saint Lawerence with the falls and beautiful masculine Hudson, do not embouchure where they spend themselves more than they embouchure into him. The blue breadth over the inland sea of Virginia and Maryland and the sea of Massachusetts and Maine and over Manhattan bay and over Champlain and Erie and over Ontario and Huron and Michigan and Superior, and over the Texan and Mexican and Floridian and Cuban seas and over the seas of California and Oregon, is not tallied by the blue breadth of the waters below more than the breadth of above and below us is tallied by him.

The nonchalant American rough is a symbol of both the variety and the unity of the United States. If for Abraham Lincoln the Civil War was on the Union side above all a struggle to "save the Union", it takes no great effort of scholarship to see that Whitman was to be one with him there. What is perhaps less immediately obvious is that there was some community of feeling also in their sense of the variety of the country whose political union was so important. There is a Whitmanesque geographical imagination at work in the last part of Lincoln's letter to James C. Conkling of 26 August, 1863.

The signs look better. The Father of Waters again goes unvexed to the sea. Thanks to the great North-West for it. Nor yet wholly to them. Three hundred miles up, they meet New-England, Empire, Key-Stone, and Jersey, hewing their way right and left. The Sunny South too, in more colors than one, also lent a hand . . . Nor must Uncle Sam's web-feet be forgotten. At all the watery margins they have been present. Not only on the deep sea, the broad bay, and the rapid river, but also up the narrow muddy bayou, and wherever the ground was a little damp, they have been, and made their tracks. Thanks to all. For the great republic—for the principle it lives by, and keeps alive—for man's vast future,—thanks to all.

This is not, of course, Whitman's idiom. Yet one sees the similarity, as well as the difference, in a passage like this from "Song of Myself"

I am of old and young, of the foolish as much as the wise,
Regardless of others, ever regardful of others,
Maternal as well as paternal, a child as well as a man,
Stuff'd with the stuff that is coarse and stuff'd with the stuff that is fine,
One of the Nation of many nations, the smallest the same and the
    largest the same,
A Southerner soon as a Northerner, a planter nonchalant and
    hospitable down by the Oconee I live,
A Yankee bound my own way ready for trade, my joints the
    limberest joints on earth and the sternest joints on earth,
A Kentuckian walking the vale of the Elkhorn in my deer-skin
    leggings, a Louisianian or Georgian,
A boatman over lakes or bays or along coasts, a Hoosier, Badger,
    Buckeye;
At home on Kanadian snow-shoes or up in the bush,
    or with fishermen off Newfoundland,
At home in the fleet of ice-boats, sailing with the rest and tacking,
At home on the hills of Vermont or in the woods of Maine, or the
    Texan ranch,
Comrade of Californians, comrade of free North-Westerners,
    (loving their big proportions,)
Comrade of raftsmen and coalmen, comrade of all who shake hands
    and welcome to drink and meat,
A learner with the simplest, a teacher of the thoughtfullest,
A novice beginning yet experient of myriads of seasons,
Of every hue and caste am I, of every rank and religion,
A farmer, mechanic, artist, gentleman, sailor, quaker,
Prisoner, fancy-man, rowdy, lawyer, physician, priest.

But let us return to Whitman's self-dramatisation as "one of the roughs", and its significance. In September 1855 there appeared in the *United States Review* a review of *Leaves of Grass* which was actually written by Whitman himself and published anonymously. (This was not the only time that Whitman produced an anonymous review of his own book : he wanted to make sure that the public understood exactly what his intentions were.) This review opens thus :

> An American bard at last! One of the roughs, large, proud, affectionate, eating, drinking, and breeding, his costume manly and free, his face sunburnt and bearded, his postures strong and erect, his voice bringing hope and prophecy to the generous races of young and old. We shall cease shamming and be what we really are. We shall start an athletic and defiant literature. We realize now how it is, and what was most lacking. The interior American republic shall also be declared free and independent.
>
> For all our intellectual people, followed by their books, poems, novels, essays, editorials, lectures, tuitions and criticisms, dress by London and Paris modes, receive what is received there, obey the authorities, settle disputes by the old tests, keep out of rain and sun, retreat to the shelter of houses and schools, trim their hair, shave, touch not the earth barefoot, and enter not the sea except in a complete bathing dress. One sees unmistakably genteel persons, travelled, college-learned, used to be served by servants, conversing without heat or vulgarity, supported on chairs, or walking through handsomely carpeted parlors, or along shelves bearing well-bound volumes, and walls adorned with curtained and collared portraits, and china things, and nick-nacks. But where in American literature is the first show of America? Where are the gristle and beards, and broad breasts, and space, and ruggedness, and nonchalance, that the souls of the people love? Where is the tremendous outdoors of these states? Where is the majesty of the federal mother, seated with more than antique grace, calm, just, indulgent to her brood of children, calling them around her, regarding the little and the large, and the younger and the older, with perfect impartiality? Where is the vehement growth of our cities? Where is the spirit of the strong rich life of the American mechanic, farmer, sailor, hunter, and miner? Where is the huge composite of all other nations, cast in a fresher and brawnier matrix, passing adolescence, and needed this day, live and arrogant, to lead the marches of the world?

The rhetorical questions indicate an unfulfilled promise. Even though he goes on immediately to suggest that Walt Whitman is the answer—"Self-reliant, with haughty eyes, assuming to himself all the attributes of his country, steps Walt Whitman into literature"—it is clear to us and it became increasingly clear to Whitman himself that he was also looking for political attitudes and actions which could respond to the kind of American challenge he describes, and that all the problems could not be solved by a new kind of poetry. An enlarged second edition of *Leaves of Grass* appeared in 1856, and the following year he became editor of the Brooklyn *Times*, to express in his editorials a growing disillusion with all existing political parties whose members were mostly "the meanest kind of bawling and blowing office-holders, office-seekers, pimps, malignants, conspirators, murderers, fancy men, custom-house clerks, contractors, kept-editors, spaniels well train'd to carry and fetch, jobbers, infidels, disunionists, terrorists, mail-riflers, slave-catchers, pushers of slavery, creatures of the would-be Presidents, spies, bribers, compromisers, lobbyers, sponges, ruin'd sports, expell'd gamblers, policy-backers, monte-dealers, duellists, carriers of concealed weapons, deaf men, pimpled men, scarr'd inside with vile disease, gaudy outside with gold chains made from the people's money and harlots' money twisted together; crawling, serpenting men, the lousy combings and born freedom-sellers of the earth." Against this vision of an American Inferno and the view that all existing political parties were, as he wrote in his pamphlet *The Eighteenth Presidency*, "played out", he set a picture of the kind he would like to see. This is in the same pamphlet. "I would be much pleased to see some heroic, shrewd, full-informed, healthy-bodied, middle-aged, beard-faced American blacksmith or boatman come down from the West across the Alleghenies and walk into the Presidency. I would certainly vote for that sort of man." So "one of the roughs" has become an ideal candidate for president. The bearded hero-workman of the 1855 frontispiece is "mixed", in the language of television technique, into a portrait curiously resembling Abraham Lincoln. In the presidential election of 1860 Whitman in fact voted for Lincoln.

In the 1856 edition of *Leaves of Grass* he included a new poem which bitterly expressed his disillusionment with the state of America. He later rejected it, and did not include it in editions of *Leaves of Grass* after 1876. The poem, which he entitled *Respondez!*, vibrates with an almost hysterical irony:

Let me bring this to a close—I pronounce openly for a new
 distribution of roles ;
Let that which stood in front go behind! and let that which was
 behind advance to the front and speak ;
Let murderers, bigots, fools, unclean persons, offer new propositions!
Let the old propositions be postponed!
Let faces and theories be turn'd inside out! let meanings be freely
 criminal, as well as results!
Let there be no suggestion above the suggestion of drudgery!
Let none be pointed toward his destination! (Say! do you know your
 destination?)
Let men and women be mock'd with bodies and mock'd with Souls!
Let the love that waits them, wait! let it die, or pass still-born to
 other spheres!
Let the sympathy that waits in every man, wait! or let it also pass, a
 dwarf, to other spheres!
Let contradictions prevail! let one thing contradict another! and
 let one line of my poem contradict another!
Let the people sprawl with yearning, aimless hands! let their tongues
 be broken! let their eyes be discouraged! let none descend into
 their hearts with the fresh lusciousness of love!
(Stifled, O days! O lands! in every public and private corruption!
Smother'd in thievery, impotence, shamelessness, mountain-high ;
Brazen effrontery, scheming, rolling like ocean's waves around and
 upon you, O my days! my lands!
For not even those thunderstorms, not fiercest lightnings of the war,
 have purified the atmosphere ;)
—Let the theory of America still be management, caste, comparison!
 (Say! what other theory would you?)
Let them that distrust birth and death still lead the rest! (Say! why
 shall they not lead you?)
Let the crust of hell be neared and trod on! let the days be darker
 than the nights! let slumber bring less slumber than waking
 time brings!
Let the world never appear to him or her for whom it was all made!
Let the heart of the young man still exile itself from the heart of the
 old man! and let the heart of the old man be exiled from that of
 the young man!
Let the sun and moon go! let scenery take the applause of the
 audience! let there be apathy under the stars!
Let freedom prove no man's inalienable right! every one who can
 tyrranize, let him tyrranize to his satisfaction!

P

Let none but infidels be countenanced!
Let the eminence of meanness, treachery, sarcasm, hate, greed,
     indecency, impotence, lust, be taken for granted above all!
     let writers, judges, governments, households, religions,
     philosophies, take such for granted above all!

It was clearly time for the "heroic, shrewd, . . . beard-faced American blacksmith" to come to the rescue.

In December 1862, some twenty months after the outbreak of the Civil War, Whitman left Brooklyn for the hospital camp in Falmouth, Virginia, to look after his brother George who had been wounded in the battle of Fredericksburg. Throughout the rest of the war he stayed in Washington, tending the wounded who were accommodated in a great variety of public buildings in the capital. After doing part-time work in the Army Paymaster's Office, he obtained a clerkship in the Indian Bureau of the Department of the Interior early in 1865, and when six months later he was discharged because of the supposed indecency of some of his poems, his friends were able to secure for him a similar position in the office of the Attorney-General, which he held until 1872, when he was transferred to a branch of the Department of Justice. He left Washington for good after his paralytic stroke of January 1873, and spent the rest of his life in Camden, New Jersey.

Whitman was thus in Washington from the end of 1862 throughout the rest of the period of the war and the remainder of Lincoln's life. "I see the President almost every day", he wrote on 12 Aug. 1863 in the rambling journal he later published as *Specimen Days*, "as I happen to live where he passes to or from his lodgings out of town. He never sleeps at the White House during the hot season, but has quarters at a healthy location some three miles north of the city, the Soldiers' home, a United States military establishment. I saw him this morning about $8\frac{1}{2}$ coming in to business, riding on Vermont avenue, near L street . . . Mr Lincoln on the saddle generally rides a good-sized, easy-going gray horse, is dress'd in plain black, somewhat rusty and dusty, wears a black stiff hat, and looks about as ordinary in attire, etc., as the commonest man . . . I see very plainly ABRAHAM LINCOLN'S dark brown face, with the deep-cut lines, the eyes, always to me with a deep latent sadness in the expression. We have got so that we exchange bows, and very cordial ones. . . Earlier in the summer I occasionally saw the President and his wife, toward the latter part of the afternoon, out in a barouche, on a pleasant ride through the city. Mrs Lincoln was dress'd in complete black, with a long crape veil. The equipage is of the plainest kind, only two horses, and they nothing extra. They pass'd me once very close, and I saw the President in the face fully, as they were moving slowly, and his look, though abstracted, happen'd to be directed steadily in my eye. He bow'd and smiled, but far beneath his smile I noticed well the expression I have alluded to. None of the artists or pictures has caught the deep, though subtle and indirect expression of this man's face. There is something else there. One of the great portrait painters of two or three centuries ago is needed."

Whitman never got closer to Lincoln than the distant exchange of bows described here. But from an early stage Whitman endowed Lincoln with some of the ideal qualities of his American rough, the "heroic, shrewd, beard-faced" blacksmith.

In his later years Whitman delivered several times a lecture on the Death of Lincoln in which he described his first sight of the President —which was not in Washington, but in New York.

In the height of all this excitement and chaos, hovering on the edge at first, and then merged in its very midst, and destined to play a leading part, appears a strange and awkward figure. I shall not easily forget the first time I ever saw Abraham Lincoln. It must have been about the 18th or 19th of February, 1861. It was rather a pleasant afternoon, in New York city, as he arrived there from the West, to remain a few hours, and then pass on to Washington, to prepare for his inauguration. I saw him in Broadway, near the site of the present Post-office. He came down, I think from Canal street, to stop at the Astor House. The broad spaces, sidewalks, and streets in the neighborhood, and for some distance, were crowded with solid masses of people, many thousands. The omnibuses and other vehicles had all been turn'd off, leaving an unusual hush in that busy part of the city. Presently two or three shabby hack barouches made their way with some difficulty through the crowd, and drew up at the Astor House entrance. A tall figure step'd out of the centre of these barouches, paus'd leisurely on the sidewalk, look'd up at the granite walls and looming architecture of the grand old hotel—then, after a relieving stretch of arms and legs, turn'd round for over a minute to slowly and good-humoredly scan the appearance of the vast and silent crowds. There were no speeches— no compliments—no welcome—as far as I could hear, not a word said. Still much anxiety was conceal'd in that quiet. Cautious persons

had fear'd some mark'd insult or indignity to the President-elect—for
he possess'd no personal popularity at all in New York city, and very little
political.   But it was evidently tactily agreed that if the few political
supporters of Mr Lincoln present would entirely abstain from any
demonstration on their side, the immense majority, who were any thing
but supporters, would abstain on their side also.   The result was a sulky,
unbroken silence, such as certainly never before characterized so great
a New York crowd.

Later in the same lecture Whitman described how Lincoln appeared
to him from the top of an omnibus on this same occasion :

From the top of an omnibus, (driven up one side, close by, and block'd
by the curbstone and the crowds,) I had, I say, a capital view of it all,
and especially of Mr Lincoln, his look and gait—his perfect composure
and coolness—his unusual and uncouth height, his dress of complete
black, stovepipe hat push'd back on the head, dark-brown complexion,
seam'd and wrinkled yet canny-looking, face, black, bushy head of hair,
disproportionately long neck, and his hands held behind as he stood
observing the people.   He look'd with curiosity upon that immense sea
of faces, and the sea of faces return'd the look with similar curiosity.
In both there was a dash of comedy, almost farce, such as Shakspere
puts in his blackest tragedies.

It seems that the process not so much of idealisation as of *symbolisa-
tion* of Lincoln kept on developing in Whitman's mind from the
moment he first saw him, and quite possibly from an even earlier
period.   Yet this process went on side by side with much shrewd
observation.   "He has a face like a Hoosier Michael Angelo", he
wrote to Nat and Fred Gray from Washington on 19 Mar., 1863,
adding immediately, "so awful ugly it becomes beautiful, with its
strange mouth, its deep cut, criss-cross lines, and its doughnut complexion.—My notion is too, that underneath his outside smutched
mannerism, and stories from third-class county barrooms (it is his
humor), Mr Lincoln keeps a fountain of first-class practical telling
wisdom.   I do not dwell on the supposed failures of his government ;
he has shown, I sometimes think an almost supernatural tact in keeping
the ship afloat at all, with head steady, not only going down, and now
certain not to, but with proud and resolute spirit, and flag flying in
sight of the world, menacing and high as ever.   [Note here the germ
of the imagery of "O Captain! My Captain!"]   I say never yet
captain, never ruler, had such a perplexing dangerous task as his, the

past two years. I more and more rely on his idiomatic western genius, careless of court dress or court decorum."

It is interesting to set this last phrase, "careless of court dress or court decorum", beside Whitman's description of himself as the new American poet in that review of his own book from which quotation has already been made : "No breath of Europe, or her monarchies or priestly conventions, or her notions of gentlemen and ladies, founded on the idea of caste, seems ever to have fanned his face or been inhaled into his lungs". There seems no doubt that bit by bit Whitman's image of Lincoln came together both with his earlier vision of the ideal American president and his vision of himself as the new kind of native American poet. This may help to explain the intensely personal nature of Whitman's attitude to Lincoln, a man whom after all he had never spoken to and never even properly met. It also throws light on a significant distinction noted by W. H. Auden in an article[2] comparing British and American poetry : "Leaving aside all questions of style", wrote Mr Auden, "there is a difference between Tennyson's *Ode on the Death of the Duke of Wellington* and Whitman's elegy for President Lincoln *When Lilacs Last in the Door-yard Bloom'd* which is significant. Tennyson, as one would expect from the title of his poem, mourns for a great public official figure, but it would be very hard to guess from the words of Whitman's poem that the man he is talking of was the head of a State ; one would naturally think that he was some close personal friend, a private individual."

On 4 March 1865 Whitman set down his impression of Lincoln's second inauguration :

> The President very quietly rode down to the capitol in his own carriage, by himself, on a shart trot, about noon, either because he wish'd to be on hand to sign bills, or to get rid of marching in line with the absurd procession, the muslin temple of liberty, and pasteboard monitor. I saw him on his return, at three o'clock, after the performance was over. He was in his plain two-horse barouche, and look'd very much worn and tired ; the lines, indeed, of vast responsibilities, intricate questions, and demands of life and death, cut deeper than ever upon his dark brown face ; yet all the old goodness, tenderness, sadness, and canny shrewdness, underneath the furrows. (I never see that man without feeling that he is one to become personally attach'd to, for his combination of purest, heartiest tenderness, and native western form of manliness.)

[2] *Anchor Review* No 1.   New York, 1955.

Here we see quite explicitly the note of personal feeling that Mr Auden finds in *When Lilacs Last* . . . The lilacs of this poem, it might be added, are quite different in origin and function from, say, the flowers that Milton strews on "the laureate hearse where Lycid lies". They derive from a real and personal memory. "I remember", wrote Whitman in his Lincoln lecture, describing the spring atmosphere of that fatal day of 14 Apr. 1865, "I remember where I was stopping at the time, the season being advanced, there were many lilacs in full bloom. By one of those caprices that enter and give tinge to events without being at all a part of them, I find myself always reminded of the great tragedy of that day by the sight and odor of these blossoms. It never fails".

Whitman was not in fact in Washington on the actual day of the murder : he was visiting his mother in Brooklyn. He later recalled their hearing the news : "The day of the murder we heard the news very early in the morning. Mother prepared breakfast—and other meals afterward—as usual ; but not a mouthful was eaten all day by either of us. We each drank half a cup of coffee ; that was all. Little was said. We got every newspaper morning and evening, and the frequent extras of that period, and pass'd them silently to each other."

Whitman's final statement of the way in which Lincoln combined for him the prophetic and the practical, the visionary and the shrewdly realistic (a combination equally important for him in his own poetry) is found in a late article on Lincoln in which he tries to sum up the President's stature. "How does this man compare with the acknow-ledg'd 'Father of his country?' " he asked, and he replied that Lincoln "was far less European, was quite thoroughly Western, original, essentially non-conventional, and had a certain sort of outdoor or prairie stamp." ("One of the roughs.") He continued :

> One of the best of the late commentators on Shakspere (Professor Dowden,) makes the height and aggregate of his quality as a poet to be, that he thoroughly blended the ideal with the practical or realistic. If this be so, I should say that what Shakspere did in poetic expression, Abraham Lincoln essentially did in his personal and official life. I should say the invisible foundations and vertebra of his character, more than any man's in history, were mystical, abstract, moral and spiritual—while upon all of them was built, and out of all of them radiated, under the control of the average of circumstances, what the

vulgar call *horse-sense*, and a life often bent by temporary but most urgent materialistic and political reasons.

The kind of character that Whitman detested above all was what he called the "dandy" or the "dandified" person, with no real character of his own, who supinely followed fashion and imitated others. He once attacked the young men of America as "a parcel of helpless dandies, who can neither fight, work, shoot, ride, run, command—some of them devout, some quite insane, some castrated—all second-hand, or third or fourth, or fifth hand—waited upon by waiters, putting not this land first, talking of art, doing the most ridiculous things for fear of being thought ridiculous, smirking and skipping along, continually taking off their hats". Lincoln in Whitman's eyes stood for everything that was opposed to the qualities here described. He was the anti-dandy, a rough, genuine, first-hand American character. The hatred of dandyism lies very close to the centre of Whitman's view of morality and of his political and social thought; thus Lincoln as the anti-dandy par excellence naturally became a potent symbolic figure for him.

But of course the greatest expression of Whitman's feeling about Lincoln is his magnificent elegy, *When Lilacs Last in the Dooryard Bloom'd*. He wrote other poems on Lincoln, too. There is the well known *O Captain! My Captain!*, a rhetorical statement of the paradox involved in the president's dying in the hour of victory. The captain, it should be noticed, is also the speaker's father :

> Here Captain! dear father!
> This arm beneath your head!
> It is some dream that on the deck,
> You've fallen cold dead.

> My Captain does not answer, his lips are pale and still,
> My father does not feel my arm, he has no pulse nor will,
> The ship is anchor'd safe and sound, its voyage closed and done,
> From fearful trip the victor ship comes in with object won ;
> Exult O shores, and ring O bells!
> But I with mournful tread,
> Walk the deck my Captain lies,
> Fallen cold and dead.

Not a characteristic nor even a very good Whitman poem, in spite of its popularity. Whitman was to change his mind about the degree to

which the ship was anchored safe and sound.   His bitter indictment of
the failures of American democracy that he wrote in 1871 under the
title *Democratic Vistas* shows all the great hopes still unrealised.   "I
say we had best look our times and lands searchingly in the face, like a
physician diagnosing some deep disease.   Never was there, perhaps,
more hollowness at heart than at present, and here in the United
States . . .   The spectacle is appalling."   Whitman observed the com-
mencement of the Gilded Age and, like many another American
writer, he did not like what he saw.   In retrospect, the figure of Lincoln
shone even brighter, but the tragic incompleteness of his achievement
was also highlighted.

Two other poems on the death of Lincoln, *Hush'd Be the Camps
To-day* and *This Dust Was Once the Man*, are slight, the latter a four-
line epitaph :

> This dust was once the man,
> Gentle, plain, just and resolute, under whose cautious hand,
> Against the foulest crime known in any land or age,
> Was saved the Union of these States.

The great Whitman Lincoln document is *When Lilacs Last*, and it is
fitting that an account of Whitman and Lincoln should end with some
discussion of this remarkable poem.

For all the deep personal feeling of this elegy, the subject is curiously
distanced.   And the paradox is that the distancing makes the poem the
more moving.   The three controlling images of the poem are the
lilacs, the "powerful western fallen star", and the singing thrush.
These have no direct connexion with Lincoln.   The lilacs are a
domestic image—they bloomed "in the dooryard" ;   the thrush is
related to that other bird in *Out of the Cradle Endlessly Rocking*, the
"solitary singer" whose song combines love and loss, passion and
elegy, comfort and sadness ;   the "great star early droop'd in the
western sky in the night" derives, like the lilacs, from a personal
recollection and association.   In a journal entry made at the time of
Lincoln's second inauguration Whitman had noted the unusual
weather of that March :

> The western star, Venus, in the earlier hours of evening, has never
> been so large, so clear ; it seems as if it told something, as it if held
> rapport indulgent with humanity, with us Americans.   Five or six

nights since, it hung close by the moon, then a little past its first quarter. The star was wonderful, the moon like a young mother. The sky, dark blue, the transparent night, the planets, the moderate west wind, the elastic temperature, the miracle of the great star, and the young and swelling moon swimming in the west, suffused the soul. Then I heard, slow and clear, the deliberate notes of a bugle come up out of the silence, sounding so good through the night's mystery, no hurry, but firm and faithful, floating along, rising, falling leisurely, with here and there a long-drawn note ; the bugle, well play'd, sounding tattoo, in one of the army hospitals near here, where the wounded (some of them personally dear to me,) are lying in their cots, and many a sick boy come down to the war from Illinois, Michigan, Wisconsin, Iowa, and the rest.

The opening six lines of the poem move from the lilac to the star and then to the dead man, who is described in simple, private terms as "him I love" :

When lilacs last in the dooryard bloom'd,
And the great star early droop'd in the western sky in the night,
I mourn'd, and yet shall mourn with ever-returning spring.

Ever-returning spring, trinity sure to me you bring,
Lilac blooming perennial and drooping star in the west,
And thought of him I love.

This is one of the very few direct, personal references to Lincoln in the whole poem, which soon moves on to describe a symbolic American spring scene :

In the dooryard fronting an old farm-house near the white-wash'd
    palings,
Stands the lilac-bush tall-growing with heart-shaped leaves of rich
    green,
With many a pointed blossom rising delicate, with the perfume strong
    I love,
With every leaf a miracle—and from this bush in the dooryard,
With delicate-color'd blossoms and heart-shaped leaves of rich green,
A sprig with its flower I break.

The poet then turns to the solitary hermit thrush singing his song in the swamp. And then, leaving the images of lilac, star, and singing

bird to echo in the reader's mind, he goes on to show the funeral train
moving through America :

> Over the breast of the spring, the land, amid cities,
> Amid lanes and through old woods, where lately the violets peep'd
>   from the ground, spotting the gray debris,
> Amid the grass in the fields each side of the lanes, passing the
>   endless grass,
> Passing the yellow-spear'd wheat, every grain from its shroud
>   in the dark-brown fields uprisen,
> Passing the apple-tree blows of white and pink in the orchards,
> Carrying a corpse to where it shall rest in the grave,
> Night and day journeys a coffin.

> Coffin that passes through lanes and streets,
> Through day and night with the great cloud darkening the land,
> With the pomp of the inloop'd flags with the cities draped in black,
> With the show of the States themselves as of crape-veil'd women
>   standing,
> With processions long and winding and the flambeaus of the night,
> With the countless torches lit, with the silent sea of faces and
>   the unbared heads,
> With the waiting depot, the arriving coffin, and the sombre faces,
> With dirges through the night, with the thousand voices rising
>   strong and solemn,
> With all the mournful voices of the dirges pour'd around the coffin,
> The dim-lit churches and the shuddering organs—
>   where amid these you journey,
> With the tolling tolling bells' perpetual clang,
> Here, coffin that slowly passes,
> I give you my sprig of lilac.

The poet now goes back to the western star—

> Now I know what you must have meant as a month since I walk'd,
> As I walk'd in silence the transparent shadowy night,
> As I saw you had something to tell as you bent to me night after
>   night, . . .

But the note of personal elegy, and the symbols of lilacs, star, and bird
which are used to orchestrate this note keep giving way before the
larger theme of America as a whole, in that counterpointing of the
personal and the national, of private feeling and large, out-going

sympathy, of psychology and geography, that is so characteristic of
Whitman's poetry.

> O what shall I hang on the chamber walls?
> And what shall the pictures be that I hang on the walls,
> To adorn the burial-house of him I love?
>
> Pictures of growing spring and farms and homes,
> With the Fourth-month eve at sundown, and the gray smoke lucid
>   and bright,
> With floods of the yellow gold of the gorgeous, indolent, sinking
>   sun, burning, expanding the air,
> With the fresh sweet herbage under foot, and the pale green leaves
>   of the trees prolific,
> In the distance the flowing glaze, the breast of the river,
>   with a wind-dapple here and there,
> With ranging hills on the banks, with many a line against the sky,
>   and shadows,
> And the city at hand with dwellings so dense, and stacks of chimneys,
> And all the scenes of life and the workshops,
>   and the workmen homeward returning.

The whole nation is evoked, with its various landscapes and its varieties
of labour :

> this land,
> My own Manhattan with spires, and the sparkling and hurrying
>   tides, and the ships,
> The varied and ample land, the South and the North in the light,
>   Ohio's shores and flashing Missouri,
> And ever the far-spreading prairies cover'd with grass and corn.

Then the singing bird arrests him again, and the other personal
symbols return also :

> O wondrous singer!
> You only I hear—yet the star holds me, (but will soon depart,)
> Yet the lilac with mastering odor holds me.

Personal elegy and national destiny : these two are counterpointed
throughout the whole poem. Whitman's characteristic out-going
feeling towards all he has seen or imagined throughout the length and
breadth of the United States provides a check to the moody, introspective note of self-indulged grief. The death that he is lamenting is

passed visually, as it were, across the vast panorama of the United
States :

> Now while I saw in the day and look'd forth,
> In the close of the day with its light and the fields of spring,
>   and the farmers preparing their crops,
> In the large unconscious scenery of my land with its lakes and forests,
> In the heavenly aerial beauty, (after the perturb'd winds and the
>   storms,)
> Under the arching of the afternoon swift passing,
>   and the voices of children and women,
> The many-moving sea-tides, and I saw the ships how they sail'd,
> And the summer approaching with richness, and the fields all busy
>   with labor,
> And the infinite separate houses, how they all went on,
>   each with its meals and minutia of daily usages,
> And the streets how their throbbings throbb'd, and the cities
>   pent, lo then and there,
> Falling upon them all and among them all, enveloping me with
>   the rest,
> Appear'd the cloud, appear'd the long black trail,
> And I knew death, its thought, and the sacred knowledge of death.

How different this is from the characteristic English Victorian mood
of elegy :

> And the stately ships go on
>   To their haven under the hill ;
> But O for the touch of a vanish'd hand,
>   And the sound of a voice that is still!

Tennyson's lines, with their suggestion of sad, introspective with-
drawal from the workaday world, are in direct contrast to Whitman's
"and I saw the ships how they sailed, / And the summer approaching
with richness, and the fields all busy with labor". Yet the private
mourning is there in Whitman's poem too ; the whole poem swings
to and fro like a pendulum, between the lilacs, the star, and the bird,
with their associated personal emotions of both death and joy, on the
one hand, and the American panorama on the other. As the poem
progresses the oscillations become shorter and quicker, until, with the
vision of the myriads of American Civil War dead fusing with the
vision of the dead Lincoln—both at peace, while it is the comrades
left behind who mourn—the pendulum's movement is arrested at

he centre. The poet is not now "the solitary singer", but the centre of a band of comrades; the personal mourning, while still personal, has become national; "lilac and star and bird" reach both inward and outward in their significance, and the poem, which began with the lilacs blooming in the farmhouse dooryard, ends in the dusk of the forest with pines and cedars :

> Yet each to keep and all, retrievements out of the night,
> The song, the wondrous chant of the gray-brown bird,
> And the tallying chant, the echo arous'd in my soul,
> With the lustrous and drooping star with the countenance full of woe,
> With the holders holding my hand nearing the call of the bird,
> Comrades mine and I in the midst, and their memory ever to keep,
>   for the dead I loved so well,
> For the sweetest, wisest soul of all my days and lands—
>   and this for his dear sake,
> Lilac and star and bird twined with the chant of my soul,
> There in the fragrant pines and the cedars dusk and dim.

From an early stage in his knowledge of Lincoln, Whitman had made the President his own, and at the same time had seen him as a potent national symbol. He had fused that "seam'd and wrinkled yet canny-looking face" with the figure on his own frontispiece of 1855 and with the imaginary beard-faced American blacksmith from the West of whom he had early formed messianic expectations. From the first fusion came that deep personal feeling he had for Lincoln, as though he had indeed been a beloved personal friend; from the second came his insistence that Lincoln represented the whole United States. In his famous lecture on the death of Lincoln he called his annual observance of the day of his death "no narrow or sectional reminiscence". "It belongs to these States in their entirety", he went on "—not the North only, but the South—perhaps most tenderly and devoutly to the South, of all; for there, really, this man's birth-stock". Later in the lecture he said :

> The final use of a heroic-eminent life—especially of a heroic-eminent death—is its indirect filtering into the nation and the race, and to give, often at many removes, but unerringly, age after age, color and fibre to the personalism of the youth and maturity of that age, and of mankind. Then there is a cement to the whole people, subtler, more underlying, than any thing in written constitution, or courts or armies—namely, the cement of a death identified thoroughly with that

people, at its head, and for its sake. Strange, (is it not?) that battles, martyrs, agonies, blood, even assassination, should so condense—perhaps only really, lastingly condense—a Nationality.

This represented a profession of faith rather than a realistic observation of what the era of the carpet-baggers was bringing to American nationhood. But the faith was real, and it has survived.

12

Cultivated Innocence[1]

Nearly twenty years ago I visited a Teachers' College in Kansas and was given some of the students' essays to read. I cannot remember now exactly what the subject of the essays was, but it involved some discussion of the value of the study of history. I was much struck by one essay which opened with the flat statement that Americans were not interested in history since, unlike the old countries of Europe, they looked to the present and the future rather than to the past. History, in fact, was un-American.

Now in a sense this is of course a very naïve and indeed a preposterous attitude ; nevertheless, it represents something very real and very deep in the American consciousness. *Homo Americanus* is, and ought to be, man without history, man responding to his immediate environment in innocence and wonder with the uncorrupted vision of a child, a primitive, a backwoodsman : this view runs with surprising continuity through American literature from Emerson (to go no further back) to J. D. Salinger. Emerson not only exclaimed, "We have listened too long to the courtly muses of Europe" ; he also held up as the ideal observer "the child with his sweet pranks, the fool of his senses, commanded by every sight and sound, without any power to compare and rank his sensations, abandoned to a whistle or a painted chip, to a lead dragoon or a ginger-bread dog, individualising everything, generalising nothing." Thoreau not only exclaimed, "How much virtue there is in simply seeing!" He also noted in his journal his belief "that we should treat our minds as innocent and ingenuous children whose guardians we are. . . . Routine, conventionality, manners, etc., etc.—how insensibly an undue attention to these matters dissipates and impoverishes the mind, robs it of its simplicity and strength, emasculates it!" Whitman not only called on his Muse

---

[1] First published in *Encounter*, October 1965.

to "migrate from Greece and Ionia" to take up her habitation in the "better, fresher, busier sphere", the "wide, untried domain" that awaited her; he also wrote, "*I loafe and invite my soul, | I lean and loafe at my ease observing a spear of summer grass.*" Whitman's loafing reminds us of Thoreau's advocacy of "a true sauntering of the eye", of Huckleberry Finn's "lazying" while employing the naïve vision of the child and the outcast, of Gertrude Stein's protest against "letting remembering mix itself with looking" and her endeavour to redeem words from history and continuity in favour of "moment to moment emphasising". We may be reminded, too, of Sherwood Anderson's deep urge to record the "odd little things" that make up experience directly and naïvely without the patterning and interpretation of the interfering mind. And we may recall the famous passage from Hemingway's *A Farewell to Arms* which concludes, "Abstract words such as glory, honour, courage or hallow were obscene beside the concrete names of villages, the numbers of roads, the names of rivers, the numbers of regiments and the dates."

There is something refreshing, and there is also something dangerous, in this American tradition. At its best it can, in Tony Tanner's words,[2] "refresh and revivify our vision of the world." To treat even the familiar as an object of wonder, to confront the external world afresh, redeemed from all the accretions of prejudice, presupposition, and tradition, can result in a genuine new vision. It can also, if set beside more conventional ways of seeing and responding, cast a dark ironic shadow on convention itself and on the whole world of gentility and indeed of organised society. (Huckleberry Finn does this in one way; the heroine of *What Maisie Knew* does it in another.) Innocence can show up civilisation as corrupt. But it can also produce facility, sentimentality, even fatuity. If every observer is to start afresh, with no help from the past experience of the race, civilisation of any kind will eventually become impossible since cumulative knowledge, on which civilisation is based, will not be allowed to develop. This is a heavy price to pay for freedom from corrupting conventions and distorting preconceptions. The price will include the loss of art, for art cannot exist long as a series of unrelated primitive productions. Gertrude Stein, for all her brilliance, and for all her influence on Sherwood Anderson and Ernest Hemingway, preached the death of

---

[2] Tony Tanner, *The Reign of Wonder : Naïvety and Reality in American Literature*, Cambridge (University Press) 1965.

language as an art medium when she urged that words should be cut
off from their history.

> A word can always express more than it means ; it has a history.
> I do not mean simply an etymology : it has a past; it has lived in
> different works and undergone the influence of its environment; it
> has had adventures ; it has had encounters ; it has been helped,
> supported by other words, or else it has come to their aid, has sustained
> them ; and it retains hazy recollections of all its former companions,
> like a halo around itself.

These words of Jacques Rivière, quoted by Dr Tanner in his
chapter on Gertrude Stein, sum up this aspect of the problem very
well.

There is also the charge that can be made against Emerson and
others of the American Transcendentalists that they sought an "un-
earned" vision ; they imagined that they could move from naïve
wonder in regarding particulars to a mystic view of the divine unity
underlying everything simply by sliding from one to the other.   Even
Thoreau, who had a grainier sense of the stubborn reality of individual
facts than Emerson, can move from "closeness to the physical fact" to
a view of the language that records those facts as "the symbol of the
spiritual" in a single sentence.   Nevertheless, the realisation "that the
writer need not surround native local facts with established 'poetry'
but can entice fresh and relevant poetry from the facts themselves,
simply by stating those facts, has had a profound influence on American
writing".   This is largely the theme of Dr Tanner's book, which
moves from the Transcendentalists to Walker Percy's novel *The
Moviegoer* in tracing this tradition in American literature.

The thesis is not, of course, new, but the intelligence and perceptive-
ness with which Dr Tanner has developed and illustrated it help to
make his book a stimulating invitation to reconsider this aspect of
American literature.   Who would have thought to see Henry James
in this company of strategic innocents?   But it is possible to look
carefully at *What Maisie Knew, The Awkward Age,* and *The Sacred
Fount* and see in all three James' deliberate placing of the innocent
observer of a corrupt or at least a complex society—not so as to indict
society or glorify simplicity but rather so as to shadow forth, in all
kinds of subtle ways, the relation of the artist (who is always to some
extent an observer and an outsider) to the material in real life out of

Q

which he shapes his art.   The artist is a special kind of innocent.   This
is an intriguing point, and persuasively argued ; Dr Tanner's accounts
of these three works of James are among the best I have read, and I
have found them genuinely helpful.   But is this equation, or partial
equation, of innocent and artist really in the great American tradition
of naïvety and wonder?   If this is so, then the argument would apply
to many more than James.   The "alienated artist" (and, so far as
society is concerned, the innocent is the alienated) is one of the commonest themes in modern literature both European and American—
indeed, more often European than American.   An American scholar
has recently published a study of the artist as hero in European and
American fiction in the late 19th and 20th centuries : there are
thousands of them.

   James, says Dr Tanner,

> took the untutored eye—so received by the Transcendentalists—and
> subjected it to a dynamic, unprogrammed education.   And watching
> the naïve person assimilating, misconstruing, digesting, regurgitating,
> concentrating, omitting, as he or she was faced with the task of visually
> appropriating the world, James learnt something profound about
> the whole question of veridical knowledge, about the whole problem
> of verifying impressions.

He concludes that in James' stories and novels we see that

> for the truly naïve eye, the habit of wonder, there is no place in the
> social centre of the world : it must either give way to some more
> worldly perspective in the world, or flee, or die.   And yet—and this
> links James with Emerson and Thoreau—it is the naïve wondering
> eye which most generously celebrates and responds to the full range of
> experience.

This is true of Maisie and Nanda, and it is illuminating to have it put
this way ; but it is only part of the truth.   Further, to argue, as Dr
Tanner does, that "Henry James was the first . . . writer to inquire into
the fate of wonder when it is introduced into the clotted complexities of
society and the turbulence of time" is to forget (or to be ignorant of)
those numerous early American novels which show the innocent
countryman confronting the complications of an urban society.   "For
early 19th-century America", observed Daniel Hoffman in his seminal
book, *Form and Fable in American Fiction*, "the Yankee villager is one

expression of the myth of innocence, the Yankee peddler of the myth of competence". These two confronted each other in American fiction before James was born, and even if the confrontation represented a much cruder version of the innocent-observer-in-society theme than we find in James, the authentic theme is certainly there. "The usual pattern of one numerous *genre* of the American novel", wrote Hoffman, "is to move an innocent character from his country home into the temptations and evils of city life. This pattern conforms not only to that found in the 'young man from the provinces' class of novels, but also to the movement of populations in the American 19th and 20th centuries". It might be at least as interesting to set James in *this* tradition as to set him beside Emerson and Thoreau.

Just as it can be argued that this aspect of James can be related to other American traditions than that traced by Dr Tanner, so it could on the other side be argued that some at least of the phenomena that Dr Tanner sees as bound up with the American tradition of the innocent eye can be seen as having an affinity with an important European movement. The imagination's kindling at objects, an almost mystic sense of reality deriving from intense perception of things which on any traditional standard can only be considered trivial (and we find this in Thoreau, Whitman, Sherwood Anderson, Hemingway, among others), reminds us irresistibly of Joyce's "epiphany" Dr Tanner does indeed suggest that Sherwood Anderson "at his best does sometimes achieve that which Joyce said short stories should aim at—an epiphany", though he denies that Hemingway's moments of clarity and meaning are epiphanies in Joyce's sense

But isn't there more to it than this? The sense of reality as a private revelation coming to one unexpectedly as a result of chance confrontation of an object or objects which at any other time would have no special meaning and even now have no special meaning to anybody else—such a sense we find developing among European novelists (including British) in response to that breakdown in the public sense of what is significant in experience out of which one might almost say the modern novel was born. The feeling of living in a private world in which one finds meaning only through the personal epiphany is common enough in the novel of the 1920s and 1930s. When novelists find tradition untenable, find that their roots do not nourish and the patterns of significance to which society pays lip service have no meaning for them, they have travelled, as it were, to an America of the mind and sensibilities. They are like those ideal pristine Americans who pitted their virgin sensations against a virgin country. "What is meant by reality?" asked Virginia Woolf in 1928. And she answered : "It would seem to be something very erratic, very undependable— now to be found in a dusty road, now in a scrap of newspaper in the street, now in a daffodil in the sun." Doesn't this remind us of Sherwood Anderson's "little things", of William Carlos William's poem "The Red Wheelbarrow" ("*so much depends / upon / a red wheel / barrow / glazed with rain / water / beside the white / chickens*"), of Thoreau's feeling that nature "must steal on us when we expect it not", of Emerson's "power to fix the momentary eminency of an object"? When traditions fail, European novelists cultivate the innocent eye : to that extent, perhaps Dr Tanner would say, they make themselves American.

But it was less the failure of tradition than the renunciation of tradition that motivated the first American proponents of wonder. Language must be geared to what is actually seen (it is remarkable how *sight* is the one sense that matters to all these writers) uncorrupted by prior formulations, and to this end "children and savages" (Emerson's phrase) are the models, and a vernacular speech more effective than worn out literary modes. The search for a workable vernacular is one of the great themes in American literature, and the central achievement here is, of course, Mark Twain's *Huckleberry Finn.* Dr Tanner's splendid chapters on this great novel are really the core of his book and constitute one of the most illuminating studies of Mark Twain I know.

> It was Clemens who finally and completely inverted the pastoral situation and perfected the vernacular-child-narrator with a fruitfully naïve perspective on life and a manner of speaking which was an adequate vehicle for the new point of view.

In doing this he was led into a deeper attack on the conventions of society than he must have been aware of. The final realisation that modern life has no place for innocence, that the American Eden which had once provoked the authentic response of wonder no longer exists and that this response is now available only to the outcast, darkened the latter part of Mark Twain's life and is surely responsible for the puzzling final section of *Huckleberry Finn.* Dr Tanner charts this movement in Twain's imagination with sensitive particularisation.

This is one of the great crises of American experience, and if we understand it, it seems to me, we understand that fluctuation between Dream and Nightmare that is so marked in American literature in the last hundred years and more. The paradox of the co-existence of the Great Society and the H-bomb is not new.

13

Mark Twain as Hamlet[1]

Mark Twain's greatest work is *Huckleberry Finn*, but in some respects his most interesting is *A Connecticut Yankee in King Arthur's Court* because in the latter book we see him trapped in the ambiguous implications of modern industrial democratic civilisation, in a way that illuminates a whole area of modern history, British as well as American. When Macaulay reviewed Southey's *Colloquies* in 1830, he rebuked Southey for his nostalgic sighing after the picturesque backwardness of earlier periods of history, and he looked forward with confident optimism to the time when "a population of fifty millions, better fed, clad, and lodged than the English of our time, will cover these islands", when "cultivation, rich as that of a flower-garden, will be carried to the very tops of Ben Nevis and Helvellyn" and "machines constructed on principles yet undiscovered will be seen in every house, . . . there will be no highways but railroads, no travelling but by steam". This would be achieved, Macaulay believed, not by state control but "by the prudence and energy of the people". "Our rulers will best promote the improvement of the nation by strictly confining themselves to their own legitimate duties, by leaving capital to find its most lucrative course, commodities their fair price, industry and intelligence their natural reward, idleness and folly their natural punishment, by maintaining peace, by defending property, by diminishing the price of law, and by observing strict economy in every department of the State. Let the Government do this : the People will assuredly do the rest." This is a classic statement of *laissez-faire* liberalism, combining a belief in progress and private enterprise with faith in machinery and an ever expanding industrialism.

The price that England paid for this sort of liberalism—and for the Industrial Revolution which partly produced it and was partly pro-

[1] First published in *Encounter*, February 1964.

duced by it—was heavy ; it was pointed out with bitter eloquence in different ways by Carlyle, Ruskin, Matthew Arnold, and William Morris. Yet Carlyle ended with his unsavoury doctrine of hero-worship ; Ruskin and Morris became involved in their own versions of the "good old days" fallacy ; Arnold, when it came to the political pinch, was with the defenders of private property against any attempt to shift the balance of power within the state. Where is progress and where is reaction? It can be argued that in the long run it is progress to accept, rather than reject, the Industrial Revolution, based though it was on a policy of "leaving capital to find its most lucrative course", and it is reactionary to wish that the Industrial Revolution had never occurred and that people were spared the benefits of modern machines. But in the short run the progressive must denounce the horrors— child labour, slums, the blackening of the countryside—that industrial-ism brings and try to temper the effects of uncontrolled private enter-prise by bringing in the state to impose certain controls and guarantee minimum working conditions. This is how things went in nineteenth-century England. A view of society based on a pre-industrial pas-toralism is bound to be reactionary, however generously based on response to the darkness and suffering involved in industrialisation. Yet if modern industrial democratic civilisation is essentially based on an economic free-for-all, with individual economic self-interest the primary motivating power in society ; if the smart operator and the unscrupulous financier are all that industrial democracy can offer in place of the feudal lord and robber baron of old and the "self-made man" the main myth that nourishes the democratic imagination ; then the generous mind will be hard put to it to choose between Macaulay and Carlyle and in the end may well choose the latter or else give up in despair. (This is to assume, of course, that he has no third or fourth choice, no Marx or Keynes. And I am discussing those to whom, for one reason or other, no such choice was available.)

This situation can be confusing enough in England. But cross it with the American Dream, the vision of the great new free classless society implacably opposed to the monarchies, aristocracies, dynastic struggles, social inequalities, and effete traditions of Europe, and you get something more confusing still. Beside Macaulay's reproach to Southey we can set the apostrophe addressed by the mid-nineteenth century American journalist J. Ross Browne to the "mighty kings and chieftains" of the European past :

If the Coliseum at Rome had accommodated fifty millions of people instead of fifty thousand, would it have taught them the blessings of peace and good government, or disseminated useful knowledge among them? If all your palaces were built of pure gold instead of marble, would it have caused thousands of human beings that you were continually embroiling in war to entertain a more fraternal spirit toward each other? . . . We don't build pyramids and coliseums, but we build railroads. The smallest steamboat that paddles its way up the Hudson is greater than the greatest monument of antiquity, and does more to promote the civilisation and happiness of mankind; the wires of our electric telegraphs carry more power in them than all the armies you ever brought into battle.

It is in this spirit that Mark Twain's Connecticut Yankee sets out to transform King Arthur's Britain. Soon after getting to work, "in various quiet nooks and corners I had the beginnings of all sorts of industries under way", and eventually "the telegraph, the telephone, the phonograph, the typewriter, the sewing-machine, and all the thousand willing and handy servants of steam and electricity were working their way into favour. We had a steamboat or two on the Thames, we had steam war-ships, and the beginnings of a steam commercial marine; I was getting ready to send out an expedition to discover America". The Old World had been given the advantages of the New, and now the two could be brought together. The pre-industrial past had been industrialised, with equality of opportunity for all. Yet neither Mark Twain nor his Yankee hero is altogether happy about this. Henry Nash Smith, in his admirable study of Mark Twain's development,[2] points out that running through *A Connecticut Yankee*, and running directly counter to its overt belief in progress and industrialism and its scorn for the backward, class-ridden society of Arthur's Britain, there is a yearning for a pre-industrial Arcadia. Professor Nash Smith quotes an entry in Mark Twain's notebook made at a time when *A Connecticut Yankee* was barely begun: "He mourns his lost land—has come to England and revisited it, but it is all changed & become old! so old!—& it was so fresh & new, so virgin before . . . Has lost all interest in life—is found dead next morning—suicide." In spite of the snobberies, ignorance, and cruelty of sixth-century Britain, its landscape has the glory and the

[2] *Mark Twain: The Development of a Writer*, Cambridge, Mass., The Belknap Press of Harvard University; London, Oxford University Press.

freshness of a dream. Now this special kind of dream-feeling, Nash Smith points out, is associated by Mark Twain both with the American South and with "the dreamlike peace and happiness of childhood". The ambiguity is fundamental, and is linked to Mark Twain's ambiguous feelings about the machine. "The machine is theoretically good but emotionally disturbing. Like most of his countrymen, Mark Twain oscillated between enthusiasm for the brave new world of science and technology, and nostalgia for the simple agrarian world that the industrial revolution was destroying before his eyes. *A Connecticut Yankee* expresses his emotions about the shattering transformation and is on this account, for all its confusions (indeed, because of them), a central document in American intellectual history."

America is committed to progress; it is the country of the future. Yet how often is Mark Twain emotionally compelled to set the Hannibal of his childhood—"the matter of Hannibal", as Nash Smith calls it, locating it precisely in the pattern of Mark Twain's work—against the screamingly competitive industrial world of his later years! The language of Wall Street is both the language of free-enterprise America, and so of progress and virtue, and the language of those smart operators whose financial buccaneering seemed a threat to everything the American Dream had stood for. Time and again Hank Morgan, Mark Twain's Yankee, reduces Arthur's Britain to size by describing its institutions in terms of financial speculation. "Knight-errantry is a most chuckle-headed trade, and it is tedious hard work, too, but I begin to see that there *is* money in it, after all, if you have luck . . . A successful whirl in the knight-errantry line—now what is it when you blow away the nonsense and come down to the cold facts? It's just a corner in pork, that's all, and you can't make anything else out of it." This financial language is reductive, reducing such an institution as knight-errantry to a money-making operation, and at the same time it is produced as evidence of the hard-headed, practical (and therefore wholly admirable) attitude of the Yankee. What Carlyle called the "cash nexus" thus both destroys and justifies : to apply it to medieval institutions is to expose them—but this is because it is the proper standard to apply. Or is it? When Dan Beard, the socialist artist who did the illustrations for *A Connecticut Yankee*, interpreted many of the incidents as attacks on American capitalists, even to the point of giving an arrogant slave driver the face of Jay Gould, the railroad millionaire and notorious financial manipulator, Mark Twain, even though he himself "was not strongly attracted toward any of the radical programmes", did not protest. Indeed, he hailed Beard's illustrations with enthusiasm.

Left-wing Americans who attacked with equal relish both British institutions and American financiers and monopolists (expressing what Nash Smith calls "the blend of jingoism and pro-labour sentiment characteristic of much grass-roots radicalism") did not see any contradiction in *A Connecticut Yankee*, but hailed it, in the words of one reviewer, as "one long satire on modern England and Englishmen". Yet England was the pioneer industrial country, and the book glorified industrialism. It was left for British reviewers, as Nash Smith shows, to point out some of the inconsistencies not only in Mark Twain's attitude but in the American attitude in general :

> The Republic is a "land of liberty", yet its commerce, its railways, and its manufactures are in the hands of a few cliques of almost irresponsible capitalists, who control tariffs, markets, and politics in order that they may be enriched, to the disadvantage of the masses. Which, then, is to be most admired—the supremacy of a knight or the success of a financier? Under which King will the Americans serve—the ideal or the real? Will they own allegiance to King ARTHUR or JAY GOULD?

This was the *Daily Telegraph*, doubtless glad to get its own back for Mark Twain's digs at England in his book ; but the writer did not realise that the dilemma was not exclusively American, even though faith in the American Dream exacerbated it. It was a dilemma inherent in an industrial democratic society. Nash Smith comments : "Mark Twain's inability to make Hank Morgan a consistent character parallels Turner's and [Henry] Adams' failure to find a basis for democracy in a world dominated by technology." The agrarian strain in American social idealism made the problem particularly acute. *A Connecticut Yankee*, Nash Smith remarks, "was an imaginative version of the central issue in American culture of the 1880s and the following decades—the need to adapt an agrarian system of values to an industrial order that was felt by thinkers as diverse as Henry George, Edward Bellamy, Frederick Jackson Turner, and especially Henry Adams." We are reminded that William Morris, socialist though he was, saw his ideal England of the future as smokeless and non-industrial. The ambiguities of progress tease most of the imaginative thinkers of the nineteenth century in both Britain and America.

"In the end, Mark Twain's uncertainty concerning the effects of the industrial revolution undercuts the ideology of progress." So Nash Smith sums up the lesson of *A Connecticut Yankee*, a book which begins as satire, proceeds partly as farce and partly as propaganda, and ends as nightmare. Mark Twain was involved in the dilemmas of his age, but he was also involved in an acutely personal dilemma. He had begun his writing career as a humorist, drawing on the native vernacular tradition, the direct experience and "horse sense" of the rural or small-town American, to undermine the genteel pretensions and unreal ideals of the official culture that came from the east but was clung to with particular tenacity by all in the Middle West who wished to vindicate their respectability. He was not, however, by nature a bold man, and he found it hard to develop an art-form which gave full expression to his deep sense of the bogus nature of much of the official culture available to Americans of his time. From the beginning he had a habit of looking nervously over his shoulder at the representatives of the genteel tradition and making placatory gestures towards them. *The Innocents Abroad*, originally written as a series of letters to the San Francisco *Alta California* and published in book form, with some cautious omissions and revisions, in 1869, shows him fluctuating between mockery and respectability, between providing his American readers with the kind of edifying guide-book to Europe they expected from their men of letters and exploiting that other American attitude to Europe which saw it as representing a burden of history to be cast off by the man of the new world. It was hard for Mark Twain to be both an American humorist and an American man of letters, for the former role tended to undermine the latter. Yet he wanted to be both. He was writing for the *Atlantic* at the same time as he was working on *Huckleberry Finn*, and the two roles were in many respects incompatible. His dilemma emerges with symbolic force in the incident of the *Atlantic* dinner for Whittier's seventieth birthday in December 1877. Whittier, Longfellow, Howells, Holmes, and Charles Eliot Norton were all present, as well as Mark Twain. When it was Twain's turn to speak he gave a carefully prepared talk—one of the funniest things he ever wrote—in which his instinct to debunk the New England sages was given fairly free range. He told of three tramps and imposters, claiming to be respectively Mr Longfellow, Mr Emerson and Mr Oliver Wendell Holmes, visiting the lonely log-cabin of a Californian miner, exploiting the miner's hospitality to the full while reeling off quotations from their namesakes' poetry in contexts which made them absurd. ("Longfellow", for example, goes off the next morning having stolen his host's boots, remarking :

> Lives of great men all remind us
>   We can make our lives sublime ;
> And departing, leave behind us
>   Footprints on the sands of Time.)

The speech, fully reported in the press, caused extreme indignation, not so much in Boston as further west, and Mark Twain himself wrote ten days later an abject apology to Messrs Emerson, Longfellow, and Holmes, beginning : "Gentlemen : I come before you, now, with the mien & posture of the guilty—not to excuse, gloss, or extenuate, but only to offer my repentance", and explaining his conduct on the grounds that, not possessing a fine nature, he had acted innocently. For the rest of his life Mark Twain wavered between thinking the whole incident a horrid scandal of which he was thoroughly ashamed and thinking that it was a first-rate speech which he could re-read with pride. Nash Smith's account of this episode rightly places it as a primary clue for an understanding of the dual forces and the dual ambitions which tugged at Twain. He had been "a victim of a demonic possession. His unconscious had uttered a truth under the guise of burlesque that was much more frightening to him than to the targets of his derision . . . Mark Twain was not consciously prepared to repudiate the conception of literature represented by Emerson and Longfellow and Holmes ; but he had a half-suppressed awareness that the role assigned to them by the official culture was false and sterile."

In *Huckleberry Finn* Mark Twain found the appropriate art form, the appropriate persons, and the moment of unstable equilibrium to enable him to use the comic vernacular tradition seriously in a work of great literature. Here the morality of experience is brought up squarely against the morality of history and convention with an ironic force which enlarges the scope and meaning of the novel far beyond the "Matter of Hannibal" to make it a profound exploration of some of the perennial problems concerning the relation between tradition and the individual consciousness. Some of the moral ambiguities in the book are planted there by the author, while others find their way there in spite of him. Huck's and Jim's quest for freedom is in the end unattainable, as Mark Twain concedes in abandoning the images of happiness with Huck and Jim on the raft and devoting the last ten chapters to Tom Sawyer and his heartlesss romantic pranks at the expense of Jim. (But neither Tom nor his creator knew that the pranks were heartless.) Thus, as Nash Smith puts it, Mark Twain acknowledges "that the vernacular values embodied in his story were mere figments of the imagination, not capable of being reconciled with social reality". What, then, are we left with? A vivid awareness of the reality (which is not the same as the social possibility) of the moral world established by Huck and Jim on the raft; an equally vivid awareness of the hollowness and sometimes the downright evil of the codes prescribed by convention and tradition; a sense of the absurdity and unconscious cruelty of a false romanticism; and an uneasy feeling—deriving from the strangely powerful incident where the murderous Colonel Sherburn dominates the mob with his cool courage—that the passive stupidity of most ordinary people perhaps makes them unredeemable after all. This last seems a very un-American notion, but it weaves like a dark streak through much of Mark Twain's later work. Hank Morgan in *A Connecticut Yankee* ends his career in Arthur's Britain with the massacre (in ten minutes, with Gatling guns) of twenty-five thousand men and with a view of the common people as "human muck"; Pudd'nhead Wilson, in the novel of that name, is another "transcendent hero" whose aloof intellectual superiority asserts a truth that "destroys both elements of the long-established pattern of dominant culture versus vernacular protest"; in "The Man That Corrupted Hadleyburg"—a story which is in essence a simple fable—the outsider-detective similarly uncovers the horrid truth beneath the town's outward show of respectability; and in the unfinished *The Mysterious Stranger* Satan seems to voice the author's own disillusionment with the possibilities of man's continuous moral improvement when he describes mankind as "dull and ignorant and trivial and conceited, . . . a shabby, poor, worthless lot all round". Here is how Nash Smith sums the matter up:

> Just as Mark Twain had poured all the capital he could muster into the typesetter, he had invested all his political enthusiasm, his humanitarian emotion, and his hope for the future of his country in the idea that the common man was the prime creative force in history. Hank Morgan's conclusion that the mass of the nation in Arthur's Britain was only "human muck", which was of course a judgment on the mass of the American nation in the 1880s, proclaimed the bankruptcy of

the writer's idealisms. The outcome had been in sight since the moment when Mark Twain confronted the fact that Huck's and Jim's quest for freedom was doomed to failure. For these protagonists had become bearers of the vernacular system of values that had sustained his writing career . . . Since Mark Twain was trying to sustain by force of will a belief that had already lost its intuitive solidity, the outcome of the story was latent in it from the beginning.

This view of Mark Twain's almost Swiftian progress may come as a surprise to many of his readers, but it is borne out by much in his unofficial writings such as the comments he wrote in the margins of books and the vast, inchoate mass of autobiographical material that he wrote and dictated throughout a long period in the latter part of his life and intended for posthumous publication only. Perhaps Mark Twain's dilemma appeared all the greater to him because of his own timidity. He conceded more than was necessary to public taste and convention ; he slashed his own writings at the request of his wife and others. He has no references at all to sex in his published writing, yet he could write in his private notes that "of the delights of *this* world man cares *most* for sexual intercourse. He will . . . risk fortune, character, reputation, life itself. And what . . . has he done? . . . you would never guess—*he has left it out of his heaven!*" This and other jottings can be found in a rather scrappy little book by Caroline Harnsberger, *Mark Twain's Views of Religion*[3], in which a somewhat perfunctory introduction is followed by a collection of extracts from Mark Twain's notebooks, marginal notes in books, essays, letters, and the autobiography. Mark Twain was not a Christian ; he believed that the Bible was a purely human book produced under no special inspiration, and he did not believe in the divinity of Jesus. He radically objected to the Bible's view of the nature of God. "If I were going to construct a God, I would furnish Him with some ways and qualities and characteristics which the present Bible One lacks. He would not stoop to *ask* for any man's compliments, praises, flatteries ; and He would be far above *exacting* them. I would have Him as self-respecting as the better sort of man in these regards . . ." He seems to have been more or less a Deist, but intermittently. He was capable of breaking out with great savagery about the Bible and Christianity, but at other times preserved a decent reticence so as not to hurt people's

³ Caroline Thomas Harnsberger : *Mark Twain's Views of Religion*. Evanston, Ill. (The Schori Press) 1961.

feelings. But he never published anything of this, and this was only one of many respects in which he remained in thrall to the genteel tradition. The more one reads Mark Twain the more the belief grows that by temperament and conviction he was more or less an anarchist as well as a religious sceptic. One does not need oneself to be an anarchist or a sceptic to regret that he never had the full courage of his convictions. Of course it is true, as Nash Smith is at pains to explain, that his convictions were themselves mixed and subject to change, and this mixture and this change produce some of the major tensions in his work. But he seems to have shied away from the full implications of his own insights. Tom Sawyer's antics at the end of *Huckleberry Finn* represent a refusal on the author's part to face his tragic vision. It would have been too shocking both for his audience and for himself. Thus he is not like the traditional comedian who longs to play Hamlet : he is rather Hamlet who puts on an antic disposition in order to save his reason. The result is sometimes disturbing, always interesting, and, on one occasion at least, truly great literature.

14

Presenting The Bible[1]

Something under four thousand years ago a troubled citizen of the
Central Mesopotamian city of Haran left the community in which
he had been born and brought up to wander westward to the
country that was later known as Palestine. The Hurrian society from
which he became a voluntary refugee had long been subject to
Babylonian influence and was part of a complex of Mesopotamian
civilisation whose nature is now reasonably well known to scholars
from a variety of records and texts. Cosmopolitan, stable, sophisticated, law-abiding, with flourishing literary and scientific activities, an
exciting architecture, enlightened agricultural methods, and prospering
commercial enterprises—this is the picture that modern scholarship
has built up. Was this a civilisation for a sensible and sensitive man to
flee from? Perhaps its very stability and prosperity oppressed him ;
perhaps the complex but smooth-running machinery of political and
ethical life left out too much. For it was a spiritual quest on which
the wanderer set out. In embarking on it he began what the late
Professor Ephraim A. Speiser, in his introduction to the Anchor Bible
Genesis,[2] calls "the biblical process". In Abraham's belief that he had
been called from his native land to seek a new way of life elsewhere lies
the beginning of that extraordinary historical and religious development that produced the story of the Patriarchs, of Joseph in Egypt, of
the Exodus, of the giving of the Law to Moses on Mount Sinai, and
the subsequent history of Israel and Judah, the progress of Judaism,
and the emergence of Christianity. The Bible, and biblical history,

---

[1] First published in *Commentary*, September 1965.

[2] *The Anchor Bible*, eds. W. F. Albright and D. N. Freedman. N.Y. (Doubleday)
1965– (38 volumes in all). "Genesis", trans. and introd. by E. A. Speiser ; "I & II
Chronicles", trans. and intro. by Jacob M. Myers ; "Jeremiah", trans and intro. by John
Bright ; "Job", trans. and intro. by Marvin H. Pope ; "Proverbs and Ecclesiastes",
trans. and intro. by R. B. Y. Scott.

and all the consequences of biblical history, begin in fact with Abraham's migration.

The great medieval Jewish biblical commentator, Rabbi Solomon ben Isaac (generally known as Rashi), looking at the five Books of Moses in traditional Jewish fashion as the Torah, the Law, remarked at the beginning of his commentary on Genesis that the Torah should really have commenced not with the story of the Creation but with the second verse of the twelfth chapter of Exodus, where the first actual precept is found. He added, however, that the earlier parts were necessary to show to the world the divine claim of the Jewish people to their Palestinian homeland. But if one looks at the whole biblical process, one is inclined to disagree both with Rashi and with those ancient biblical writers and editors who apparently adapted Babylonian accounts of primeval history to provide as it were a cosmic introduction to the story of Abraham's quest and its consequences. "The biblical process" begins neither with chapter 1 of Genesis nor with chapter 12 of Exodus : it begins with the divine words recorded in Genesis 12 : 1-3 as having sounded in Abraham's ears while he still lived in his native Haran. *Lech lecha*—"Get thee out of thy country, and from thy kindred, and from thy father's house, unto the land that I will show thee." That is the familiar Authorised Version rendering, and certainly "get thee out" captures the pithy forcefulness of the Hebrew *lech lecha*. Speiser, rightly seeing this divine message as a little inset poem, translates thus :

> Go forth from your native land
> And from your father's home
> To a land that I will show you.
> I will make of you a great nation,
> Bless you, and make great your name,
> That it may be a blessing.
> I will bless those who bless you,
> And curse those who curse you ;
> And through you shall bless themselves
> All the communities on earth.

So Abraham and his wife and his nephew, with all their possessions, "set out for the land of Canaan and arrived in the land of Canaan".

But is it true? Was there a real, historical Abraham who really did leave his native Haran for the land of Canaan in obedience to a sense of divine call to engage in a spiritual quest? The paradox is that the

R

evidence provided by all those modern tools of research into the Bible that are so shunned by right-wing Jewish Orthodoxy—the evidence of history, anthropology, textual criticism, comparative religion, linguistic scholarship—is on Abraham's side.   The Bible says that Abraham migrated from Haran to the land of Canaan, and there is abundant evidence in the text of Genesis that the narrator of the story of the patriarchs was dealing with an original Hurrian character in a non-Hurrian context so that he did not understand the meaning of the Hurrian customs that he was recording.   Abraham twice, and Isaac once, claimed that his wife was his sister when visiting a foreign notable.   The three accounts in the Bible remain puzzling, and cast little credit on either patriarch.   But Speiser explains that "in Hurrian society a wife enjoyed special standing and protection when the law recognised her simultaneously as her husband's sister, regardless of actual blood ties.   Such cases are attested by two separate legal documents, one dealing with the marriage and the other with the woman's adoption as sister.   This dual role conferred on the wife a superior position in society."   Now Abraham, who originally came from the old Hurrian centre of Haran, was of course familiar with Hurrian social practices.   "Hence when he and his son, in visits to foreign lands, spoke of their wives as sisters, they were apparently intent not so much on improving their own prospects as on extolling and protecting their wives."   It is important to note that "these particular wife-sister customs were peculiar to the Hurrians".   The author of the accounts in Genesis of Abraham and Isaac claiming that their wives were their sisters clearly hadn't a clue as to what it all meant and was forced to invent the only plausible (and unfortunately rather discreditable) reason for this odd behaviour that he could think of.   Only if we imagine a later writer producing in the land of Israel (Canaan) an account of genuine old traditions some of which, being Hurrian, he could not understand, can we find any convincing explanation of this and other oddities in Genesis.

The Hurrian origin of the patriarchs is further evidenced by the puzzling story of Jacob's tricking Esau out of the eldest son's blessing. "On this point we now have pertinent illustrations in the Hurrian sources from Nuzi, which in turn mirror social conditions and customs in the patriarchal centre at Haran.   Birthright in Hurrian society was often a matter of the father's discretion rather than chronological priority.   Moreover, of all the paternal dispositions, the one that took

the form of a death-bed declaration carried the greatest weight." The
whole situation recorded in the 27th chapter of Genesis, continues
Speiser, reflects "an old and authentic usage", and he refers to the
relevant supporting documents in the Annual of the American Schools
of Oriental Research and elsewhere. "On the socio-legal level . . . the
account is a correct measure of early relations between Hurrians and
Hebrews."

Again, in chapter 28 of Genesis Jacob leaves Beer-sheba and sets
out for his grandfather's birthplace, Haran, to escape Esau's anger and
find a wife (as his father had done) from among his relations there. He
returns, that is, to Mesopotamia, though of course only temporarily.
It is on his way there that he has his famous dream in which he sees
a stairway set on the ground, with its top reaching the sky. On
waking, he exclaims : "How awesome is this place! This is none
other than the abode of God, and that is the gateway to heaven!"
(Speiser's translation.) He calls the place where he had the dream
Bethel, or House of God. Is it a coincidence that on this journey to
Mesopotamia Jacob dreams of something remarkably like a Mesopotamian temple tower or ziggurat? "For a ziggurat rose hard by the
main temple on the ground . . . to provide on its summit a place for
the deity to visit . . . and communicate there with mortals : a spiritual
symbol, in short, of man's efforts to reach out to heaven." So Speiser
comments, and he adds : "The phraseology is much too typical of
the temple tower to be merely coincidental, and the underlying
imagery cannot be mistaken." The irresistible conclusion is that the
author of this passage is reporting an authentic tradition.

In chapter 29, similarly, we are told how Laban, Jacob's maternal
uncle, gives Jacob his daughter Leah in marriage, though Jacob was
really in love with her younger sister Rachel ; later in the same chapter
Jacob gets Rachel too. In each case the narrator sticks in the paren-
thetical note that with the daughter Laban handed over a maid to wait
on her. "Laban had assigned his maid-servant Zilpah as maid to his
daughter Leah." "Laban had assigned his maid-servant Bilhah as
maid to his daughter Rachel." These brief interpolated sentences
have their exact parallel in the Nuzi tablets ; in a document printed in
the Harvard Semitic Series (V. no. 67), dealing in part "with a marriage
involving a young woman of high standing in the local community", we
find that, after all the relevant details have been set out, the text adds
parenthetically: "Moreover, Yalampa [a slave girl] is herewith assigned

to Gilimninu [the bride] as her maid." The authenticity of the custom is thus vouched for.

Lastly, in chapter 31 we find the puzzling story of Rachel stealing her father's household images when Jacob and his family return from Haran to Canaan. The significance of the incident can now be seen to derive "from underlying social practices as they bear on the nature of the patriarchal narratives in general. According to the Nuzi documents, which have been found to reflect time and again the social customs of Haran, possession of the house gods could signify legal title to a given estate, particularly in cases out of the ordinary, involving daughters, sons-in-law, or adopted sons."

This is only a selection of those passages in Genesis which remain puzzling or meaningless until seen as the recording of Hurrian customs by a Hebrew writer who had lost touch with their original meaning and purpose. If all this does not prove beyond any possible doubt that a man called Abraham (or Abram, as we are told his name originally was) left Haran for the land of Canaan about 1700 B.C., it certainly helps to authenticate the traditions recorded in Genesis and confirms the biblical view of Abraham's origins. Nothing, in fact, in Genesis is inconsistent with the historicity of Abraham, and there is considerable external supporting evidence for the basic truth of the biblical account of the patriarchs' migrations and questings.

It is this deft and scholarly use of supporting material out of the abundance of his own knowledge of the whole world of the ancient Middle East that makes Speiser's notes and comments in the first volume of the enormously ambitious Anchor Bible so illuminating and indeed so exciting. To translate the text afresh in the light of the best modern knowledge and to reconstruct the background with every available tool of scholarship is the aim of this series, and it could not have got off to a better start. On the question of translation, the editor of each volume has had to make his own decision. On the whole the editors of the six Old Testament volumes here considered agree in preferring accuracy to liturgical grace, in jettisoning the antique if beautiful forms of the Authorised Version and its later revisions in favour of starting from scratch with an appropriate modern English and at the same time in giving some clear indication of the nature of the literary form to be found in the original.

Some surprises result. It may come as a shock to the layman to be told that the very first words of the Bible do not mean "In the beginning." The test as vocalised by the Masorites (the Jewish editors who preserved and normalised the text of the Hebrew Bible, which they fixed about the 2nd century A.D., though they did not develop the full vocalisation for another four centuries or so) shows the opening word as clearly in the "construct" form, meaning "in the beginning of". Speiser renders the opening thus : "When God set about to create heaven and earth—the world being then a formless waste, with darkness over the seas and only an awesome wind sweeping over the water—God said, 'Let there be light.' And there was light." This should not disturb Jewish scholars who know (or should know) that both Rashi and Ibn Ezra suggested a similar rendering. "In the beginning of God's creating the heaven and earth . . ." is the meaning according to Rashi, which is also how Speiser understands it—though he does not give Rashi's further reason for repudiating the traditional translation, "In the beginning God created the heaven and the earth," which was that it is clear from verse 2 that God did *not* first create heaven and earth, but rather the waters. The modern scholar is less concerned to eliminate apparent inconsistencies than to use them as evidence of different hands engaged in the composition of the narrative.

No modern scholar can discuss Genesis without giving some account of the cogent evidence suggesting the different hands in the book. Speiser presents a scholarly and balanced summary of this evidence, and while some of his attributions must inevitably remain problematical, there can be little doubt in the mind of the unprejudiced reader that the different versions of the same story, differences in style and vocabularly, differences in main preoccupations and attitude, and differences in point of view (such as the extraordinary chapter 14, where we suddenly, and for the only time, get an outside view of "Abram the Hebrew" as a prosperous chief who can mobilise his own army at short notice), all add up to proof of multiplicity of authorship. Genesis, like all of the first books of the Bible, is a carefully wrought compilation from a variety of sources. Once again we are faced with the paradox that a recognition of this increases our admiration for what has actually been achieved in that remarkable book, just as our awareness of the Babylonian origins of the Creation and the Flood stories enhances our wonder at the radically different tone and meaning imposed on the material by the biblical authors. Speiser links these differences with Abraham's protest against the Mesopotamian civilisation from which he withdrew. "The migration . . . was in protest against the local religious solution [*sic.* "situation"?]. And reflexions of that protest can still be detected throughout the account of Primeval History. *P's*[3] statement about Creation differs from its Mesopotamian analogue by its overriding concept of an omnipotent Creator. *J's* version of the Flood receives a moral motivation. Most revealing of all is the same writer's narrative about the Tower of Babel. The scene of the episode is Babylon itself, and some passages in that story read as though the author had had the Babylonian prototype before him. Yet the purpose of the tale is not a direct though unacknowledged transcript, but a stern criticism of the builders' monumental presumption."

Of the three main authors of Genesis who can be identified, *P* is distinguished by his use of *Elohim* and *El Shaddai* for God, by his interest in genealogies, and by his concern for the purity of the line through which God implemented His purpose ; *J* is the great story-teller, who handles the Joseph story so magnificently, and he uses the tetragrammaton YHWH for God ; *E* is also a good storyteller, though not so lively and individual as *J*, interested in dreams as God's way of communicating with man, and inclined to elaborate explanation and justification of the actions of his characters. The mysterious name of God, YHWH, has traditionally been translated "the Lord" in English versions, following the age-old Jewish custom of reading it as "*Adonai*," "my lord (s)". The name itself was in Jewish tradition ineffable and not to be spoken except once a year in a moment of great awe by the High Priest. Whether it was ever pronounced "Yahweh" by the earliest readers of any part of the Bible is surely doubtful. The old Hebrew tradition of putting the vowels of "*Adonai*" under the consonants YHWH to show that the word should be read "*Adonai*" suggests an ancient inhibition. (It was a misunderstanding of this shorthand device that led Renaissance Christian Hebraists to read the word as "Jehovah", a non-existent name and a philological monstrosity.) The translators of all these volumes regularly render YHWH as "Yahweh" : I confess that this makes me feel slightly uncomfortable.

The general problem presented by translating from biblical Hebrew into modern English is difficult. The two languages are so very different in sound, structure, and behaviour. By means of a system of prefixes and suffixes Hebrew can compress into a single word what it may take three or four to express in English. The whole concept

---

[3] See below for an explanation of P, J, and E.

of verbal tenses is radically different from English and indeed from Indo-European languages in general. Many idioms, if rendered literally, may sound picturesque but may well give quite a wrong impression of the true meaning. A word or even a phrase may change its meaning in virtue of a difference in context, and to render them identically on each occasion when they occur may result in mistranslation.

In addition to these and similar problems, there are the problems presented by the state of the text itself. For the fixing of the Hebrew text by the Masorites, while it provided a stable text, did not necessarily provide a consistently accurate one. A long process of transmission, some of it originally oral, had been going on for many centuries before the Masorites got to work; such an extended interval always implies some degree of corruption. The problems presented by the text of the Hebrew Bible are bound up with the history and the transmission of this diverse anthology of Hebrew religious literature (for the Hebrew Bible is nothing less than that). The Masoretic text (MT) represents a late stage in the development of the biblical text and it has come down to us in manuscripts of no great antiquity. The Septuagint, the Greek translation made from a pre-Masoretic Hebrew text centuries before MT was established, points to an underlying Hebrew which sometimes differs from and sometimes may be superior to MT. One of the problems of the modern translator is to get behind MT where it is obviously or even possibly corrupt. So long as MT is regarded as sacrosanct, as it is by Jewish Orthodoxy (even though there are cases where pre-Masoretic readings are preserved in the Talmud), textual scholarship is limited.

Among the numerous differences between the Anchor Bible and the attractively produced Soncino Books of the Bible put out by the Soncino Press in England in the 1940s is that the latter, edited by Jewish rabbis and ministers throughout, sticks to MT and never seeks to emend or get behind it. The Soncino Bible prints the Hebrew as well as the English (in the translation of the Jewish Publication Society of America) and its commentary is less academic, or at least less rigorously professional, aimed more at the religious layman. In this respect it resembles more the volumes of the Pentateuch put out under the general editorship of the late J. H. Hertz, British Chief Rabbi, which are conservative and edifying rather than genuinely scholarly and, while attractively produced for the worshipper, skate over and sometimes simply ignore the really difficult and disturbing problems. It

must be admitted that, with some notable exceptions, of which the
Anchor Genesis is one, Christian scholarship on the Hebrew Bible has
been more enterprising and often more genuinely scholarly than
Jewish scholarship on the same subject has been. The Anchor Bible,
where Jewish scholars contribute some volumes and Protestant and
Catholic scholars contribute others, provides a fine proving ground
for the biblical scholarship of all three groups.

Genesis is the first book of the Bible for both Jews and Christians.
The name "Genesis" is of course Greek, and was first given to it by
the Greek translators of the Septuagint in the 3rd century B.C.   In
Hebrew it is known by its first word, *bereshit*, "In the beginning" (or,
more accurately, as we have seen, "In the beginning of"—a good
example of how Hebrew can get into one word what English has to do
in four). It combines Primeval History with Partiarchal History and
brings the story up to the settlement of the Children of Israel in the
land of Goshen and the death of Joseph. The three following books
of the Hebrew Bible deal with the Exodus from Egypt, the giving of
the Law on Mt. Sinai, the wandering in the wilderness, and further
details of legal and ritual enactments. But the fifth book—the last
book of the Pentateuch, the last of the so-called Five Books of Moses,
the final volume of the Torah in the Orthodox Jewish view—is rather
different. While in many respects the first four constitute a unity and
the same hands can be traced in each of them, the fifth, Deuteronomy,
appears as we have it to be the work of a writer who was trying to
recall Israel to the fundamental principles of the Mosaic Law and
worship of the one God ; it was a reformist manifesto gathering up,
recapitulating, classifying, reaffirming the religion of Moses partly
under the inspiration of the idealism of the prophets Hosea and
Isaiah.

It is important to recall the historical background. The Children of
Israel (to give them the traditional biblical name) finally conquered the
original inhabitants of Canaan and settled there, in accordance with
the primal promise made to Abraham. Their Golden Age was the era
of David and Solomon (tenth century B.C.) when those great kings
successively ruled over an Israelite empire which fell apart on the death
of Solomon (c. 922 B.C.) into the northern kindgom of Israel with its
capital eventually at Samaria and the southern kingdom of Judah with
its capital at Jerusalem. For two hundred years those tiny (by modern
standards) kingdoms survived side by side, sometimes in enmity and

sometimes in alliance, enabled to do so because, as Professor John Bright points out in his introduction to the Anchor Jeremiah, the world situation permitted it. "One must realise that Israel's entire history since her occupation of Palestine had until this time been spun out in a great power vacuum ; it was one of those interludes in which no world empire existed—neither in the Nile Valley, nor in Mesopotamia, nor elsewhere."

But in the second half of the 8th century B.C. things began to change : the accession to the Assyrian throne of Tiglath-pileser III inaugurated Assyria's period of empire. Israel, reduced to a tributary kingdom by Tiglath-pileser in the course of that king's conquest of all western Asia, was finally destroyed by Tiglath-pileser's successor Shalmaneser V in c. 722 B.C. Samaria was totally destroyed, and the inhabitants of Israel carried off into exile whence they never returned : they were eventually absorbed into their new environment and disappear from history—though some may have trickled into Judah later. Judah carried on, but as an Assyrian dependency after 734 B.C., its kings alternately vainly trying to throw off Assyrian domination by alliance with Egypt or (like King Manasseh, so detested by the author of the Book of Kings) submitting voluntarily to Assyria and imitating Assyrian ways.

This naturally threatened the traditional religion, for the Jews seem to have been only too ready to give way at almost any time to idolatrous practices and cults from other nations. It was Manasseh's grandson Josiah who tried to stop the rot and restore his people to the true religion of the God of Israel. In the eighteenth year of Josiah's reign (i.e. 622), according to Kings, a copy of "the book of the law" was discovered in the Temple while repairs were being made there. The book was read to the king, and it gave further impetus to his religious reforms. It was clearly some form of Deuteronomy, whose reformist author or reviser went on to produce the historical books of the Bible from Joshua through II Kings. The work of the Deuteronomist (as this author is now called) had as its aim, in the words of Professor Jacob M. Myers, editor of the Anchor Chronicles, "to exhibit the effectiveness of the word of the Lord in Israel's history, both as judgment and salvation, and to foster the hope of a revitalisation of the promise to David, in the face of a weakening Assyria if king and people heeded the lessons of the past". For Assyria, at the very moment of her greatest expansion, was beginning her decline and fall.

Religious reform and feeling for national independence went together, as so often in Israel's history. (It should be noted that although the northern kingdom of Israel had now disappeared, the term "Israel" still existed and was still in use—as it is today—to describe those of the ancient people who retained their identity. The "ten lost tribes" of the northern kingdom were not in fact ten distinct tribes at the time of the Assyrian conquest; the inhabitants of Judah took over the whole inheritance of Israel.)

The work of the Deuteronomist presented Israel with a problem that was to engage the attention of many of the Hebrew Prophets. Would adherence to the Mosaic Law, as recapitulated and reaffirmed in Deuteronomy, ensure the preservation of national independence and identity? And if, in spite of Josiah's reforms, Assyria or some other pagan foreign power were to subdue the country and overthrow its institutions, would this mean that God's promises were false and the confidence that He would look after His people if they did His will had all all along been misplaced?

Meanwhile, the political situation was worsening. Assyria joined with Egypt in an attempt to check the rising power of Babylon; Josiah, either alone or in alliance with Babylon, tried to stop the joint Assyrian-Egyptian army, and was defeated and killed. In 598–7 the Babylonians marched against Judah and conquered it, though Nebuchadnezzar allowed the state to exist under Babylonian suzerainty; in 587, after a final Jewish rebellion, the Babylonians destroyed Jerusalem and deported the population to Babylon. In 539 the conquering Cyrus the Great of Persia subdued Babylon and issued an edict allowing all the Jewish deportees and their descendants who so desired to return to Judah. The author of Chronicles wrote that it was the Lord who aroused the spirit of Cyrus to do this, and records his decree in this way: "Thus has Cyrus the king of Persia said: Yahweh God of the heavens has given me all the kingdoms of the earth and he has appointed me to build for him a house in Jerusalem which is in Judah. Whoever among you belongs to all his people, may Yahweh his God be with him and let him go up." (Myers's translation.)

The Deuteronomist had tried to prove to the people that obedience to the Mosaic Law would preserve them in freedom and security. Professor Myers comments: "Deuteronomy may have contributed [to the religious and moral decline that followed the death of Josiah]

by the creation of a misdirected sense of security on the part of officials
who trusted in externals to the exclusion, or nearly so, of a deep inner
commitment to the will of God." At any rate, Josiah's reforms had
not preserved national independence. The author of Chronicles ("the
Chronicler") set himself to rewrite the history of Israel from the death
of Saul and the accession of David to the decree of Cyrus in order to
serve the needs of the returned exiles. His object was threefold : "to
demonstrate that the true Israel was the one perpetuated in Judah—
the one which began in the Davidic kingdom, continued right through
the history of Judah, and more to the point, was now represented in
the exilic community" ; to create the proper conditions for true
religious worship and centralise it in Jerusalem ; and to provide an
institutional structure that could resist "the manifest political and
social pressures exerted upon the new community". He drew on a
variety of sources, including, of course, the historical books of the
Deuteronomist, but selected, organised, and emphasised in his own
way for his own purpose. "He did not", says Professor Myers,
"deliberately distort history to fit his purpose ; he employed those
phases that were apropos and, at numerous points, he manifestly
relied on sources sometimes more accurate than those used by the
Deuteronomist. In view of that fact one cannot accuse him of writing
imaginative history, as has been charged so often. That he had his
own way of filling in the gaps, with some embellishments no doubt,
was due to the interests of the cause. The political aspects of the
Davidic line had come to an end and there was no hope of re-establishment, at least not so far as he could see. Hope for Israel lay in the
fortification of the religious institutions that survived the tragic
experiences of 587 B.C. and the long years of the Exile."

It is fascinating to go through Chronicles and, with the aid of
Professor Myers's notes, see how the Chronicler has focused attention
on David, Solomon, and the Temple cult in order to present to his
people the kind of history that would best serve them in their crisis.
The Chronicler was, says Professor Myers, "above all else a churchman
of the highest order" whose aim was to help his people by strengthening "a living religious institution rather than through the royal
messianism proclaimed by the prophets—a messianism which had
signally failed in the early stages of the post-exilic community". The
Hebrew Bible in its traditional Jewish ordering ends with Chronicles :
this makes sense, for the Chronicler (who was probably also the

author of Ezra and Nehemiah) recapitulated Jewish history in such a way as to provide the basis for the survival of the Jewish people as essentially a religious community, thus preparing them for the greater *Galut*. It is surely ironical that a work designed to help the exiles returned from Babylon to re-develop their national religious life in their own country should have in fact helped to prepare their descendants for permanent exile.

Professor Myers's edition of Chronicles lacks the fine verbal grace we find in Speiser's Genesis (both in introduction and translation) : no one who persistently uses the word "returnees" can claim the highest linguistic sensitivity. But the translation of Chronicles does not call for any great stylistic subtlety, and Myers does a scholarly and workmanlike job. His introduction, if not a model of English prose, is consistently illuminating. He perhaps exaggerates, in the interests of clarity of presentation, the difference between the Chronicler's position and that of the prophets, whose message can certainly not be adequately summed up in the phrase "royal messianism". The prophets saw the little states of Judah and Israel caught up in the great power struggles of the time, and counselled a contracting out of the whole game of power politics in favor of concentration on prasticing justice, mercy, and righteousness. Between the decline of the Davidic empire and the final fall of Jerusalem to Babylon, these extraordinary men, speaking with total conviction in the name of God, exhorted, warned, castigated, and comforted their people in the firm belief that goodness rather than political strength or cunning would save the nation. By the same token, if Israel was oppressed by an outside power, it was by the will of God, and the duty of the people was to return to God rather than to rebel. This was the anguished message of Jeremiah, who prophesied in Judah from the beginning of the period of Babylonian domination of the country until after the final Babylonian conquest and the carrying off of so many of the people into exile. In a sense he was a Quisling, a traitor, counselling submission to Babylon because he saw no way out through political or military resistance. Babylon was God's instrument : he was convinced of this. Yet the knowledge tortured him, and he spoke out only because he felt that God was urging him to do so. After the final victory of the Babylonians, the victors offered him specially favourable treatment if he would come to Babylon with them. They misunderstood him, as so many of his own people misunderstood him. He stayed with the remnant of his people in devastated Judah until forcibly taken to Egypt.

Professor John Bright, in his Anchor Jeremiah, paints in the historical background with a vigorous brush, covering some of the same material dealt with by Professor Myers in his introduction to Chronicles but with a different focus. The center of the picture remains Jeremiah, the reluctant prophet, castigating his people for their faithlessness to their God and for preferring mere ritual to ethical action, prophesying with horrified conviction the defeat and destruction that God had prepared for His faithless people, protesting against his own prophetic mission and cursing his fate that he should be born into such a world and entrusted with such a message, and in the end advising the exiles in Babylon to seek the welfare of the country to which they had been deported and comforting them with visions of future restoration.

The Book of Jeremiah, with its prophetic poems, its historical and biographical narrative, and its terrifying autobiographical outbursts, is far from orderly (either chronologically or logically) as we now have it, and Professor Bright does some useful explaining and rearranging, sorting out the different strands and relating them to their background. In his translation he seeks a mean between a wooden literalness and a paraphrase, endeavouring to put the sense of the original into clear modern English and at the same time, in the poetic passages, trying to give the reader some impression of the effect of Hebrew poetry by keeping the lines at about the same length as the original and keeping the same number of accented syllables. This last aim sometimes leads him to use contractions that sound a bit too colloquial, but more often there is an immense gain in immediacy. Compare the following :

A.V. Be not dismayed at them.
BRIGHT. Don't lose your nerve because of them.

* * *

A.V. And they shall fight against
thee ; but they shall not
prevail against thee.
BRIGHT. Attack you they will ; overcome you they can't.

* * *

A.V. And send unto Kedar and consider
diligently ; and see if there hath
been such a thing.

BRIGHT.   Send out to Kedar and closely observe!
      And see—was there ever the like?

* * *

A.V.   And my people love to have it so ;
      and what will ye do in the end
      thereof?

BRIGHT.   And my people—they love it that way.
      But what will you do when it ends?

* * *

A.V.   Oh that I had in the wilderness
      a lodging place of wayfaring men ;
      that I might leave my people, and go
      from them! for they be all adulterers,
      an assembly of treacherous men.

BRIGHT.   O that I had in the desert
      A wayfarer's lodge,
      And so could leave my people,
      Get away from them!
      For they're all adulterers,
      A gang of crooks.

"A gang of crooks" is an admirable rendering of the Hebrew *atseret bog'dim* and brings the phrase immediately out of the realm of the antique-poetic into that of vigorous market-place talk, which, after all, is what Jeremiah was engaged in.

The question of whether the prophets were right in believing that the practice of virtue could have saved the people from foreign domination—what does a small nation *do* when ringed round by mighty military powers?—may bother the modern reader, but it is worth noting that, in Professor Bright's words, "precisely in that Jeremiah's was a message of judgment, it was a saving message. By ruthlessly destroying false hope, by ceaselessly asserting that the tragedy was Yahweh's doing, his righteous judgment on the nation for its sin, Jeremiah as it were drew the national disaster within the framework of faith, and thus prevented it from destroying faith". The disaster proved not the death of God but the very present existence of God. In making the people see this, Jeremiah helped to lay down a basic article of creed that the Jewish people clung to through subsequent centuries. "And because of our sins we were exiled from our land" is a phrase repeated by Orthodox Jews every New Year (in the *musaph* service). Two thousand years of exile and intermittent persecution, culminating in the murder of the six million by Hitler, because of the sins of some remote ancestors? If Jeremiah had seen further into the future he would surely have been appalled, and been even more reluctant to prophesy than he in fact was, and the eloquent messages of future comfort that we find in chapters 30 and 31 might never have been announced.

Jeremiah did not, however, accept the word of the Lord tamely ; he not only protested against the burden laid on him but also questioned God directly about His treatment of him. But it was in a different kind of context that the intractable question of the prosperity of the wicked and the suffering of the innocent was most fully treated in biblical literature. Among the third division of the Hebrew Bible (the traditional division is into Law, Prophets, and "Writings") we find that curiously attractive yet oddly anomalous group of books which belong to the "Wisdom" literature—that somewhat sophisticated, international, sometimes apparently agnostic, often worldly-wise, sometimes hedonistic, sometimes sad and world-weary to the point occasionally of anguish, trilogy of works, Job, Proverbs, and Kohelet (Ecclesiastes). Job, essentially a dialogue on theodicy inserted into the framework of an old folk tale, raises in a way so straightforward as to amount almost to blasphemy the question of unmerited suffering and challenges squarely the older doctrine that sin brings physical punishment and that the virtuous prosper. "I have been young and now I am old ; yet have I not seen the righteous forsaken, nor his seed begging for bread", wrote the Psalmist. Nonsense, replies the author of Job. Life isn't like that at all. And of course it isn't. Suffering does not prove antecedent sin, nor does righteous living guarantee happiness. While Job's friends try to persuade him that since he has been afflicted with such misfortunes he must have sinned, Job flatly refuses to accept this and keeps asking God to show him the indictment against him, to give him a proper trial instead of punishing him without even letting him know what he stands accused of. God replies, oddly enough, by castigating Job's friends and praising Job, yet at the same time humiliating Job by reciting a chain of natural wonders which God has created and which Job cannot possibly understand or control. The solution lies in wonder. God's ways are mysterious ; we cannot hope to understand them. His is the power and the mystery, and we must just trust that He knows what He is doing.

The text of Job is difficult and sometimes corrupt, and the matter is made worse by the attempts of the Masorites to smooth away some of Job's more daring outbursts. Thus the exclamation ". . . he will slay me ; I shall have nothing to hope for" was changed by reading the Hebrew *lo*, meaning "not", as the word *lo*, meaning "to him" (same sound, difference in spelling of one letter), with the result that it could be translated, as the Authorised Version has it : "Though he slay me, yet will I wait for him." (Professor Marvin H. Pope, in the Anchor Job, renders it : "He may slay me, I'll not quaver.") Job is full of such passages which Professor Pope's edition lucidly explains and clarifies. Some of the most famous sentences attributed to Job, which have rung down the ages as professions of faith, are clearly misreadings of the Hebrew, though they have developed a life of their own in religious thought and literature.

Like Professor Bright with Jeremiah, Professor Pope makes a good attempt to capture the feeling of the original poetry, using a much shorter line than more traditional translations. Here are some examples :

A.V.

As God liveth, who has taken away my right ;
And the Almighty, who hath vexed my soul ;
(For my life is yet whole in me,
And the spirit of God is in my nostrils ;)
Surely my lips shall not speak unrighteousness,
Neither shall my tongue utter deceit.

POPE.

As God lives, who withholds my right,
Shaddai who has embittered my soul,
While I have life in me,
God's breath in my nostrils,
My lips will not speak falsehood,
Nor my tongue utter deceit.

* * *

A.V.

Let the day perish wherein I was born.
And the night which said, there is a man child conceived.

POPE.

Damn the day I was born,
The night that said, 'A boy is begot.'

Pope's rhythms are much more like those of the Hebrew.

Job sounds fevered and desperate beside the mellow scepticism of Kohelet, that curiously unbiblical work which is the best and most characteristic representative of straight Wisdom literature to manage to get into the canon. It didn't get in without a struggle, and the addition of an editorial conclusion to turn the genial scepticism of the author into a reason for faith and obedience. (One is reminded of the fun David Hume had with the idea of scepticism as the basis of faith in his *Dialogues on Natural Religion*.) Professor R. B. Y. Scott, who edits the Anchor Proverbs and Ecclesiastes (in a single volume), gives us a scholarly and workmanlike translation preceded by a clear if far from concise account of the background of the Wisdom literature. Some of the information he provides duplicates the material provided in Professor Pope's Job, but this is inevitable if each volume is to be regarded as independent. He does tend to be verbose, though, not only in his introduction but also occasionally in his translation. I can see no conceivable reason why that fine verse in Proverbs traditionally (and absolutely literally) translated :

> Her ways are ways of pleasantness,
> And all her paths are peace

should be rendered by Professor Scott as :

> Her ways are ways to delight
> And all her paths lead to felicity.

"Ways to delight" might just be defended on the grounds that it gives the sense of the Hebrew more accurately (though "ways of pleasantness" is both literal and charming, if considerably longer than the Hebrew), but what can possibly be said for changing "all her paths are peace" to "all her paths lead to felicity"? Scott admits in his notes that the substitution "seems literary sacrilege" but defends it on the grounds that it makes the meaning a little clearer. I confess that I cannot see how it does that. He tells us in an earlier note that the Hebrew *shalom* really means "wholeness, harmonious well-being". It is indeed true that *shalom* is etymologically associated with the concept of wholeness and harmony; but I can't help wondering what would happen if, the next time I visited Israel, I greeted someone there with : "Harmonious well-being to you!"

But this is a minor point. To present Proverbs and Kohelet together in a single volume with a translation which, even if occasionally infelicitous, does genuinely clear up (particularly with respect to the latter book) some of the beautiful mystifications of the Authorised Version translators and sets both works in their time and place and in

S

the whole context of Wisdom literature of the Near East is a fine and welcome achievement. It is interesting to put the present translation beside that of Robert Gordis, whose work on Kohelet is one of the noblest monuments of American Jewish biblical scholarship. Gordis emends MT less frequently than Pope, but his translation is sometimes even freer. Gordis renders "Cast thy bread upon the waters" as "Send your goods overseas", which is not what the Hebrew says, though it may well be its implication ; Pope renders with absolute literalness : "Throw your bread on the surface of the water", and in doing so gives us nine English words for the five Hebrew.

The whole question of how to render the imagery of Kohelet is beset with difficulties ; sometimes the idiom rendered literally is meaningless ; sometimes it is suggestive but in the wrong way ; sometimes again (as, surely, with the example just quoted) the literal translation can be left to achieve its own suggestion. Sometimes emendation is absolutely necessary to achieve any sense at all ; at other times it may improve the sense or at least make it seem more logical. A.V. renders the opening of the last chapter, "Remember also thy Creator in the days of thy youth ". Gordis has, " Remember your Creator in the days of your youth" (the Jewish Publication Society's version retains the dubious force of the Hebrew prefix *u-* by rendering "Remember *then* thy Creator in the days of thy youth"). But Scott decides to emend MT *bor'ēcha* ("your creator") to read *bor'cha* ("your grave")—thought the common meaning of *bor* is "pit"—and renders, "In the days of your youth, remember your grave", which *is* more logical, since the passage goes on to describe the coming of old age and death. But this whole chapter is full of problems. Let anyone compare the mysteriously eloquent Authorised Version with those of Gordis and Scott, and he will realise that the poetry of A.V. often produces a pleasing fuzz of meaning which is nevertheless fuzz.

As for Proverbs, they are an interesting collection of secular and religious sayings and didactic poems reflecting many of the characteristics of Near Eastern Wisdom literature. Many of the sayings keep reminding me of that bogus oriental proverb we used to joke about as schoolboys : "The rich man is kind to his dog, but the poor man rises early in the morning." After re-reading the whole book of Proverbs more carefully than I have ever done before, and pondering on one of the categories of proverbs listed by Professor Scott (the pattern of "*non-identity, contrast,* or *paradox*"), I realise that this fake oriental proverb of my childhood really makes sense : the rich can afford the luxury of indulging animals, while the poor are too busy scratching a living to be able to afford that kind of indulgence. But I prefer the snappier sayings, some of which Professor Scott renders most incisively. "Go to the ant, thou sluggard," the well known A.V. rendering, does not leap out of the pages like :

Go watch an ant, you loafer!

Now that is something you can really say to people.

Sof davar hakol nishma (Kohelet, 12 :13, rendered by Professor Scott as "The sum of the matter when all has been heard is this") is that the Anchor Bible is the most exciting development in biblical studies in the English-speaking world at the present time. The endeavour to give a new rendering of each book of the Bible in the light of the knowledge now possessed by the sum of biblical scholars and to set that translation in an account of the context and background drawn similarly from every relevant branch of knowledge from archaeology to textual criticism must be warmly welcomed by anybody who considers himself in any degree literate. The Bible is a quite extraordinary anthology of religious literature which, quite apart from the special part it has played in the history of Judaism and Christianity, is of the highest literary, historical, anthropological, and general human interest. It is good that expert knowledge about its nature and meaning should be released from the pages of learned journals and made available to the layman. For myself, I would have preferred an edition with the original text facing the translation. (In reviewing these volumes I have had to have a semicircle of Hebrew texts around me.) But that is probably a special taste. Of more universal value would have been the provision of maps and full indexes to each volume. One must not complain, though. This is a remarkable and quite exceptionally valuable series, and I look forward to its future volumes.

15

The Book of Job[1]

The Book of Job continues to fascinate and challenge scholars. Last year, we had Marvin Pope's translation and commentary in the Anchor Bible, and now we have Robert Gordis, the distinguished Jewish authority on Hebrew Wisdom literature, presenting a study, a commentary, and a translation.[2] Gordis puts the book into its historical setting, demonstrating its relation to the principal strands of ancient Hebrew religion and culture as well as to the whole corpus of Wisdom literature produced by the various nations of the Fertile Crescent. He assigns the book to the early post-Exilic period, after Deutero-Isaiah, between 500 and 300 B.C. and sees it as part of the concern with the fate of the individual (as distinct from the nation or the family) shown by upper-class writers in that unstable period. The lower classes, facing their unvaried lot of poverty and oppression at the hands of both domestic and foreign masters, began to look to a future life to redress the balance, or to await some great supernatural cataclysm which would usher in a new order. Out of this came apocalyptic movements, frowned on by official Judaism but highly influential in the development of Christianity. But the Book of Job is not apocalyptic, and it specifically denies belief in an after-life. It is the work of a great upper-class poet, obsessed with the problem of personal suffering and the apparent injustice of God in dealing with individuals. Though its theme is personal rather than national, it is also universal, not concerned with the survival of the people of Israel (neither the setting nor the characters of the book are Israelite) but deeply worried about the problem of theodicy, God's justice in dealing with men.

[1] First published in *Commentary*, May 1966.
[2] Robert Gordis, *The Book of God and Man : A Study of the Book of Job.* Chicago (University of Chicago Press), 1966.

Using as a framework a simple folk-tale written in a clear, direct, classical Hebrew, the author has built up a dialogue between Job and his "comforters" in an extraordinary rich and difficult vocabulary which goes beyond the range of normal biblical Hebrew. The original folk-tale tells of a prosperous man who was visited with great afflictions but who, in spite of everything, resisted the temptation to "curse God and die", and was rewarded for his patience in the end by a restoration of more than his former prosperity. It is interesting that until relatively recently in the history of both Judaism and Christianity, it is the simple moral of the folk-tale that was dwelt on : we still talk of "the patience of Job" as though we had never read beyond Chapter One of the forty-two chapters of the book. However, in a development of the dialogue by the great poet who used the original folk-tale merely as a starting point, Job is shown as far from patient. Emboldened by his agony and his outraged sense of injustice, he asserts that God's power is not matched by His equity and he challenges God to face him and tell him what he has done wrong that he has been made to suffer so. He sees the world full of the prosperous wicked and the tortured innocent, and will not accept for a moment the simple equation between suffering and guilt that his friends try to force on him—nor will he even accept Elihu's more sophisticated view that God sometimes sends suffering to test character and prevent future evildoing by shaking moral complacency. He does not doubt God's omnipotence ; he does doubt His justice. Yet running through his anguished cries of despair and anger, and his contemptuous dismissal of his friends conventional arguments, is another argument : If only Job could get God to face him properly, he would somehow find his advocate, his defender.

In a curious way, Job seems to appeal from God to God—either from one aspect of God to another, or even to a principle beyond God. When he cries that in spite of everything "I know that my Redeemer lives" (and the Hebrew word go'el, traditionally translated as "re- deemer", originally meant the nearest kinsman who had the duty of exacting vengeance in a blood feud, and then took on an extended meaning of defender or deliverer), is he saying that in spite of every- thing he believes that God, whom he has been attacking as his perse- cutor, is really on his side, or is he looking to some power behind God? Earlier, Job had said : "Yes. He may slay me ; I have no hope, but I will justify my ways to His face"[3] and we get the feeling that if only

[3] Gordis's translation.

he could force a confrontation with God, he would find God, the unjust wielder of power, and God, the redeemer, identical. Sometimes a curiously elegiac note rises up : here is Gordis's rendering of one such passage :

> If a man die, can he live again?
>> all the days of my service I would wait,
>> till my hour of release should come.
> You would call and I would answer You ;
>> You would be longing for the work of Your hands.

That's the sort of God Job would like, a God who would enable a man to live again after death (which Job did not believe God could or would do), when a loving reconciliation between the creator and the creature could take place. But nowhere in the poem is it suggested that this will actually occur. Even though, in the astonishing con-clusion of the poem, God does appear out of the whirlwind and con-front Job, it is to assert the unfathomable diversity, wonder, and splendour of the universe and God's unknowable power in creating it. Job is abashed, but God does not reprove him for his near-blasphemous words : on the contrary, he reproves his friends (who had maintained throughout the discussion the conventional doctrine that suffering must imply prior sin) for having talked nonsense.

Job gets his confrontation, then. But it is not the kind he had demanded, with a clear statement of what he was supposed to have done wrong so that he could disprove it in open court, as it were. God's voice, speaking marvellous poetry, gives a tremendous picture of the great non-human forces in the universe, almost as though to suggest that man hardly counts. The memorable portraits of *behemoth* and *leviathan* (the hippopotamus and the crocodile) suggests two things, says Gordis. "First, man, who is only one of God's creatures, is *not* the measure of all things and the sole test of creation. Second, man's suffering must be seen in its proper perspective within the framework of the cosmos." And Gordis goes on to say that "evil will then seem less pervasive in the universe than Job's anguished cries have made it appear". To this, one can reply that surely in any higher religion man has a special relationship to God which cannot be blurred by dwelling on the magnificence of the non-human creation ; and secondly, that if man suffers unjustly, his suffering—whatever proportion it happens to occupy of the sum-total of activity in the universe—still represents injustice, and God should not be unjust. One is reminded of the servant girl who pleaded that her illegitimate baby was a very little one. The size is not relevant to the issue.

I cannot myself feel that what is going on in this extraordinary final part of Job is quite what Gordis says it is. For he then goes on to say that God's second speech to Job teaches Job "to recognise both the mystery and the harmony of the world". The mystery, yes ; the power, the diversity, the sheer scope, and even monstrousness of creation, yes. But harmony? I can find nothing in the original text which suggests this notion. In other words, it seems to me that Gordis is rationalising a bit. God says that His creation is mysterious and wonderful and that man cannot begin to understand it. That is all the answer Job gets. God does *not* say to Job that if he could see the creation as a whole he would recognise its harmony and justice. He does *not* say that man's suffering is justified because it is so small a part of the totality of the universe (which is a pretty dangerous position theologically and morally anyway). He calls attention to Job's inability to command the morning, tread on the sea-bed, discover the home of light, bind the chains of the Pleiades, seize leviathan with a net, and do many other things ; and it is true that the list of these things is absolutely stunning in its suggestion of power and glory, so that it does exalt the spirit to read it. But the only answer to Job's question is that there is no answer : the universe is more complicated than man can ever hope to understand, so he had better refrain from discussing the principles on which it is run. Yet Job is not punished for having raised the question ; instead, his friends are reproved for having given the neat, conventional answers. There are no answers that man can understand.

One can argue forever about the real meaning of the last part of the book, and if I have some minor disagreements with Dr Gordis it is not because I do not appreciate the scholarship and the qualities of mind and imagination that reveal themselves again and again in his commentary. I was particularly impressed by his solution to some of the perennial textual problems presented by this difficult work, one part of which is clearly incomplete and out of order but which, on the whole, is much less in need of radical emendation than earlier scholars, in the heyday of textual reconstruction, believed. In a perceptive chapter on "the rhetoric of allusion and analogy" Gordis draws attention to the great demands made on the reader in the ancient

Semitic world, not only in vocalising a consonantal alphabet in the
process of reading, and in supplying punctuation, but also in following
what is often a highly allusive line of thought, and in making sense of
parallels and contrasts which are set going by imagery lacking either
cumulative or antithetical conjunctions.   By the simple process of
recognising certain sentences as quotations, existing within unwritten
quotation marks, he makes impressive sense of entire chapters that had
been truncated or scrapped by earlier editors.   In his translation, he
helps the reader by putting into Job's mouth, as he addresses his
friends, such phrases as "*You* say . . . but *I* maintain" and immediately
the whole pattern of the speech becomes clear and we no longer are
bewildered by arguments of Job's opponents emerging intermittently
from the mouth of Job with disturbing lack of logic.   Similarly, Job
may cite a well-known proverb before going on to confute it with
reference to his own experience.   If we do not recognise that proverb
as a quotation, we are puzzled by Job's saying one thing and then
going on to say the precise opposite.

The translation itself is always interesting and often illuminating,
though the scope of the book does not allow detailed textual notes
defending a given rendering.   Occasionally Gordis, in his desire to
make the point absolutely clear, adds a word not in the original, and I
am not sure that this does not weaken rather than strengthen the effect.
For example, the second verse of Chapter 12 is rendered thus both by
the Authorised Version and the Jewish Publication Society translation:

> No doubt but ye are the people,
> And wisdom shall die with you.

Marvin Pope (who takes the Hebrew word *am* to be a technical social
term meaning upper-class landowners, though its basic and more
general sense is simply "people") renders :

> No doubt you are the gentry,
> And with you wisdom will die.

Gordis renders :

> No doubt you are the people that count,
>   and with you all wisdom will die!

In his desire to spell out what the original means, Gordis adds "that
count" (not in the Hebrew), thus blunting the sly irony of the original,

and adds the word "all" (also not in the Hebrew) before "wisdom".
It is true that this results in a crystal-clear statement of the intention of
the original, but it lacks its compression and thus its power.   Again,
let us compare the opening on Chapter 3 in the three versions (A.V.,
Pope, and Gordis) :

> Let the day perish wherein I was born,
> And the night wherein it was said :
>   'A man-child is brought forth.'
> Let that day be darkness ; . . .

> Damn the day I was born,
> The night that said, "A boy is begot."
> That day—let it be darkness.

> Perish the day when I was born,
>   and the night which said :
> "A man-child is conceived."
> That day—may it be utter darkness !

Only Gordis adds the unnecessary word "utter", which is not in the
Hebrew. (The Hebrew word *choshekh* is simply the ordinary word
for darkness : there is another Hebrew word for darkness, *arafel*, used
in Isaiah and usually translated "thick darkness", but it is not the
word used here.)   Nevertheless, Gordis's is a clear and vivid translation, and a conservative one in the sense that he does not emend the
masoretic text unnecessarily.   Here is a final example of different
renderings of the same passage, nicely illustrating not only some of the
linguistic difficulties but also the way in which the doctrinal element
can affect the translation.   The first is from the Authorised Version,
the second from the Jewish Publication Society, the third is Pope's,
and the fourth Gordis's :

> For I know that my Redeemer liveth, and that He shall stand at the
>   latter day upon the earth :
> And though after my skin worms destroy this body, yet in my flesh
>   shall I see God.

> But as for me, I know that my Redeemer liveth,
> And that he will witness at the last upon the dust :
> And when after my skin this is destroyed,
> Then without my flesh shall I see God.

I know that my vindicator lives,
A guarantor upon the dust will stand :
Even after my skin is flayed,
Without my flesh I shall see God.

For I know that my Redeemer lives,
   though He be the last to arise upon earth!
Deep in my skin this has been marked,
   and in my very flesh do I see God.

Pope gets "guarantor" by reading the Hebrew word *acharon*, which normally means "last", in the light of the Mishnaic and Talmudic term *achar'y* (responsible). But he adds that it makes little real difference whichever way we take the word, "since the crucial point is that the vindicator and guarantor is not God but rather a mediator, an arbiter who will eventually prove Job's innocence before God". But Gordis returns to the older view that the *go'el* is God, seeing Job as appealing from God to God, from the God of power to the God of justice. It is, for Gordis, a mystical vision which Job has for an instant and cannot sustain : "In this moment of mystical exaltation, Job feels his ultimate reconciliation with God engraved on his very flesh. He yearns to hold fast to the ecstatic experience, but it flees. The vision of the future fades as quickly as it has come, and there remains only the agony of the present." Much of Gordis's interpretation depends on his seeing swiftly changing moods succeeding themselves in Job's consciousness. This enables him to retain as authentic many passages earlier editors threw out as illogical excrescences.

The argument will go on. No study of this fascinating book can be final : but this is an impressive and illuminating contribution.

DATE DUE
